MW01472435

THE LETTERS OF THOMAS CHANDLER HALIBURTON

Bust of Haliburton at the Isleworth Branch Library, Middlesex

EDITED BY RICHARD A. DAVIES

The Letters of
Thomas Chandler Haliburton

UNIVERSITY OF TORONTO PRESS
Toronto Buffalo London

© University of Toronto Press 1988
Toronto Buffalo London
Printed in Canada

ISBN 0-8020-2628-1

∞

Printed on acid-free paper

Canadian Cataloguing in Publication Data

Haliburton, Thomas Chandler, 1796–1865
  The letters of Thomas Chandler Haliburton

Includes index.
ISBN 0-8020-2628-1

1. Haliburton, Thomas Chandler, 1796–1865 –
Correspondence. 2. Authors, Canadian (English) –
19th century – Correspondence.* I. Davies, Richard A.
II. Title.

PS8415.A38Z54 1988   C818'.309   C87-094959-4
PR9199.2.H34Z48 1988

This book has been published with the help of a grant from the Canadian Federation for the Humanities, using funds provided by the Social Sciences and Humanities Research Council of Canada.

To Beverly, Harriet, and Emily

Contents

ILLUSTRATIONS viii

ACKNOWLEDGMENTS ix

ABBREVIATIONS xiii

CHRONOLOGY OF HALIBURTON'S LIFE xv

EDITORIAL PROCEDURES xix

1 The Early Years, 1796–1829 3

2 The Young Judge, 1829–1837 49

3 *The Clockmaker* and England, 1838–1840 86

4 A Literary Career, 1840–1856 113

5 A New Life, 1856–1859 179

6 Parliamentary and Business Interests, 1859–1865 212

LETTERS OF UNCERTAIN DATE 259

MISCELLANEOUS ADDITIONAL LETTERS 263

HALIBURTON'S SPEECHES IN ENGLAND, 1856–1865 269

SOURCES OF LETTERS 271

PICTURE CREDITS 275

INDEX 277

Illustrations

Bust of Haliburton ii
Haliburton, *c.* 1831 50
'Clifton,' Judge Haliburton's residence at Windsor, NS, in 1842 51
Haliburton in 1838 101
Gordon House, Isleworth, 1869 180
Haliburton and his wife, Sarah Harriet, at Gordon House 180
Haliburton, *c.* 1860 213
Haliburton, photographed by Parish and Co., Halifax 214
Wood-engraved portrait of Haliburton, *c.* 1865 215
A letter in Haliburton's hand 248

Acknowledgments

The Social Sciences and Humanities Research Council of Canada supported this work with two awards: a summer research grant in 1979 that enabled me to annotate a substantial proportion of Haliburton's English correspondence and a leave fellowship during the 1983-4 academic year that enabled me to complete the manuscript. Without this support, it would have been impossible to proceed. I am also grateful to the referees who supported my application for the summer research grant and the leave fellowship. As the manuscript evolved, it was read by two readers appointed by the Canadian Federation for the Humanities, and their suggestions and corrections have been very useful.

The work of collecting and annotating these letters was begun in 1977. The search for letters involved writing to several hundred libraries over the course of seven years, and I am grateful to the vast number of librarians and archivists who took time to reply and who frequently enclosed complimentary photocopies of single letters they possessed and were often full of ideas as to where else I might look. Lisa Fink of the Maine Historical Society and Richard M. Ludwig of Princeton University Library were particularly helpful. I would also like to thank the Ewart Library, Dumfries, Scotland; the Liverpool Public Library, England; and J. Richard Abell of the Public Library, Cincinnati and Hamilton County, Ohio, USA, for responding to inquiries. In all of the libraries I used regularly, especially those close to home – the Acadia University Library and the Public Archives of Nova Scotia – I found the staff members uniformly helpful. Over the years, the following people provided valuable information: Peter Booth, Gwendolyn Davies, Toby Foshay, Gordon Haliburton, Douglas Lochhead, Barry Moody, Cecil Price, and M. Brook Taylor.

Mrs Virginia Barrington, great granddaughter of Thomas Haliburton, acted as spokesperson for the descendants of Haliburton's daughters and communicated with other family members in England on my behalf. For this invaluable help and for her expressions of interest in the project I am most grateful. Thanks are also due to my brother, John Atterbury.

In 1976 and 1983 Acadia University provided small grants for travel and photocopying. In 1979, an Ontario Arts Council grant encouraged me at a stage when encouragement was needed. A SEED grant during the summer of 1986 provided money for an assistant. I am indebted to Anne Perkin for scholarly assistance in preparing the final version of the manuscript and in checking the text. Nova Morine and Andrew Chodakowski also helped to check the text. Mrs Elizabeth Grigg, Kim Leonard, Lynn Connors, and, particularly, Paul Steele provided assistance in using the word-processing facilities at Acadia University.

I am grateful to the following individuals and institutions for granting permission to publish Haliburton letters in their possession: Vaughan Memorial Library, Acadia University; Rare Books and Manuscripts Department, Boston Public Library; DesBrisay Museum, Bridgewater, Nova Scotia; Department of Manuscripts, British Library; Brotherton Collection, University of Leeds; James Fraser Gluck Collection, Buffalo and Erie County Public Library; Department of Special Collections, University of California Research Library, Los Angeles; Chicago Public Library Special Collections Division; Rare Book and Manuscript Library, Columbia University; University Archives, William Inglis Morse Collection, Dalhousie University Library; Manuscript Department, William R. Perkins Library, Duke University; Rare Books and Manuscripts Department, Mitchell Library, Glasgow; Houghton Library, Harvard University; Charles Roberts Autograph Letters Collection, Haverford College, Pennsylvania; Huntington Library, San Marino, California; University of Iowa; Rare Book Room, University of Illinois at Urbana-Champaign; University of King's College, Halifax; the Hon. David Lytton Cobbold, Knebworth House, Knebworth, Hertfordshire; the Officers and Trustees of the Maine Historical Society; the Master and Fellows of Massey College, Toronto; Miscellaneous Papers, Manuscript and Archives Division, New York Public Library, Astor, Lenox, and Tilden Foundations; Elmer Holmes Bobst Library / Fales Library, New York University; University Libraries, Pennsylvania State University; Rare Book Department, Free Library of Philadelphia; Historical Society of Pennsylvania, Philadelphia; Pierpont Morgan Library, New York; Public Archives of Canada; Public Record Office, Chancery Lane and Kew Gardens, London; the Trustees of the National Library of Scotland; Thomas Chandler Haliburton Collection,

Acknowledgments

Barrett Library, University of Virginia Library; and Collection of American Literature, Beinecke Rare Book and Manuscript Library, Yale University. I am also grateful to Charles Ritchie for permission to quote from the King-Stewart Family Papers at the Public Archives of Canada.

I regret that I have been unable to locate Professor Raymond Bennett, the owner of Haliburton's letter to Cecilia Tilley, 18 July 1843. Professor Bennett sent a copy of the letter in his possession to Professor Douglas Lochhead, who at one time was contemplating an edition of Haliburton's letters. Professor Lochhead sent me the copy when I started work on the edition, and I have included it.

I would also like to thank Professor Allen Penney of the Technical University of Nova Scotia in Halifax for his generosity in allowing me access to his fine collection of Haliburton illustrations. For additional help with the illustrations, I am grateful to Deborah Trask of the Nova Scotia Museum, Halifax, and Gary Boates of the Audio-Visual Department at Acadia University. Anne Doucet helped to check the proofs.

At the University of Toronto Press, editor Gerry Hallowell, a reader appointed by the Press (who remained anonymous to me), and copy-editor Margaret Woollard all significantly influenced the form of the final manuscript. The first two concentrated on its general design and editorial procedures; Margaret Woollard expertly copy-edited the final version.

My wife, Beverly, encouraged and sustained me from start to finish. She has always been my firmest and friendliest critic.

Richard A. Davies
Department of English
Acadia University, Wolfville, NS

Abbreviations

Belcher's	*Belcher's Farmers Almanack* (various dates)
BL Add. MS	British Library, Additional Manuscript
Calnek	W.A. Calnek, *History of the County of Annapolis* [1897]. Belleville, Ont.: Mika Studio 1972
Chittick	V.L.O. Chittick, *Thomas Chandler Haliburton ('Sam Slick'): A Study in Provincial Toryism*. New York: Columbia University Press 1924
Coward	Elizabeth Ruggles Coward, *Bridgetown, Nova Scotia; Its History to 1900*. Kentville 1955
DAH	*Dictionary of American History*
DCB	*Dictionary of Canadian Biography*
Deveau	J. Alphonse Deveau, *Along the Shores of Saint Mary's Bay: The Story of a Unique Community*. 2 vols Church Point: Université Sainte-Anne 1977
DNB	*Dictionary of National Biography*
Fales Family	DeCoursey Fales, *The Fales Family of Bristol, Rhode Island*. Privately printed 1919
Gettman	Royal A. Gettman, *A Victorian Publisher: A Study of the Bentley Papers*. London 1960
Harvard	The Houghton Library, Harvard University, Cambridge, Mass.
Historical ... Account	*An Historical and Statistical Account of Nova Scotia*. 2 vols Halifax 1829
ed. Morse, W.I.	'The Correspondence of Thomas Chandler Haliburton and Richard Bentley,' *The Canadian Collection at Harvard University, Bulletin* IV. Ed. William Inglis Morse. Cambridge, Mass.: Harvard University Press 1947, 48–105

Abbreviations

PAC	Public Archives of Canada
PANS	Public Archives of Nova Scotia
Parks, M.G.	Joseph Howe, *Western and Eastern Rambles: Travel Sketches of Nova Scotia.* Ed. Malcolm G. Parks. Toronto: University of Toronto Press 1973
PRO	Public Record Office (Chancery Lane or Kew Gardens, London)
Raddall	Thomas H. Raddall, *Halifax, Warden of the North.* Toronto: McClelland and Stewart 1971
Shand	Gwendolyn D. Shand, *Historic Hants County.* Windsor: Petheric Press 1979
UCLA	University of California, Los Angeles
Yale	Beinecke Library, Yale University, New Haven, Conn.

Chronology of Haliburton's Life

1796	17 December	Born in Windsor, Nova Scotia
1815		Graduates BA from King's College, Windsor, Nova Scotia
1816	28 May	Marries Louisa Neville at Henley-on-Thames, Oxfordshire, England
1819	24 October	Applies to be a notary
1821	July	Moves to Annapolis Royal
1823		Publishes *A General Description of Nova Scotia*
1824	13 December	Appointed Judge of the Probate Court at Annapolis Royal
1826	22 May	Elected Member of the Legislative Assembly for Annapolis County
1829	7 July	Death of father, W.H.O. Haliburton, aged sixty-two, at Windsor
	26 August	*An Historical and Statistical Account of Nova Scotia*, 2 vols, published by Joseph Howe at Halifax
	1 October	Succeeds father as First Justice of the Inferior Court of Common Pleas for the Middle Division of Nova Scotia
1830	February	Returns to live in Windsor
1835	24 September	Weekly serialization of *The Clockmaker* begins in the *Novascotian*
1836	10 February	Serialization of *The Clockmaker* in the *Novascotian* ends with no. XXI, 'Setting Up for Governor'
1837	4 January	*The Clockmaker* advertised in the *Novascotian*

		as 'just issued from the Press.' It contains 'eleven Numbers not hitherto published.'
	27 March	*The Clockmaker* published by Richard Bentley in London
1838	26 April	Sails for England on the *Tyrian*
	16 July	*The Clockmaker*, Second Series, published by Richard Bentley in London
1839	9 January	*The Bubbles of Canada* published by Richard Bentley
	18–26 February	'Reply to the Report of the Earl of Durham. By A Colonist,' seven letters, published in *The Times*
	23 March	Embarks for Halifax on the *Great Western* steamship from Bristol
1840	3 January	*The Letter-Bag of the Great Western* published by Richard Bentley
	30 October	*The Clockmaker*, Third Series, published by Richard Bentley
1841	29 March	Appointed Judge of the Supreme Court of Nova Scotia
	29 November	Death of his wife, Louisa
1843	18 May	Embarks for England
	1 July	*The Attaché*, First Series, published by Richard Bentley
	3 September	Returns to Nova Scotia
1844	21 October	*The Attaché*, Second Series, published by Richard Bentley
1846	May	'The Lone House' published in *Fraser's Magazine*
1847	February–December	*The Old Judge* serialized in *Fraser's Magazine*
	4 November	Death of his son Thomas, in Boston
1849	January	*The Old Judge* published by Henry Colburn and Co., London
1851	31 March	*The English in America* published by Henry Colburn and Co., London. The work is retitled *Rule and Misrule of the English in America* to prevent confusion with a similarly titled work.
1852		*Traits of American Humour by Native Authors*, 3 vols, published by Henry Colburn and Co., London

1853		*Sam Slick's Wise Saws and Modern Instances* published by Hurst and Blackett, London
	3 September	Embarks at Liverpool for Halifax
1854		*The Americans at Home or, Byeways, Backwoods, and Prairies*, 3 vols, published by Hurst and Blackett, London
1855		*Nature and Human Nature* published by Hurst and Blackett
1856	11 August	Tenders resignation as a Supreme Court judge
	30 September	Marries Sarah Harriet Williams at St George's Church, Hanover Square, London
1857	26 March	*Address on the Present Condition, Resources and Prospects of British North America* published in London by Hurst and Blackett
1858	16 June	Receives Hon. DCL at Oxford University
1859	March	Serialization of the *The Season Ticket* begins in the *Dublin University Magazine*
	29 April	'Elected' Member of Parliament for Launceston, North Cornwall
1860	6 March	*The Season Ticket* published in London by Richard Bentley
	21 April	*Speech of the Hon. Mr. Justice Haliburton, M.P. in the House of Commons, on Tuesday, the 21st April, 1860, on the Repeal of the Differential Duties on Foreign and Colonial Wood* published in London by Edward Stanford
	27 August–10 October	Visits North America
1861	*c.* 25 August–November	Visits Nova Scotia
1865	4 July	Resigns his parliamentary seat
	27 August	Dies at Gordon House, aged sixty-nine

Editorial Procedures

The letters are arranged in chronological order and numbered consecutively. They derive from three sources: manuscripts, copies in another hand, and printed versions. Where a letter survives in manuscript it has authority over all other versions. Letters existing only in a printed form have been reprinted from the earliest published version. An abbreviated note is placed at the foot of each letter indicating whether the source of the letter is a manuscript, copy, or printed version. The note also indicates whether the letter has been transcribed directly from the holograph or from a photocopy of the manuscript. '[Ph.]' is used in the second case. Previous publication of the letter, if any, is also indicated.

The advantages of preparing a text directly from the original manuscript have always been apparent. In the case of the large collection of Haliburton-Bentley manuscript letters at the Houghton Library, Harvard University, first transcribed by W.H. Bond in 1947,[1] proper archival care of the manuscripts has rendered legible areas of the correspondence that were previously illegible because of mould. As a result, I am able to provide many readings that were unavailable to W.H. Bond.

The text of the manuscript letters has been minimally amended. Editorial emendations to the literal text are designed to reduce the visual confusion for the reader. Minimal emendation means, in this instance, that the letters of Haliburton reprinted in this edition differ from the originals in the following ways:

1 The place and date of writing is always positioned at the head of a letter. Haliburton often included such information at the end. Information not supplied by Haliburton is placed within square brackets [ ].

2 Superior letters wherever they occur are lowered to the line. Both M^r and M^r are rendered as 'Mr.' M^{rs} has been rendered as 'Mrs.'

3 Haliburton's punctuation in his manuscripts has been retained. No attempt has been made to remove the dashes from the ends of his sentences and to replace them by periods. Many strong defences of retaining the dash in nineteenth-century correspondence have been made by editors more eloquent than myself, and I direct the reader to them.[2] Haliburton's frequent omission of the dash at the end of the paragraph, and occasional lapses in the body of the letter itself have been silently amended. Haliburton's double quotation marks have been regularized.

4 Haliburton's spelling has not been corrected. Therefore idiosyncrasies in the MS letters will occur, and the reader will be neither consoled nor annoyed by the use of 'sic.' Haliburton's use of the ampersand (&) has also been retained.

5 The indentation of paragraphs has been standardized. A new paragraph not clearly indicated in the manuscript is rendered clearly in the text.

6 Inadvertent repetition of words has been silently amended. Words inadvertently omitted in the MS have been included in [ ].

7 I have ensured that his sentences open with capital letters and have regularized his capitalization within sentences. Haliburton's practice in his manuscripts is often inconsistent by modern standards. His 't,' 's,' 'm,' and 'c,' are larger in size than the surrounding letters. A line that looks as if it literally reads: 'I dine out Tomorrow So if you can Manage to Come early on Sunday etc' (letter 163) has been rendered 'I dine out tomorrow so if you can manage to come early on Sunday etc.'

8 Cancellations have not been recorded. Their presence in the printed text would add nothing significant to the content of the letters.

9 Letters and words not visible (for whatever reason), but that can be inferred, are included within square brackets [ ]. The addition of a question mark inside the square brackets [?] implies a doubtful reading. Words that cannot be deciphered are indicated by [?].

10 Three dots ... indicate a hiatus in the manuscript.

The notes to the letters concern only matters essential to understanding the letters themselves. The first occurrence of a name only is noted. Readers should then consult the index for the first reference. When I confess to being unable to identify a name, it is usually only after a long search. The letters themselves have been divided into chronological groups – prefaced by brief introductions – to represent convenient stages in Haliburton's life. Letters that I have been unable to date precisely are grouped under 'Letters of Uncertain Date.' Letters of joint authorship or concealed authorship have been grouped under 'Miscellaneous Additional Letters,' along with letter 240, which arrived too late for insertion in the main body of the text. It is the editor's hope that more Haliburton letters will come to light as a result of this edition, which is the result of a long and diligent search for extant correspondence.

1 W.H. Bond, 'The Correspondence of Thomas Chandler Haliburton and Richard Bentley,' *The Canadian Collection at Harvard University, Bulletin IV*, ed. W.I. Morse (Cambridge, Mass. 1947) 48–105
2 See *The Letters of John Ruskin to Lord and Lady Mount-Temple*, ed. John Lewis Bradley (Columbus, Ohio: Ohio State University Press 1964) x; *The Winnington Letters*, ed. Van Akin Burd (Cambridge, Mass.: Belknap Press of Harvard University Press 1969) 87; and *The Letters of Sara Hutchinson from 1800 to 1835*, ed. Kathleen Coburn (London: Routledge and Kegan Paul 1954) xii.

THE LETTERS OF THOMAS CHANDLER HALIBURTON

1
The Early Years, 1796–1829

Thomas Chandler Haliburton was born in Windsor, Nova Scotia. His mother, Lucy (c. 1774–97), died a few months after bringing him into the world, and he never knew her. Four years later his father, William Hersey Otis Haliburton, married Susanna Boutineau (Francklin) Davis, a widow. She was the daughter of the former lieutenant-governor of Nova Scotia, Michael Francklin. Haliburton's father, a lawyer, aided by his socially advantageous second marriage, entered politics and represented Hants County in the House of Assembly. In 1824, he was appointed one of the three newly created judges of the Inferior Court of Common Pleas for the Middle Division of the province.

The fortunes of the family were not always so secure. Haliburton's paternal grandfather, W.H. Haliburton, was a talented, restless man, whose early years in Nova Scotia (after 1761) were dogged by ill fortune. He survived bankruptcy in 1774 when a trading venture failed.[1] Later, he sought the security of the legal profession and was a judge of the Probate Court at Windsor, 'a local office of profit' (Thomas Chandler's words describing his own similar position at Annapolis Royal in 1824).

Thomas Chandler Haliburton was educated in Windsor, first at the Anglican Grammar School, then at King's College. Haliburton felt great nostalgia for King's later in his life even though the fortunes of the college declined as the century advanced. Luigi Mariotti, who wrote of his time at King's in 1842, maintained that most local people sent their children abroad to complete their education because of the college's inadequacies.[2]

Haliburton graduated with a BA in 1815, a year later than his exact contemporary Robert Parker (1796–1865), a fact explained perhaps by his departure for England in 1814 (mentioned in *The Attaché*), to stay with his stepmother's sister, Mrs Ann Piercy, who lived at Henley-on-Thames,

Oxfordshire. We do not know for certain how long he stayed. What we do know is that at Henley-on-Thames, in 1816, he married Louisa Neville,[3] the daughter of a paymaster in the Dragoon Guards, Captain Laurence Neville.[4]

Laurence Neville died at Henley-on-Thames in 1812. His will (written in February 1812) is the only source of information for the Neville family prior to the time of Haliburton's marriage to Louisa.[5] Captain Richard Piercy, husband of Haliburton's step-aunt, died in April 1815. After Richard Piercy's death, Louisa probably continued to live with Haliburton's step-aunt, because Ann Piercy was one of the three witnesses to the marriage of Thomas Chandler Haliburton and Louisa Neville, solemnized on 28 May 1816.

Haliburton returned to Nova Scotia with his bride in July 1816. On 24 September 1816, his application to be permitted to keep his terms for his master's degree at King's without residing in college was rejected, for he gave no reason.[6] His newly married state could well have been the explanation. The presumption must be that Thomas Chandler was studying law in the office of his father at Windsor at this time, although more evidence survives of Haliburton's entrepreneurial activities in this period than of his activity as a student of the law. Upon his return from England, he promptly bought, for a considerable sum, the Old Stone House in Avondale not far from Windsor and embarked on a venture to develop the potential of the surrounding land for gypsum mining, buying the right of way across his neighbour's land so that the gypsum could be removed, taken to the nearby wharf at Avondale, and loaded aboard ship.[7]

The adventure in gypsum did not pay. The ending of the Napoleonic Wars created a world-wide economic depression. Gypsum prices slumped, and Haliburton was not able to recoup the cost of his land, which he sold at a loss in 1834, along with the rights to mine gypsum that he had acquired in 1817 and 1818. In October 1819, he penned the first letter in this collection, an application to the lieutenant-governor to be granted the status of a notary.

In July 1821, Haliburton moved to Annapolis Royal, where he commenced what he later described as a lucrative law practice, and where his first literary ambitions were fulfilled. Annapolis Royal was the old capital of the province before the centre of government moved to Halifax in 1751. It was a small port nestling on both sides of the Annapolis River where the river flowed into the Annapolis Basin. The area, once of strategic importance to the warring British and French, was now a peaceful, forgotten place, linked by ferry to Saint John, New Brunswick, and the site of one of the oldest garrisons in British North America. The garrison dominated the town. Most of the houses were huddled near to it, and Haliburton's house was a stone's throw from the fort, near the water.

The glories of Annapolis were of the past, and Haliburton found it a quiet place compared to Windsor: 'want of society here has driven me to seek for sources of amusement at home,' he wrote of these years. In the course of Haliburton's daily business as a lawyer at Annapolis he soon established a working relationship with George K. Nichols. Several hasty business notes and a few letters to Nichols have survived. In contrast to these brief notes to Nichols are Haliburton's long letters to Judge Peleg Wiswall (1763–1836), his neighbour at Digby. Haliburton sought the advice of the older man because the two shared an interest in the history and present state of the province. The old judge became Haliburton's confidant during the years when the two-volume *Historical ... Account* (1829) grew out of the *General Description* (1823).

Peleg Wiswall was the son of John Wiswall (1731–1836), an Anglican clergyman at Annapolis Royal. Peleg was born in Falmouth, Maine, but was brought up in Nova Scotia. Wiswall represented Digby township in the Legislature from 1812 to 1816, then became an associate circuit judge of the Supreme Court. He was a man with considerable knowledge of the history and politics of Nova Scotia.

Haliburton sent Wiswall chapters of the *Historical ... Account* for comment as they were finished and was relieved whenever he received Wiswall's nod of approval. As the task of compiling the book grew – and the yearning for credit with it – Haliburton's debts to Wiswall increased. Wiswall even started to pen portions of the *Historical ... Account* for Haliburton when pressure of legal work and a new post as a judge of the Probate Court for Annapolis consumed more and more of the younger man's time.[8]

In 1826, Haliburton was elected to represent Annapolis County in the House of Assembly. He owed his election to the Abbé Jean-Mandé Sigogne (1763–1844), parish priest at Clare, Annapolis County: 'as a stranger I was favored with the unanimous support of all your people, in a manner so cordial and so friendly that I shall ever retain a most grateful remembrance of it.' Haliburton's political impact was considerable. Wiswall defended him in the *Novascotian*: 'The influence of the young Member – very few men, in two Sessions, have ever acquired so much ... Profound research – logical acuteness – classic fare – impassioned eloquence – habitual good humour – and a fearless, independent bearing, are so rarely united, that they ought, I think, to excuse a few errors in judgment.'[9] Haliburton's name is also linked, at this time, to 'The Club,' a society of bon vivants and political pundits, first announced in the *Novascotian*, 13 March 1828. The papers of 'The Club' appeared weekly during each political season for the next three years, and Haliburton's early involvement in its activities meant less time to complete the *Historical ... Account*. Lacking the details of New Brunswick and Cape Breton needed to conclude the volume as he originally intended it, he enlisted the support of others, editing their contributions. He was still seeking help in October 1828. Not until 1829, at the close of Haliburton's legislative career, was the *Historical ... Account* finally finished and published. The crowning achievement of nearly a decade's work on the *Historical ... Account* was somewhat dimmed by the death of his father in July 1829. The two events, the death of his father followed by the publication of the *Historical ... Account*, altered the course of his life.

1 Hants County Registry of Deeds, Windsor, Book 3, 298, 21 January 1774
2 Antonio Carlo Napoleone Gallenga [pseud. L. Mariotti], *Episodes of My Second Life*, 2 vols (London 1884) 2: 114–35
3 Parish register transcripts, Henley-on-Thames, 1813–23, MS Oxf. Diosc. Papers d. 303, no. 62 (Bodleian Library, Oxford)
4 He served as 'adjutant' and 'riding master' in the Nineteenth Light Dragoons, mostly on foreign service, for twenty-five years, before ending his military career as a paymaster. PRO records at Kew Gardens, London, indicate that Neville resigned on 22 November 1809 and was succeeded as paymaster by his son, William Frederick (WO 12, Paymaster's Records).
5 PRO (Chancery Lane), PROB 11/Aug. 390
6 *King's College Board Minutes, 1787–1814*, I: 14 September 1816
7 See Shand, 95–7
8 Haliburton was appointed in December 1823.
9 1 May 1828: 140, 'Digby's' reply to 'Amicus' on the subject of the 'Pictou Academy'

---

1 To George, Earl of Dalhousie[1]   Halifax
24th Octr [18]19

To

His Excellency Lieutenant General the Right Honorable George Earl of Dalhousie Lieutenant Governor and Commander in Chief in and over His Majestys province of Nova Scotia and its dependencies &c &c. &c. &c.

The Petition of Thomas C Haliburton humbly sheweth that your petitioner is one of the barristers and attornies of His Majestys Supreme Court of and for this province, and that being desirous of practising as a

1796–1829

Notary & Tabellion Public[2] at Windsor in the county of Hants, your petitioner humbly prays that your Lordship will be pleased to grant him a commission for that purpose and as in duty &c.

Thos C Haliburton

PANS MS

1 George Ramsey, Earl of Dalhousie (1770–1838), ninth lieutenant-governor of Nova Scotia, 1816–19. The letter is docketed, 'I beg leave to recommend/the petitioner for the Office he seeks/S.S. Blowers.' Sampson Salter Blowers (1742–1842) was chief justice of Nova Scotia from 1797 to 1833.
2 A subordinate notary

---

2 To G.K. Nichols

Windsor
22 July 1820

My dear sir

You were kind enough to say to me when at Annapolis, that you would give me some information as to the value of some lands to which I am entitled in Digby – and the present condition of them – By referring to the papers I find that half of No 78 letter O St Marys Bay is mine – Moody owns the other half – the whole including Moodys contains 200 acres – No 31 letter N in the Digby Neck[1] consists of 500 acres an undivided half of which belongs to me – of the situation value, and other articles, such as timber, coves, &c I will thank you to inform me of and whether it would be most to my advantage to sell, settle or keep it as it is – I hope you will excuse the liberty I have taken, in imposing so much trouble upon you, and that you will at all times command the services of your

Most obt sert
Thos C Haliburton

PANS MS

1 Digby Neck is a distinctive thirty-mile peninsula of land parallel to Nova Scotia's northwest shore. Between the neck and the mainland is St Mary's Bay. Haliburton inherited the land on Digby Neck from his mother's family. See Deveau, 61 and 64. The half lot, no. 78, was at Dunbar Lake. The Moody referred to here was John Moody, son of Colonel James Moody, the original grantee. Lot no. 31 was located at Tiddville. Haliburton sold the land on 21 April 1831 (Bridgetown Record Office, Book 29: 124).

3 To G.K. Nichols

[Annapolis Royal]
2 Jany. 1822.

My dear sir

Coming away sooner than I expected I forgot to return your silver pencil case & knife which I will send by some safe conveyance at my return. I wrote to Mr. Ritchie[1] stateing to him that the language he had made use of was of a nature impossible to be passed over, and that I required him to retract his words as fully and as amply as he had made them. He answers that he has *no recollection* of having made *use of* the expressions, but that if he had it was unintentional and he was sorry to have occasioned me any uneasiness on that account.

> Adieux,
> Yrs.
> Thos. C. Haliburton

Please to present for me the compliments of this season to Mrs. Nichols.[2]

Pub.: Chittick, 47

1 Hon. Thomas Ritchie (1777–1852), lawyer, judge, and MLA for Annapolis County, 1806–24
2 Nichols married a 'daughter of Elisha Budd' (Calnek, 557).

4 To Asa Porter[1]

Annapolis [Royal], 11th Jany. 1822.

Sir –

I understand that you have not sent home Spechts wife and children, under the pretence that you wont turn them out of your house – Now sir unless you immediately sease to harbour them I will give yourself and your wife a trip to Halifax for your amusement under a writ of Habeas Corpus.

> Thos. C. Haliburton.

Fort Anne MS *Pub.*: Chittick, 48

1 Asa Porter and Anthony Specht were grantees of adjacent lots (nos 48 and 49), each of two hundred acres, at Plympton on St Mary's Bay (Deveau, 61). Haliburton refers here to their descendants, Asa Porter, Jr, and William Specht. Specht's wife and children were Asa Porter's daughter and grandchildren.

5 To Peleg Wiswall

[Annapolis Royal]
Friday evening [1823]

Dear sir –

I received a letter from my father by the last post, in which he wished me to communicate with you on the subject of the appointment of a judge at Cape Breton[1] – He would wish to retire from the fatigues of the profession, but is so situated that a removal from Windsor, owing to the state of his private business, is impracticable, he is therefore anxious to know (if not an impertinent quere) whether you are inclined to accept of the appointment – Or whether if he were to seek it, any arrangement could take place between you and him as to an exchange –

He would have written to you on the subject himself, but the idea did not occur to him until it was too late to write by the last post –

Will you therefore be so good as to write me a few lines by return of post on Monday that I may communicate with him – He desires me also to request the favor of you to consider the affair as a confidential one –

> I am dr sir
> Your most obt
> Tho C Haliburton

PANS MS

1 Financial provisions for the position of judge of the Inferior Court of Common Pleas for Cape Breton Island were debated by the House of Assembly on 12 March 1823. When a motion was placed before the House naming a stipend of £500, Haliburton's father suggested it be reduced to £100.

6 To G.K. Nichols

[Annapolis Royal]
24th March 1823

My dear Nichols –

I received your note respecting Gavasa[1] & before I could answer it finding that you had sent up a [?], thought it not worth while to [p]ut you to the expence of postage –

Geo Winniett,[2] has been long time on a *party of pleasure* at Halifax and as it is the fashion for business to be postponed to pleasure, you must not be surprised at your affair not being attended to with Saunders[3] – But I have now directed to sell the property he has taken – He goes up tomorrow –

Do for the love of God – tell Morton[4] to close that execution – The sheriffs will ruin my business – I will be damned if I can get anything done –

Tell Morton to bring White[5] up to Capn. Roaches[6] –

Will Wiswall accept the 500 per annum at Cape Britain?[7]

                             Yours
                             Tho. C. Haliburton –

Private Collection MS

1 Antonio Gavaza (1774–1848) was a property owner and businessman at Annapolis Royal.
2 George Gilbert Totten Winniett (b. 1801, d. unm.), sixth child of William Winniett (1765–1824), sheriff of Annapolis County
3 Possibly John Saunders (1755–1842)
4 Elkanah Morton (1761–1848) was a judge of the Inferior Court of Common Pleas, as well as a judge of the Probate Court at Digby.
5 Possibly Thomas White, collector of customs at Weymouth (Calnek, 410)
6 William H. Roach (1784–1861), MLA for Digby Township, 1818–26, and Annapolis County, 1826–36
7 Haliburton obviously means 'Cape Breton.'

---

7 To G.K. Nichols   Annapolis [Royal] May 2nd 1823

My dear Nichols

I did not preserve the mem [or?] money you paid me – Please send it – Also *100* grape vines by next packet – dont forget – as I have promised these to my friends at Halifax – I will chearfully pay the black-man what is proper –

                             Yours
                             Th C Haliburton

Fort Anne MS

8 To G.K. Nichols

Annapolis [Royal]
12th July 1823

My dear Nichols –

I have just arrived from Halifax where I spoke to the Atty Gen the Chief Justice & Stewart[1] upon the subject of the Sisisboo[2] registry office – It seems nothing can be done without petition to the Council & the impression seems to be as far as I could gather their opinions, that if the Sisisboo office is not convenient it is better to do it away & have only *one* in the county say at Annapolis – there is great aversion manifested to the extension or alteration of this department – I should, as you wished have addressed Sir James[3] on the subject but the Chief Justice said it was unavailing, without petitions in Council –

Will you be so good as to drive your sheriff on with [Bu?]ckcupps vs. Dr. White – Do drive him on if you please – I will see Winniett to day about yours or Saunders[4] –

I have heard that Judge Wiswall has written a statistical account of this province, which he has in manuscript, knowing, how fully able he is to accomplish such a work, & how original and apt his remarks are upon all subjects, I have a great desire & curiosity to see this one of his – I will take it as a most particular favor if you will procure me a sight of it by next post, send it by the mail I will gladly pay the postage & return it safe as soon as perused – I shall look out anxiously for the next post to bring it to me so pray do not disappoint me in this particular –

There is nothing new in town, the blades of the army drive 4 horses a breast & six in hand, with a boy on a seventh horse, holding a leathern thong which is fastend to the front pair –

This has given occasion to the wise-acres to say that our most noble legislature frame laws thro which *a coach & six may be driven* alluding to the late Tandem Law[5] –

       Yours truly
       Tho C Haliburton

I shall look into Tristram Shandy[6] for his oath of three pages & a half to damn you with if you forget the judges manuscript by next post, or sooner if you get a safe conveyance –

Private Collection MS

1 Richard John Uniacke (1753–1830) was attorney-general of Nova Scotia; S.S. Blowers was chief justice, and James Stewart (1765–1830) was MLA for Halifax County, 1798–1800 and an assistant judge of the Supreme Court of NS, 1815–30.
2 Sissiboo is the old Indian name for the Weymouth area.
3 Sir James Kempt (1765–1855) lieutenant-governor of Nova Scotia, 1820–8
4 These legal cases are unidentified.
5 In 1823, the House of Assembly passed 'An act to prevent disorderly riding, and to regulate the driving of carriages on the streets of Halifax or other towns, or on the public roads of this province, and for repealing certain acts therein mentioned.' *Revised Statutes of Nova-Scotia* (Halifax: Richard Nugent 1851) 507
6 'The Curse of Ernulphus,' in Laurence Sterne's *Tristram Shandy,* ed. M. New and J. New, 2 vols (Gainesville: University of Florida Press 1978) 1: 203–12

---

9 To Peleg Wiswall   Annapolis [Royal] 31st. Decr. 1823

Dear sir –

I send you the correspondence upon the subject of the Sheriffs security, marked according to the respective dates of the letters No 1,, 2,, 3,, – You will observe that it was not my intention to institute a regular series of charges against Mr Winnutt,[1] but merely to shew grounds why good security should be filed – The Governor thought that my letter contained such assertions as Mr Winnutt ought in justice to be made acquainted with – In this way it has confined me to *those assertions* whereas had I intended to make a regular accusation it would have borne a very different appearance – I think I have fully substantiated all I have advanced but am well prepared to hear 'that I have been actuated by motives of personal hostility, and have made cruel charges which I have been unable to prove' –

I gladly turn from this topic to something of a more agreeable nature – When I was last in Digby you were so good as to say you would correspond with me on subjects of general interest to the province – Such an intimation was the more acceptable to me as I intended to have solicited the favor – Want of society here has driven me to seek for sources of amusement at home and it occurred to me that I might find some employment for leisure hours in compiling a History of Nova Scotia – When I was in Halifax last winter I communicated my intention to Bromley[2] from whom I wanted to ascertain the number of Indians in the province, and told him I had traced an outline of such a work which I should complete as time & materials might enable me –

He informed me that he had an unemployed press and solicited me to throw some of my materials into the shape of an emigrants guide[3] and offered to remunerate himself for his labours by the sales – I enclose one of the books of which I beg your acceptance – The hasty manner in which this sudden & inconsiderate alteration of my plan was executed, unavoidably permitted many errors to escape detection until it was too late to think of their correction – I have however steadily advanced with my original undertaking and have got into a state of considerable forwardness – I shall retain the division observed in the pamphlet, but the matter will be differently arranged & remoulded, – There are two chapters which I find it difficult to complete as I could wish – the 6th, and 11th, and shall be extremely obliged to you for your observations upon them – Your topographical knowledge of the province will enable you to furnish much useful & statistical information upon the different townships for chapr. 6th.[4] and I know you are intimately acquainted with the politicks of the period treated of in the eleventh[5] – Upon these parts, & such other as you feel inclined to add to, I shall receive your remarks and contributions as a very *particular personal favor* –

The pamphlet you will perceive I have not publickly acknowledged as belonging to myself, for I knew its defects to be numerous, and although I feel that I can execute the work I have in hand in a much better manner, yet I am sensible I have undertaken a task which is above my abilities, and had it not grown to so large a size I should be tempted to relinquish the undertaking – I hope to finish it [in] the course of a year or 18 months[6] –

I suppose you will be of the same opinion with my father, that I might be much better employed at my profession, I think so too, and when I once extricate myself from this scrape my highest flight shall never exceed a [decon?] or plea –

With best respects to Mrs & Miss Wiswall I remain yours very truly

Th C Haliburton

If you come across Belknapp biography[7] I shall feel much oblige[d] to you for the loan of it – When you retur[n Winn]utts papers, please to enclose them to Goldsmith[h[8] –]

PANS MS *Pub.: Report of the P.A.N.S.* (1946), Appendix C, 36–7 (excluding first paragraph)

1 William Winniett (1765–1824), sheriff of Annapolis County and registrar of deeds. In October 1823, he was the subject of two petitions to Sir James Kempt, the lieutenant-governor, as a result of debts he had collected but failed to remit.

14						The Early Years

2 Walter Bromley (1775– ?), teacher, humanitarian, and printer, who arrived in Nova Scotia in 1813 to promote the British and Foreign School Society. For a full account of Bromley's career see Judith Fingard, 'English Humanitarianism and the Colonial Mind: Walter Bromley in Nova Scotia, 1813–25,' *Canadian Historical Review* 54 (1973): 123–51.
3 *A General Description of Nova Scotia, Illustrated by a New and Correct Map* (Halifax: Printed at the Royal Acadian School 1823)
4 Chapter VI of the *General Description* considers 'Chief Towns and Rivers.'
5 Chapter XI of the *General Description* offers 'A Brief Sketch of the State of the Province during the Administration of Sir George Prevost, Sir John Sherbrooke, the Earl of Dalhousie, and Sir James Kempt.'
6 The writing took longer than anticipated. The book was eventually published by subscription in August 1829.
7 Jeremy Belknap (1744–98), *American Biography*, 2 vols (Boston 1794–8)
8 Henry Goldsmith (1786–1845), barrister-at-law and collector of customs at Annapolis

---

10 To Peleg Wiswall   Annapolis-Royal 7th. January 1824

Dear sir

I received your obligeing letter by the last post, for which I beg you to accept my best thanks – By the Halifax mail I received no reply to my last communication to the Governor who seems disposed to act in the manner prescribed by Lord Bacon although your researches have supplied with a higher and better authority to support his measures than he is himself aware of – As he has however commenced with all due regard to Lord Bacons advice I hope he will pursue it, 'and voluntarily take some future occasion to redress this grievance'[1] –

I fully agree with you that there is in fact no history of Nova Scotia to relate, and that the few military events which might have happened here have as little bearing on the true history of the country as the Battle of Trafalga[r][2] of which it can only be said that it was fought in a particular latitude & longitude and of which the sole remaining trace is a point on the general chart of the world – These occurrences resemble duels, for which the parties for political purposes sought our wilderness as the most convenient place of rendevouz – When I therefore called the work I had in hand the history of the country I did not mean to apply it in its usual acceptation as a narrative of political events, but in a more enlarged sense as an account of whatever of interest might be found in the colony – Indeed it is not the name of it which is 'An Historical Geographical & Statistical Account of Nova Scotia' – The division of the work I intended to make the same as the pamphlet – Devoting the first chapter of 50 or 60 pages to an historical narrative – a connected but suxcinct view of the discovery settlement & transfers of the country until the peace of Paris in 1763 at which period the French yielded all their territorial possessions in North America to Great Britain[3] – After that period the 'short & simple annals of the poor'[4] afoard no materials for a continuation, and a history of the province subsequent to that epoch would be about as interesting as one of Dalhousie Settlement[5] – Having in the first chapter traced our tittle to the province, I would then attempt a geographical sketch[6] and then proceed to statisticks – It is upon the last I shall bestow the most labour as by far the most important part. Our climate population trade towns & rivers government institutions agriculture natural resources & political advantages are really subjects worthy of consideration & I hope an account of them if drawn up with tolerable care & accuracy will meet with a favorable reception from the public.[7]

The last chapter will be a completion of the outline of the 11th, in the pamphlet and is intended to answer a double purpose – First it shews the manner in which our little colonial machine is put into motion, the objects that attract the attention of its government, the mode of conducting public business and the gradual and progressive improvement of the colony – Secondly it shews the actual state of the country its revenue & the purposes to which it is applied together with the customs feelings & habits of the people and admits room for the introduction of such general remarks and observations as may not so properly be given under any of the preceding chapters – Your suggestion of publishing the work in numbers is one which I ought to have adopted in the first instance – It is possessed of many advantages – As you observe, the errors would not then have been beyond recall or correction, and if the performance attracted criticism much advantage might have been derived even from its enemies – It is also not improbable I might have received contributions of valuable matter from those who know the difficulty of the task & the value of it if properly executed – these and many other reasons which might be urged shew at once the advantage & necessity of that way of appearing before the public – But it is now I fear too late to make a second experiment upon our community which is far from being a reading society, and particularly as the new will embrace most of the old work – Whoever is known in this province as the author of any publication must consider that he has voluntarily brought himself to the stake to be baited by the empty barking of some and the stings & bites of others – If he is not known & his work attains to mediocrity it will not be censured for fear that it should be the work of some *established* character, nor praised for fear that applause should fall upon *an unknown*, whom the generality of wits if they have not considered as their inferior are at all events not disposed to place higher than on an exact level with themselves – The price of printing, too, at Halifax is beyond all reason & failure would be ruin – My intention was to go on progressively but steadily till I had finished the entire work, when I should send a correct copy to my friend Francklin[8] in London and desire him to sell it to a bookseller for the best price he could obtain if he could not sell it to give it to the printer if he would publish it at his own cost, & if he could not dispose of it to light his pipe with it – For I am not one who would rebel at the decision of the booksellers & say 'Sdeath Ill print it & shame the fools' – I think their judgement infallible – They have administered so long to the literary appetite of the public that they understand as it were by instinct what will be palatable and what will be removed from the table untoutched – Everything however which has America for its subject, (how dull or absurd soever it may be) is read in England with avidity, and I am not altogether without hopes of being able to dispose of my labours in some way or other –

Upon the subject of emigration I agree purfectly with you that we are ourselves too poor to maintain or receive the paupers of other countries and that low Irish – disbanded soldiers – hungry adventurers, & Chesapeac blacks[9] are not the class of emigrants we want, and that so far from courting their approach to our shores we have already many who could well be spared from among us – But I conceive that a limited emigration of mechanicks & practical farmers possessing a property of from 500 to 1500 pounds each would be of infinite service to us – Such is the feeling of the *mob* of all countries, that if we wanted emigrants, the proper method to obtain them would be instead of courting them & holding out alluring prospects, to circulate thorough Great Britain printed copies of a law forbidding any access of strangers as settlers to our shores – I am of opinion that such a law (not enforced) would soon people our wilderness with inhabitants –

There is an event (if a politician I could calculate its approach with as much exactness as an astronomer fixes the period of an eclipse) which we all know must happen – I mean the conquest or purchase of all these colonies by the United States (I am only expressing thoughts not wishes) – Till then no great change will take place in Nova Scotia, however much people may flatter themselves – But the day of our transfer marks the moment of our manhood – We shall then become an integral part of a large nation, and start in life with an immense estate entailed by nature on our posterity I question whether our 'iron, lead manganese, ochre, lime, grindstone sulphur slate coal plaister & freestone, our healthy climate, capacious & numerous harbours, situation amid the fisheries &c. &c.' – will not then render us the most populous part of America – *We have every thing America wants, & we want all it raises* – Till that period all these resources must inevitably lie idle –

But the limits of my paper warn me that I am trespassing too far upon your indulgence – I shall as you request consider both our correspondence, and the purport of it strictly confidential – Indeed you are almost the only person, Goldsmith excepted, who knows who the author of that work is, or that I am still employed on the same subject – For the 6th. & 11th chapters I shall be most particularly obliged to you for your contributions, and for such other parts as you think proper, and shall deem myself most happy on being favoured with your confidence & counsel – If not asking too great a favor I should be glad to submit the draft of the several chapters as they become finished, for your perusal & correction previous to their being finally engrossed –

With many thanks for your goodness & condescension I am dear sir

Yours truly
Tho C Haliburton

I rather think you will find that you took the mem of sale with you for I do not see it among my papers –

PANS MS *Pub.: Report of the P.A.N.S.* (1946), Appendix C, 37–41; Chittick, 52, 61–2, 126–9

1 The quotation marks suggest that Haliburton is quoting from Sir James's letter to him.
2 The manuscript reads 'Trafalgal.'
3 The account comprises the first 242 pages (five chapters) of the *Historical ... Account*, vol. 1, from which point it proceeds as a 'Chronological Table of Events.'
4 Thomas Gray, *Elegy Written in a Country Churchyard* (1751), line 33: 'The short and simple annals of the poor'
5 On 12 July 1817, a number of disbanded soldiers began cultivation of an area known as Dalhousie Settlement, inland from Annapolis (Calnek, 260).
6 The 'Geographical Sketch' opens vol. 2 of the *Historical ... Account.*
7 Joseph Howe, the publisher of the *Historical ... Account,* puffed it in the columns of his newspaper, the *Novascotian,* quoting favourable reviews that appeared in the *American Traveller* and *North American Review* (6 January 1830 and 20 January 1830).

8 His step-uncle, Michael Nickelson Franklin (1773–1849), who at this time lived in London
9 Wiswall discussed his ideas on immigration with S.G.W. Archibald in a letter dated 14 March 1818. See D.C. Harvey, 'A Blueprint for Nova Scotia in 1818,' *CHR* 24 (1943): 397–409.

11 To Peleg Wiswall [Annapolis Royal]
[late January / early February 1824?]

... I received your communications by last post, and have to return you my best thanks for the very friendly manner in which you have interested yourself in my undertaking – I am now under weigh for Halifax and on my return will answer you fully – If I can be of any service to you at Halifax a line by return of post addressed to me at Mrs Duffis[1] will reach me & I shall take great pleasure in executing any commission for Mrs W. or yourself – We have no news here – I received a line from town which states that Archibald[2] goes to England ... spoken of that the Governor[3] will recommend to the House the erection of three C. Pleas Circuits & the appointment of as many judges to preside in those districts[4] –

> I am yours in haste
> Very truly
> Th. C. Haliburton

PANS MS; fragment only

1 Susannah Murdoch (1772–1858), wife of William Duffis (1762–1845). Her daughter married Samuel Cunard.
2 S.G.W. Archibald (1777–1846), lawyer, master of the rolls and a judge in the Vice-Admiralty Court. He was MLA for Halifax County, 1806–35, and for Colchester County, 1836–44. He held the posts of Speaker of the House of Assembly, 1825–40; chief justice of Prince Edward Island, 1824–8; solicitor-general of Nova Scotia, 1826–31; and attorney-general, 1831–41.
3 Sir James Kempt
4 The bill authorizing these changes in the judicial system became law on 6 March 1824.

12 To Peleg Wiswall Annapolis [Royal] *19th. Feby 1824*

Dear sir –

Mr Goldsmith & myself were so fortunate as to return at the moment the man was leaving us last week, after a long & tedious journey in which he lost his valuable mare at Windsor –

I received your letter at Halifax and made enquiries for the news-paper you wished – A regular file is not to be obtained there but I left orders for it to be sent for with a regular continuance –

The House has not been doing much, as the court interfered with it,[1] to use Mr. Archibalds phrase many of the members were playing between hawk and *buzzard*, I presume he applied the latter appelation to the *House of Assembly* – Mr. Blair[2] introduced certain resolutions relative to the appointment of Circuit Judges for C Pleas – The advocates for the measure felt so strong that they did not think it necessary to apply to the Governor for his recommendation, but when they came to discuss the subject, they found several, who had always spoken in favour of it, voting against it, the consideration of it therefore was postponed to Monday week past[3] – Among the rest was Mr Ritchie,[4] who opened the subject with many eulogiums on its benefit & remarks on the necessity that existed for the alteration, but to the surprise of all ended by saying as the country was not ripe for it he would vote against it – The friends to the bill count on a majority, but the House appeared to me so nearly balanced that I think it very doubtful whether it will pass, this post will probably bring the result – I had a very satisfactory conversation with Sir James on the subject of the correspondence I transmitted for your perusal, who promises redress at the next appointment[5] – I was very much alarmed at the appearance of my father, whom I found greatly altered, in addition to a bad cold, he had a severe fall on the ice, which rendered it necessary for him to be bled – The lassitude consequent on the loss of blood has affected his spirits, and he looks more depressed & weaker than I ever saw him –

Mr. Archibald talks of going to England still & will if possible leave Halifax in April,[6] the Governor hopes to be in London by the birth-day[7] –

When you are at leisure I shall be proud to hear from you on the subject of the History of Nova Scotia – In the Friday paper of the 9th. January last there appeared some remarks upon it[8] – I have endeavoured to discover the author who is either Dr Cochran[9] or Mr Uniacke[10] I think – Mr Minns[11] promised to communicate with him on the subject & ascertain whether he would give his name – Whoever he is he appears to have given the subject considrable attention and could no doubt afoard me assistance – I have the 2d. chapter of the historical part all drafted – Tis from the year 1748 to 62 as also the 3d.[12] – The first is attended with much difficulty, the authorities are obscure & contradictory in several places, and require to be collated with great care, before I begin to compile –

I will send you the 2d chapter, and shall feel much obliged by your opinion as to the mode of compilation adopted in it – It will of course undergo much alteration & *finish* before it is finally engrossed – I have considered with great attention the alteration in the plan proposed i.e. to publish it in numbers, but am afraid to venture on it, for reasons of a private nature which I will detail to you when we meet, and which I think will appear to you insurmountable – I cannot sufficiently express my obligation to you for your assistance and beg to be favoured with a continuance of it, whenever you find it convenient or agreeable – With best respects to Mrs Wiswall I remain

>Your obt servt
>Tho C Haliburton

PANS MS *Pub.*: *Report of the P.A.N.S.* (1946), Appendix C, 41–2, paragraph five only

1 I have been unable to discover the background to this remark.
2 Richard Blair (*c.* 1782–1861), a judge of the Inferior Court of Common Pleas, and MLA for Cumberland County, 1821–5. A public dinner was given in his honour on 4 May 1825, when he departed for England.
3 There were several attempts to postpone the bill, which was passed by a vote of eighteen to seventeen in a Committee of the Whole on 4 March.
4 Thomas Ritchie was one of the beneficiaries of the bill, along with Jared Chipman and W.H.O. Haliburton.
5 Haliburton was appointed a judge of the Probate Court at Annapolis on 13 December 1824.
6 Mr Archibald spent the summer months in England, returning in November, having been appointed chief justice of Prince Edward Island in August.
7 According to Haliburton's *Historical ... Account*, Kempt visited England on 19 May.
8 In *The Weekly Chronicle*, Friday, 9 January 1824, a letter to the editor, by 'CANDIDUS,' reviews *A General Description of Nova Scotia*.
9 Dr William Cochran (1757–1833), native of Omagh, County Tyrone, Ireland, educated at Trinity College, Dublin. He was a missionary for the Church of England in Nova Scotia for forty years, and for the same period a professor of languages and moral science, as well as vice-president, King's College, Windsor. He had prepared materials for a history but died before it came to fruition (Calnek, 422). Two MS volumes of his history survive at PANS.
10 'James Uniacke's' name appears in the list of acknowledgments in the preface to the *Historical ... Account* (vii), i.e., James Boyle Uniacke (1800–58), who became commissioner of Crown lands, a member of the Executive Council, and attorney-general of Nova Scotia.
11 William Minns (*c.* 1762–1827), printer of Halifax, proprietor of the *Weekly Chronicle*. His publishing house was at the intersection of Barrington and Duke streets, opposite the south-east corner of Dalhousie College.

12 Haliburton's work went through tremendous revisions before it was ready for the press. He divided this period, from 1748 to 1763, into two parts, but it was no longer his second chapter. Chapter 2 in the *Historical ... Account* (1829) covers the period, from 1623 to 1713; Chapter 3, from 1713 to 1748; Chapter 4, from 1748 to 1755; and Chapter 5, from 1755 to 1763. His third chapter, in his original scheme, was probably the period covered by Chapter 6, from 1763 to 1828.

---

13 To G.K. Nichols [Annapolis Royal]
[1824][1]

If [Winnutt?][2] serves writ – rather a new note for debt & costs for one of your pleas, in Bogarts[3] cause

Yours in haste
Th C Haliburton

PANS MS

1 The letter is docketed '1824.'
2 William Winniett
3 The Bogarts were a family of Dutch extraction who settled in Lower Granville (Calnek, 482–3). I have been unable to trace the cause Haliburton is alluding to here.

---

14 To Peleg Wiswall [Annapolis Royal]
1 Dcr. 1824

Dear sir –

I received your favor by post, and I assure you it has given me very great pleasure to find that the manuscript has met your approbation – I had fagged and worried over it so much (for it is impossible to convey an idea of the labour it has cost me, in searching, translating, selecting, and composing it, more indeed than would be *sufficient to acquire any one modern language*) that I had wearied of every subject in it & feared it would prove a task even to read it – It has therefore relieved me of great anxiety to find you think, I have not altogether failed in the attempt –

I am much indebted to you for the hint of continuing it as a summary, which I shall adopt – I have in the old-work a chapter entitled 'Sketch of the Administration of Sir Geo Prevost – Sherbroke – Dalhousie & Kempt'[1] –

I will in pursuance of your suggestion take all the narrative part of it, which begins in 1807, and, with some alterations make it form a part of the summary from – 63 to – 24[2] – If I can get access to the Council Books[3] I can easily do it, and perhaps if you would, be kind enough to give me a letter, this winter when at Digby, to Judge Stewart he would obtain me a sight of them – I think their perusal indispensable to this part of the work –

Your directions about the map, are also noted, and will be strictly followed – I feel pleased you have mentioned it to me so soon, for I have in my possession *Judge Chipmans*[4] map, published expressly for him by government to guide him as commissioner in settling the lines,[5] embracing the territory from Labrador to Chesapeake, with old, & new names of places – With a little alteration of interior part of Nova Scotia (for it includes Cape Breton) it will just answer the purpose – I should have returned it if you had not mentioned it – I will now set a surveyor, I know at Windsor (Anson)[6] who is a beautiful draftsman, and was actually employed by commissioners, to copy this map – I forget whether I mentioned to you that I intended to enlarge the plan of the work – I shall give it the following title page

An
Historical Geographical & Statistical
Account
of
Nova Scotia
to which is added A General Description
of
New Brunswick &
Cape Breton –
Illustrated by a map and several engravings[7]

One additional chapter for New Brunswick and another for Cape Breton will be sufficient, I think I can procure materials, from my friends, which with a good deal which I am in possession of, will be sufficient to complete the work – Its tittle therefore professing to treat of so great a portion of the British Dominions here (all indeed except Canada) will attract perhaps some attention to the book from an English public – It will doubtless render the whole more perfect and acceptable – I am intimately acquainted with the Scotch clergyman at St. Andrews,[8] who will gladly give me the particulars of that place & vicinity – Robert Parker[9] of St. John – and perhaps Judge Marshall[10] will help me to particulars of his island –

You are now, dear sir, in possession of all my plans the particular division of my subject into chapters, and of the manner in which I propose executing it – I will now tell you where I am deficient of materials 1st – from 1763 to 1824 – 2y – Chief town, rivers, &c. of Nova Scotia particularly eastern parts – 3y – New Brunswick & Cape Breton 4y – For account of particular trade & several kind of fishing, mode of catch, expence of outfit, returns &c[11] –

In these four departments I am at a loss, and have got to learn before I can instruct – In all the other parts of the work I have a great mass of matter collected, & partly arranged –

I feel like the man who walked by land to the East Indies (Capn. Campbell),[12] got half way, and find the other half appearing a great deal longer, than the whole did at first – It is too much for one person, who has any other business to do, and who has no public library in reach –

When you were here, you were kind enough to say you would help me in the statistics of the eastern part of the province – In this particular I must trust to your kindness not to forget me, and any hints, additions advice, on parts of the work, you find leisure and inclination to furnish me with will confer an everlasting obligation on me, for I feel great ambition to have this book do justice to our country, and some little credit to myself –

>I am dear sir
>Yours very truly
>Th C Haliburton

PANS MS *Pub.*: *Report of the P.A.N.S.* (1946), Appendix C, 42–4; Chittick, 62, 129–31

1 Chapter XI of the *General Description* (1823)
2 He did not use the narrative portion of Chapter XI of the *General Description* for his chronological summary in the *Historical ... Account* despite his promise to do so here.
3 The council was established at Annapolis Royal in 1719, to manage the civic affairs of the province. It was reconstituted in Halifax in 1748. Haliburton consulted the records in the provincial secretary's office at Halifax.
4 Ward Chipman, Jr (1787–1851), solicitor-general of New Brunswick, 1823; chief justice, 1834–50. Judge Chipman and his father, Ward Chipman, Sr, were agents for New Brunswick in the boundary dispute with the United States. See *Collections of the New Brunswick Historical Society*, no. 20 (Saint John, NB 1971) 30–4.
5 The mandate of the commissioners (one from each side) was to determine 'The Northwest angle of Nova Scotia and the north-western-most head of the Connecticut River' (according to the fifth article of the Treaty of Utrecht).

6 H.J.W. Anson is listed as one of those who received expenses for survey work carried out for the boundary commissioners: see a receipt dated 'N. York 31 Aug 1820' at PAC, MG 23, D 1, Series 1, vol. 60, 431.
7 The actual title page reads: *An Historical and Statistical Account of Nova-Scotia, in Two Volumes. Illustrated by a Map of the Province, and Several Engravings.* Haliburton dropped his plan to include New Brunswick.
8 Rev. John Cassilis, Presbyterian minister and schoolteacher at St Andrews, NB, 1818–38
9 Robert Parker (1796–1865), Haliburton's school friend at King's College, Windsor
10 John George Marshall (1787–1880), chief justice of the Inferior Court of Common Pleas for Cape Breton, 1824–41. Marshall published prolifically on Nova Scotian subjects and later in his life lectured extensively on temperance subjects. His publications include *Industries and Resources of Nova Scotia* (1819), *A Patriotic Call* (1819), and *A Guide to Justices of the Peace* (1837).
11 Haliburton included 'The Island of Cape Breton' as part of I, Chapter II, section V, 201. He confessed that his difficulties in obtaining information on Cape Breton were resolved by Rev. Mr Trotter, Judge Marshall, and W.H. Crawley. His final account was a compilation of information supplied by all three.
12 Possibly Donald Campbell of Barbreck (1751–1804), soldier

---

15 To Peleg Wiswall [Annapolis Royal]
[1825][1]

Dear sir –

On my return from Halifax I found the 1st. chapter of History of Nova Scotia under cover of your letter accompanied by the preface and corrections which you have done me the favor to prepare – I can hardly find words to express my obligations to you for the very great trouble you have taken and for the very extensive nature of the assistance you have afforded, so far exceeding any thing I had any pretensions to expect from any friend, much less from you to whom the mere literal labour (independant of the enquiry & research) must have been personally inconvenient – Accept dear sir, all I have to offer, my most sincere thanks – If any thing can inspire me with renewed exertions it will be not to disappoint your expectations – The prefatory remarks[2] are adapted in a peculiar manner to the work, and are perhaps the best apology that could have been composed, for the present backward state of the country – Since I returned, I have been incessantly employed in assorting, filing, &c the confused papers of probate office,[3] which I had not previously touched, so that I have not been able to resume the work, but so soon as I can with propriety get at it I will write to you on that subject more fully –

There was but little to do at the January term – but 4 trials I think two only of which had any thing of interest – Forresters & Cross[4] – The latter notwithstanding all that has appeared in the papers[5] was a very mysterious affair, and tho Judge Haliburton[6] when he discharged Mr Cross told him 'He returned to an honourable profession an unspotted man & free from suspicion' yet I confess, (and I took down for amusement every tittle of evidence) that I could see nothing to remove the *suspicion* arising from the blood traced to Cross' door from the body (which was distinctly proved) nor the *suspicion* arising from the declaration of two surgeons that the wound *exactly* corresponded to that made by a regulation sword – Nor could I see any contradiction in the testimony – Tho there was nothing to *convict* there was much to induce *suspicion* and many think the officers saw what they deposed to 1st. turning away of deceased – The blackwoman what she swore to the 2d [thrusting?] out of the house and that the unfortunate man returned a *third* time & recieved his death when no human eye witnessd it – His bloody cloaths were an apalling spectacle – Of news there is but little – Government have given to Newfoundland a constitution[7] – Sir Thomas Cochran[8] (formerly a captain in the navy at Halifax to the leniency of whose command 7 gibbets at Maugers Beach[9] bore testimony) goes out Governor, and Mr Brenton[10] whom you know a relative of Judge Stewart secretary with salary of 800 a year – The office of Atty General was offered to him but declined on acct of poor health, or disinclination for the fag of office – That place is still vacant, and might it is thought be obtained by some of the seniors of the bar of N.S. if aided by Sir James Kempt – Mr. Archibald[11] is Speaker elect, the others having withdrawn their pretensions to the chair, he has returned in good health & spirits, has many anecdotes of the old world, having seen much of it as Sadler crossed the English channel in a balloon[12] – He *saw* Paris, *touched* at Brussels, *spoke* [at] Strasburg, *provisioned* at *Whitehall* &c, – He seems to feel some uneasiness from the dissatisfaction felt at the Island of St John, on the score of non residence,[13] which his natural affability and knowledge of men & manners has not been sufficient to allay, – There is an apparent jealousy also among his fellows at the bar at Halifax of his continuing in practice, and he will hereafter hear some wag inform their *honors* on the bench that his *Lordship* the *Chief Justice* of Edward Island is wrong in law &c – I saw Mr Fitzgerald Uniacke[14] at Halifax who informed me he saw Robie[15] who was all delight at what he saw, he had been on Loc-Katrine with the Lady of the Lake, in Rob Roy[16] [came?] with Scotts novel in his hand, had viewed Melrose by moonlight with Marmion &c.[17] Evry thing he saw increased his wonder and avidity to travel, and he intends not to return until the latest period of the autumn – There is a report in town which I hear Judge Haliburton takes much pain to contradict & which all his friends deny, that at Liverpool while in presence of Adl. Murray,[18] he was, as usual exalting the American navy & publishing the disgrace of the British, when he was roughly handled by the admiral, and taught to know the difference between being in the great world and a little circle of friends like Lawson[19] & Maynard[20] at Halifax – It is so characteristic of the paradox of the one & the violent temper of the other I cannot help thinking there is some truth in it –

The old subjects – *Bank*[21] – Shubenacadie *Canal*[22] & *Schools*[23] will occupy the house this winter, – Some people anticipate a stormy session, but I think it will pass over as usual with a little scolding – The two alterations of the Halifax Road – that from Fenerty's to Fultz[24] avoiding the hills by Mitchell, and that by Shaws tavern are two of the best ever made in this province – A rout has been explored to avoid Ardoise and the great hill 7 miles from Windsor which will be effected next summer, when there will be no hill except at Mount Uniack between Halifax & Falmouth Bridge – with best respects to Mrs Wiswall & Miss Wiswall in which Mrs H begs to join

> I am dear sir
> Yours very truly
> Tho. C. Haliburton

PANS MS *Report of the P.A.N.S.* (1946), Appendix C, 44–6; Chittick, 49–51, 132

1 The letter is docketed '1825.'
2 The preface to the *Historical ... Account* is by Haliburton and is not the piece of writing alluded to here.
3 Haliburton was appointed a judge of the Probate Court at Annapolis in December 1824.
4 'Forresters' was a notorious libel trial of the day. 'Cross' alludes to a murder trial, widely reported in the newspapers (see note 5). The story of the trial of Thomas Forrester, for fraud, is told in I. Longworth, *Life of S.G.W. Archibald* (Halifax 1881) 32–8.
5 The murder trial of Lieutenant Richard Cross, of His Majesty's Ninety-sixth Regiment of Foot, took place on Tuesday, 18 January 1824, before Judge Brenton Halliburton and Judge James Stewart.
6 Sir Brenton Halliburton (1775–1860), chief justice of Nova Scotia, 1833–60. He was no relation to Thomas Chandler.
7 In June 1824, acts of Parliament were passed that had the effect of bringing Newfoundland out of 'an ancient system of government based on custom and tradition' (A.H. McLintock, *The Establishment of Constitutional Government in Newfoundland, 1783–1832* [London 1941] 158).

8 Sir Thomas Cochrane (1789–1872) was governor of Newfoundland, 1825–34. He succeeded Sir Charles Hamilton. Joseph Howe alludes to this notorious martinet in his *Travel Sketches* (see Parks, M.G., 56).
9 Near Halifax, named after Joshua Mauger (*c.* 1725–88), sea captain, businessman, politician, and rum smuggler. He was given a grant of land on McNab's Island in 1756.
10 Edward Brenton is listed in *Belcher's Almanack* (1826) as colonial secretary for Newfoundland, but he did not hold the post long. He was appointed an assistant judge on 26 September 1826 (McLintock, Appendix II).
11 S.G.W. Archibald became Speaker on 15 February 1825.
12 The reference is to the remarkable inventor and astronaut, James Sadler of Oxford.
13 S.G.W. Archibald was chief justice of Prince Edward Island (1824–8), while also holding the position of Speaker of the Nova Scotia House of Assembly. His non-residence on the island caused some consternation.
14 Fitzgerald Uniacke (1797–1870), rector of St George's Church, Halifax, fourth son of Solicitor-General Uniacke
15 Simon Bradstreet Robie (1770–1858), Speaker of the House of Assembly, 1817–25; solicitor-general of Nova Scotia, 1815–26; president of the Legislative Council of Nova Scotia, 1827–38
16 *The Lady of the Lake* (1810) made the Trossachs a popular tourist attraction. Sir Walter Scott's famous novel *Rob Roy* was published in December 1817.
17 *Marmion, A Tale of Flodden Field*, a poetic romance (1808)
18 Admiral Robert Murray was the husband of Rebecca Halliburton, Judge Brenton Halliburton's sister.
19 William Lawson (1772–1848), MLA for Halifax County, 1806–36, and first president of the Bank of Nova Scotia, 1832–7. His father, John (1749–1828), was a wealthy Halifax merchant.
20 Captain Thomas Maynard, RN (1769–1857), commissioner of lighthouses, high sheriff for the County of Halifax
21 In 1825 a group of merchants formed the Halifax Banking Company (see Victor Ross, *A History of the Canadian Bank of Commerce*, 2 vols [Toronto 1920] I: 50). The Halifax Bank Bill was given its first reading in the House of Assembly on Saturday, 5 March 1825.
22 The Shubenacadie Canal scheme was an ambitious one to link Halifax and the Bay of Fundy by water. As M.G. Parks notes, in 1825, the canal was in the process of being surveyed again (*Travel Sketches*, 124, n.13).
23 A lengthy report from a joint committee on schools was laid before the House on Monday, 7 March 1825 (*Journals*, 441–3).
24 See Parks, M.G., 62: 'The first thing that strikes the eye after leaving Fultz's is the alteration of the Road, by which so many hills are avoided, and so many houses left in the rear ...'

---

16 To G.K. Nichols [Annapolis Royal]
30th March 1825

My dear Nichols –

I received your letter and am really much surprised at Old Morehouse[1] refusing to sign the deed – No such idea was entertained by me as to entrap him to convey more than he sold, and as for the notion of outrunning Bakewell[2] I did not know he was in that part of the country, but I did know for Judge Stewart told me who had seen his papers, that he was not authorised to make any purchases in behalf of the company,[3] but merly to report, his bankers have failed & he is now ordered home so there is an end of that bubble – Morehouse has sold his ore *well*, for I doubt the existence of any body, I wish he would sign the deed, but if he will not, send them up to me & they shall be rewritten – Pray do lend a hand to get this business fixed – Bonnell[4] is acting very foolishly about Miss Robertson[5] bond, in attempting to stave off the judgement, he is only irritating her, & giving me unnecessary trouble, and when the judgement comes as come it will this term, he will find it not easy to allay those angry feelings he is now so foolishly exciting – You had better advise him to act a more prudent part –

Will you be so good as to say to Judge Wiswall that I have no other papers from Halifax in Mossman v. Mossman[6] than what I sent him, and that I suppose the bill will be taked[?] them,[7] for I have not seen it, will therefore thank him to make return of report as soon as convenient to me, and to send a minute of what I am to pay him, as also in Robn v Bonnell of his fees, for I believe they are unpaid, and I will send him amount by return of post, of both sums – I am quite pleased to hear he did not go to Saint Johns,[8] the season of the year is too far advanced, to render a voyage either safe or pleasant, and I believe after 25, every body more or less feels the effects of our springs – I do not mind the winter but really I dread the spring, the cold is so raw & damp, so penetrating & yet heavy on the nerves, the ground so wet & chill, and the weather so variable, that I swear I feel in a shiver from 10th. March to 10th. of May – Ritchie has not yet returned, that unfortunate man has his heart lodged in the *House*, it was the temple in which he worshipped the Speakers chair, the idol of his ambition, and now that he has lost his *cast*, he wanders thro the gallerys, and strays in the porticos, & lingers on the steps, as if both to lose sight of an object, which is perhaps dearer to him, in proportion, as it is unattainable. I believe he is to be pitied, for he is far from being a happy man, therefore like a true Christian I will pray for a herd of swine, to receive the seven devils with which he is possessed –

There is very little doing here just nothing – By the bye-election[9] – Poor Annapolis County, how folorn, when John Bath[10] Wm Davies,[11] William Roach &c. &c are to be candidates – They may talk as they will of Nova Scotia but it is deteriorating – The Assembly is not to be compared to what it was, the bar not to be named with the old one, for law, sense, manner, liberality, or anything good, and the state of society, I mean in the country, will not be so good these 100 years to come, ask the judge if he does not think so – Remember me most kindly to him, & Mrs Wiswall and ask him if he received the Canadian Review[12] from D Carter[13] & a note requesting the loan of the odd vol: of Belknaps biography

In haste sincerely yours
T C Haliburton

PANS MS *Pub.*: Chittick, 46–7, portions only

1 Either James Moorhouse (who died, aged eighty-seven, on 1 April 1844) or John Moorhouse (d. 1847)
2 Charles Lyell, in *Travels in North America; with Geological Observations on the United States, Canada and Nova Scotia*, 2 vols (London 1845) 2: 235, alludes to 'Mr Bakewell Jun., ... son of the distinguished geologist of that name.'
3 Possibly the London-based General Mining Association
4 W.F. Bonnell, an assistant judge
5 Deborah Robinson was the complainant, W.F. Bonnell and Anna, his wife, were the defendants in the High Court of Chancery decree, dated 5 May 1825, ordering the Drake farm in Digby Township to be sold at a public auction on 25 July 1825.
6 An indenture foreclosing on the property of Andrew Mossman the younger, 'merchant' of Annapolis, was drawn up by Peleg Wiswall on 3 December 1825 (Annapolis County Registry of Deeds, Book 24, 403). The property, in the town of Annapolis, was duly advertised in the *Royal Gazette* and sold at public auction on 1 March 1826.
7 The land was near the garrison at Annapolis.
8 Haliburton's own maternal grandmother died in the woods near Saint John, New Brunswick, on 11 March 1787, after being shipwrecked on her way to a Loyalist land-commission meeting.
9 The election in the county that saw Abraham Gesner, uncle of the famous inventor, elected to the House of Assembly to replace Thomas Ritchie (Calnek, 312)
10 John Bath (1779–?), who came from Yorkshire, England, and settled in Granville (see Coward, 67)
11 Haliburton and a 'William Davis' were trustees for the estate of Mrs Henrietta Macara in 1822
12 *The Canadian Review and Literary and Historical Journal* was published in Montreal.
13 Unidentified

17 To Peleg Wiswall

[Annapolis Royal]
10th. May 1825

My dear sir –

I had the pleasure to receive your letter by Mr. Nichols, and feel greatly obliged to you for the interest you continue to take in the History, as well as for matter you are preparing for chapter containing the outline of our colonial constitution[1] – It is a more difficult subject than is generally thought and less understood even by colonial lawyers, than they might perhaps admit, – I shall therefore receive with very great pleasure your remarks on this subject, and shall leave what I have prepared on that head statu quo until I see you – I am sorry to say, various private affairs have prevented me this spring from making much progress, for which I feel the greater regret as the winter in the country can so easily be employed by a professional man without in the least interfering with his business – As the June court is always a *triable* term I suppose I shall not get fairly to work again until that is over – I have the materials (such as can be got) *hewn out* and *partly fitted*, so that when I sit up in *the stocks* I hope to finish it for a voyage across the Atlantic when Lockyer[2] goes to England in December next – I will at least try very hard – According to your desire I enquired when at Halifax for Stokes,[3] which I found in the library in Halifax, and think a valuable, tho ill arranged book – there is a great deal of colonial law in it – precedents of plantations – forms – commissions, &c. and many other matters which are only to [be] found there – I made no extracts as Mr. Uniacke promised to lend me his – He also furnished me with a reference of page & book, to the Council Books of such subjects as I might require –

We have no news here, all attention is taken up with death and funeral of Mrs Ritchie – I suppose you have particulars of that melancholy affair – It appears she had a miscarriage of a violent and extremely sudden nature, and that first debility and then convulsion fits ensued – I believe she had 30 fits and in the last a violent discharge from her head took place, forcing itself thru the nostril, apparently the contents of an absys which had been forming there – Her death which took place a few days after is by the regt. surgeon attributed wholly to the disorder in her head, which he thinks would have at all events terminated her existence, before long, and that any illness which could have put it in motion would have led to the same result – She is represented by those who knew her, as a very amiable (tho weak woman). This funeral takes place today, and by the arrangements which have been made, is calculated to be a 'spectacle' –

You had I suppose seen some English papers of late and have noticed the wonderful changes of colonial policy[4] – As far as we can judge the system seems wise, whether it is viewed as removing the only badge of dependance we bear, as enriching the colonies, benefiting the mother country, or drawing more close those bonds of natural affection between the two countries – Nothing seems better calculated to preserve the colonies, for it leaves us nothing to obtain by independance but what we now possess – So far thus much of the novelties of the present day is for our advantage, but the spirit itself is a dangerous one, and when let loose, as it is now, may be difficult to manage – Of all the mad bubbles, the society which is formed, of a capital of one million sterling to be cmded in New B. & N. Scotia,[5] is the most absurd, but cannot fail of being of advantage to us, as not one peny of it will ever be again recalled by the society which invests it here – I presume however that we are to view it rather in the light of a subscription for our benefit than a serious association to employ capital, in the hopes of gain or profit – It is one however of the many instances to prove the unbounded wealth of our parent country, of that monstrous capital which seeking rent in the most remote parts of the world – It would seem as if our notions of national grandeur were too limited for us to concieve the idea of greatness to which Great Britain is destined, and that if she were merly at the enhancing of a fate of which history gives no example, and imagination can find no paralel –

Of domestic occurrences, the only one of interest here is that Col-Barclay[6] is calling in all his money from Nova Scotia, and the lash of law is applied to the tardy, that together, with the added lnds of Delancey's which is also wanted, has put money into great requisition here – the notice has been very brief – Our iron work are like to fail –

Mr. Shaw[7] complains of ill usage – It appears Mr Ritchie was his great advisor & prompter, & promised strenuous support, but has lately found iron on his land up Eassons brook[8] – In conveyance of which he procured the act of association to be drawn up not for 'Shaw & others' as was expected but for 'certain persons', and not for Shaws place in Clements but 'The County of Annapolis' – And wishes to step in & sell[?] his ore & land to the company & share the premium instead of Shaw whom it is intended to give the go-bye to – This is certainly not fair play, and it is unfortunate as it has set them quarreling whose efforts ought to be united – Shaw has completely verified the old proverb – 'He has beat the bush while another has caught the bird' – but what is most extraordinry he never discovered that he had been made a tool of until Ritchie explained to him a few days since – Will you do me the favor to inform me by return of post if you expect to be here in June as I wish to have a sale before you then? –

         Yours very truly
         Th C Haliburton

PANS MS *Pub.*: *Report of the P.A.N.S.* (1946), 46–7, the first paragraph only

1 *Historical ... Account*, vol. 2, Chapter V, 'Various Kinds of Colonial Governments,' 307–47
2 Henry Lockyer (d. 1864), a dry-goods merchant of Halifax
3 Anthony Stokes, *A View of the Constitution of the British Colonies, in North-America and the West Indies* (London 1783)
4 The *Free Press*, Tuesday, 26 April 1825, reported the arrival of British newspapers informing the colonies that the British government was removing restrictions from colonial trade. There were celebrations at Province House and the Exchange, as well as a public dinner.
5 'The Nova-Scotia and New Brunswick Company' had a capital of one million pounds (10,000 shares of 100 pounds each) to buy land and encourage emigrants.
6 Colonel Delancey Barclay (d. 1826) was aide-de-camp to George IV, and son of Thomas Barclay (1753–1830), lawyer, politician, and adjutant-general of the militia. The Barclays owned 5,000 acres of land in Aylesford, Nova Scotia (Calnek, 347). Both father and son were known as 'Colonel.'
7 Moses Shaw (*c.* 1766–1851), pioneer of the lumbering and milling industry in New Brunswick, inventor, originator of the Annapolis Iron Works and Foundry. Moses Shaw purchased 900 acres from Israel Potter on 30 July 1825. The deed was witnessed by 'Thomas C. Haliburton' (Annapolis County Registry of Deeds, Book 24, 107–10).
8 Probably named after John Easson or Easton, a young Scotsman, who was granted 520 acres of land in 1759. See *Seasoned Timbers. A Sampling of Historic Buildings Unique to Western Nova Scotia*, 2 vols (Halifax: Heritage Trust of Nova Scotia 1972) 1: 93.

18 To Peleg Wiswall

[Annapolis Royal]
23d July [1825]

My dear sir

Enclosed are the papers in cause of Robertson vs. Bonnell which is for sale on Mondy 25th. – I regret the extreme heat will prevent my coming to Digby as intended – I have written to Mrs. R. to get Muir[1] to attend for her to bid at sale –

I hope you have returned in good health –

Yours very truly
Tho C Haliburton

You will observe by the Saturday paper[2] some meddling and impertinent person has taken the liberty to republish the 'Gen. Description of Nova Scotia' not only without my consent but without my knowledge –

PANS MS

1 W. Muir was the postmaster at Digby.
2 The advertisement appeared in the *Acadian Recorder*, Saturday, 16 July 1825.

19 To Abbé Sigogne

[Annapolis Royal]
5th Sepr. 1825

My dear sir –

I had the pleasure to receive your letter respecting the suit between Davoust and Doucett[1] – Since then one of the Robisheaus[2] has come to me for a writ –

It is not however by any means proper for me to hurry these poor people into a lawsuit, without a more intimate knowledge of their case, an inspection of their titles, and a sight of the award & bond of reference – Law is extremely expensive, whoever loses this suit, will lose much money, and as they look to me for candid advice, I think I should be deficient in that candour, if I encouraged a precipitancy in the plaintiff to rush into a costly suit, before I can well understand the grounds of his claim – Much will depend on his tittle being definite including the spot in question, without reservation, and much more on the length of the possession – As neighbours I could wish they would settle it themselves, but if that is impossible, I hope they will do me the justice to suppose that this delay originates in a sincere desire, to serve *them effectually* and not in any negligence of their interest – Will you do me the favor, my dear sir, to convey this my opinion to them, and at the same time to explain to them that the expence of bringing witnesses from so great a distance will make this suit more expensive to the losing party than they have any idea of, and in short more than the land is worth – I wish to see the plaintiff, at Digby Court and hope he will bring me all his papers, when I will give him a writ for next Supreme Court,[3] which will decide the affair before the period of mowing –

When I was last in town, I saw some of your friends there, who were making enquiries after your health – The book[4] you see advertised in the papers, is, strange to say, nothing more than a reprinted copy of the old one, which an unprincipled bookseller has pirated from me, thinking no doubt a very clever thing to avail himself of the profits of my labour – I knew nothing of it till I saw it advertised – The second edition which I am preparing will take nearly a year to compleat in a way to satisfy myself, as soon as it is printed I will send you a copy –

Mrs Haliburton desires to unite with me in begging you to accept the assurance of

My great esteem
Yours most truly
Tho. C. Haliburton

Acadia University MS *Pub.*: Chittick, 54–5

1 The dispute appears to have been settled outside the law.
2 The Deveau, Doucet, and Robicheau families settled land grants in close proximity to one another.
3 The last day in September
4 An unauthorized reprint of *A General Description*

---

20 To G.K. Nichols   [Annapolis Royal] [1826][1]

My dear Nichols –

I send you the petition of Smith[2] – Will you have it signed by Ritchie & Morton[3] and serve copy of summons on Goldsmith for Friday or Saturdy – Also let somebody serve subpaenas on Hayt[4] and make affidt. – before Judge Wiswall –

I am half dead, worne out with fatigue & tooth ache or I would come down, but in course of July or August will see you and talk over matters –

Will you give order to Cutler[5] who returns immediately so that Smith may be brought down –

                    Adieu in haste
                    T.C.H.

Excuse the trouble I have given you –

PANS MS

1 The letter is docketed '1826.'
2 Unidentified
3 Thomas Ritchie and Elkanah Morton were judges of the Inferior Court of Common Pleas.
4 Possibly one of the children of Captain Jesse Hoyt (1744–1822), a Loyalist who settled at Annapolis Royal, NS. Both Silas Hoyt (1766–1838) and Jesse Hoyt (1767–1838) dealt in land at this time, according to the records at the Annapolis County Registry of Deeds.
5 Either Edward H. Cutler, sheriff of Annapolis County, or his father, Ebenezer Cutler (1740–1831), who was protonotary of Annapolis County

---

21 To John George Marshall   Annapolis [Royal] 7th Dr. 1826

My dear sir –

In the year 1823 I published at the Acadian School at Halifax a small pamphlet entitled 'A General Description of Nova Scotia' designing it as a sort of emigrant's guide – The researches which I made when engaged on that compilation furnished me with materials and suggested the idea of undertaking a work of a similar nature upon a much more extended plan 'An Historical & Statistical Account of Nova Scotia' which I have now nearly ready for the press –

In a work embracing such a variety of topics the assistance of friends becomes essentially necessary, and I have taken the liberty of requesting the favor of you to give me a graphic description of Cape Breton – an account of the extent population & resources of Sydney, and some particulars relative to the coal mines –

I have derived much information from your valuable 'Practical Call'[1] of which I have made an acknowledgement in the prefatory part of this book, and I feel fully convinced from the close attention which you have evidently given to every subject connected with the interests of Nova Scotia that you can, if your avocations permit, furnish me with many interesting statistical information respecting Cape Breton –

On this subject I am sadly deficient, and have no friend capable of the task, to whom I can apply but yourself, and I trust to your goodness to favor me with some communication relative to it –

You will add materially to the obligation, by forwarding your reply to me at Halifax before the close of the legislature[2] –

> I am dear sir
> With much respect
> Yours try
> Tho. C. Haliburton

PANS MS *Pub.*: In facsimile, Allan C. Dunlop, 'A General Description of Nova Scotia,' *Canadian Notes and Queries* 24 (1979): 10–11

1 *A Patriotic Call* (Halifax 1819)
2 The Legislature closed on Tuesday, 17 April 1827.

---

22 To Abbé Sigogne

[Halifax?]
23d Jany 1827

Reverend & dear sir –

I have to acknowldge the recipt of your favor of the 10th instant, and am much obliged to you for the communication – On the score of schools[1] there is such a diversity of opinions, that it is impossible to say what plan will be adopted, although the general [vo]ice of the county is in favor of some better one than that proposed last year – The great difficulty seems to arise in the large sum of money which any general system will require – I know too well the nature of legislative bodies, to place much confidence in succeeding in a scheme which I have formed fot that purpose but let whatever one be selected that may, rest assured, I will do all that lays in my power, to have Clare district, and its proportion of money for schools put under your sole direction as trustee – There is something so peculiar and distinctive, in the condition, feelings, language habits and uniform religion of its inhabitants as to claim the exclusive privledg of exception – I will endeavour to interest all my friends on its behalf –

I was aware of the expence you had personaly incurred on behalf of the Indians, by far too much for any individual, and had been requested by our mutual friend Mr. McCarthy[2] to make some effort for the [re]lief of those poor neglected, people, whose vices are borrowd from the whites with an ease that the arts of civilised life, defy – We owe them much for they have derived many misfortunes, and but very little benefit from any intercourse with us – It is however a subject replete with difficulties, but somethg at least ought to be done, to prevent their becoming too great a burthen to you & your friends – I will make it my business to talk to Sir James upon the subject and if any thing effective is likely to be done I will take an early opportunity of acquainting you –

When the decision of a subject rests with many one person can do but little, but what little I can do I shall take a particular pleasure in promoting your views –

> I am dear sir
> With great respect
> Your most obt
> Tho. C. Haliburton

PANS MS

1 On 20 March 1827, Haliburton introduced a bill into the Legislature for the establishment of common schools. The bill passed. The bill, however, was rejected by the council and Haliburton reintroduced it into the Legislature with a scathing attack on the council.
2 Charles W. McCarthy, commissioner of roads for the lower district of Clare

23 To Abbé Sigogne

[Halifax?]
10 March 1827

Rev & dear sir.

I received your second letter on the subject of the roads[1] and have given it as the basis of what has been done, although when there are so many to consult in the division, I have not been able in all points to meet it so fully as either you or I could wish. There has been an application made to remove all test oaths from Roman Catholics, and I could assure you it gave me sincere pleasure to raise my feeble voice in its favor. I enclose to you a garbled report of the debate.[2] Many ill disposed persons have said my zeal carried me too far, who would have gladly availed themselves of any excuse to vote against the measure, but I had two reasons for adopting the course. 1st, My judgement and feelings both concurred in it, and 2ndly, As a stranger, I was favored with the unanimous support of all your people, in a manner so cordial and so friendly that I shall ever retain a most grateful remembrance of it, and shall feel most happy when any occasion offers, to testify my host hearty acknowledgement of a kindness shown to me when I stood in need of it.[3] I trust that you and my friends in Clare will find that I am not disposed to make a convenience of them at an election, and forget the remembrance of their kindness, when the necessity for their support ceases to exist. In my friend Mr Uniacke[4] they found a most zealous advocate and the Catholics of Nova Scotia have been gratified by the spectacle of a *Protestant* Assembly (for Kavanagh[5] was not there) giving a unanimous vote in their favor – with respect to the Indians, and the means of providing for them, I think you will be pleased to hear that Sir James has given a special recommendation of their case to the House, and some permanant plan will now be adopted and an annual sum voted.[6] He is fully aware and duly appreciates the laborious undeviating and zealous exertions you have ever made for their religious instruction. Charles Glode[7] came down and I went with him to Sir James, who has returned to him the expenses of his grant, and given orders for furnishing him in the spring with implements. As soon as any thing definite is agreed upon I shall not fail to acquaint you.

With great respect
Your obed.
Thos. C. Haliburton

PAC copy

1 When Haliburton spoke in the debate on financial appropriations for roads on 16 February 1827, he admitted he had been sent to guard 'local interest,' but he also declared himself concerned about the 'provincial interest.'
2 Haliburton spoke at length in support of R.J. Uniacke's motion in the House of Assembly 'for the Remission of Test Oaths' (Monday, 26 February 1827) as 'the unsolicited and voluntary friend of the Catholic' (the *Novascotian*, 24 February 1827, 27).
3 Exactly the point Haliburton made in his speech to the House
4 Richard John Uniacke, Jr (1789–1834), son of R.J. Uniacke, Sr (1753–1830)
5 Lawrence Kavanagh, Roman Catholic representative for Cape Breton. When he was sworn in on 5 April 1823 there was considerable debate as to whether he should take the declaration against popery and transubstantiation (see the *Acadian Recorder*). Attempts to exclude him, however, were defeated.
6 Sir James Kempt wished to give each family 'Lots' on the land set aside for Indians, hoping that the Assembly would pay for allotting and surveying their lands. In addition, each family would receive an axe, a hoe, and a few seeds. Sir James also requested that the Assembly afford a 'moderate supply of Provisions and coarse Clothing' for the 'weak and sickly' (*Journals and Proceedings of the House of Assembly* [1827] 74–5).
7 Charles Glode (listed by Deveau I: 26 as 'Charley Claude'), Mic-Mac chief

---

24 To Abbé Sigogne

[Annapolis Royal]
18th. June 1827

Revd. & dear sir –

Tibido[1] has complained to me of some scandalous reports spread by one of Amero's daughters concerning a child of his & requested me to bring a suit thereon –

Considering the enormous expence of these suits to poor people and that they had better settle them at home I beg leave to call your attention to page 31 of 1st. vol of Province Laws, being the *last clause* of an act entitled 'An act for punishing criminal offenders'[2] –

By that act you will find you have the power to send for the girl by summons (as a Justice of Peace) and fine her as high as 5 pounds –

It is an excellent law, and while it gives speedy justice, offers a cheap mode of getting at it,

Your most obt
Tho. C. Haliburton

PANS MS

1 The names 'Tibedo' and 'Amero' are anglicizations of the French surnames 'Thibodeau' and 'Amerault.' Nevertheless, mention is made of a Joseph Tibedo of the Township of Digby in Book 12, 46, of the Digby County Registry of Deeds.

2 *Statutes at Large* (Halifax 1805) I CAP XX, 'An Act for punishing Criminal Offenders,' sec. XV, clauses XI, XII, XIII, XIV, and XV, relates to perjury and the handling of such offenders. Although the mode of justice might be speedy and cheap, the judge could choose among a wide range of punishments, from placing the offender in the stocks for three hours to whipping.

---

25 To George Renny Young[1] [1 September 1827]

As the first permanent European settlement in North America was made at Annapolis, every thing connected with that remote event is exceedingly interesting.[2] The first settlers were poor, and their attention was directed more to the fur-trade and fisheries, than to the colonisation of the country. Their buildings and their fortifications were of a temporary nature, and their settlements were no sooner abandoned than they were covered with a new growth of wood, which in a few years, was not to be distinguished from other parts of the forest that covered the face of the country. While we cannot therefore wonder at the few traces which have survived them, we naturally place a much higher value upon those which are occasionally discovered. In my last letter I mentioned to you the report of some persons in this neighbourhood having accidentally found the monument left by those who visited the country in 1604. I have this remarkable stone, together with another of a subsequent date, now in my possession, and shall give you the most probable conjecture which has occurred to me respecting the persons by whom they were engraved, and the object which they had in view at the time. The first is a stone about 2½ feet long and two feet broad, of the same kind of hard iron stone, which forms the substratum of Granville mountain. On the top of it are engraved apparently the square and compass of a free mason, and below in very large and deep figures 1606. These latter are the arabic figures. The stone does not appear to have been what masons call dressed, but merely one of those smooth faced stones which are so frequently found in our fields. The surface of it seems, at the time it was engraved upon, to have suffered by the effects of the weather, and to have [spawled] a little under the chisel. When we consider the very great antiquity of the description, we are at first induced to doubt, whether it has not been made at a subsequent period; but a close inspection soon removes all scruples about its authenticity. The interior of the figures have suffered in the same unequal manner with the surface, the 1 is still as deep as we may suppose it to have been originally, but the 0 is worn down about one half, and the upper part of the latter 6 nearly as much. The stone itself has yielded to the power of the climate, the seams on the back part of it have opened, and from their capacity to hold water, and the operation of frost upon it when thus confined, it is probable that in a few years it would have crumbled to pieces. This stone was found in Granville, nearly opposite to Goat Island, and about 30 feet from the ledge of the river. The first question which naturally occurs to us, is, how it came there? and what was the object of the inscription? and the difficulty of answering these questions is not a little increased by the fact, that the first settlement was made where the fort at Annapolis now stands, and not in Granville. You are aware that De Monts explored this part of the country in 1604. He arrived on the 4th of May, in that year, at Rossignol (Port-Royal)[3] from thence he coasted the peninsula to the Bay of St. Mary, and shortly afterwards discovered St. George's channel, or Digby Gut, and sailed up the harbour as far as the point of land where Annapolis now stands. In this expedition he was accompanied by a gentleman of the name of Pontrincourt, who had been long desirous of visiting America – Pontrincourt was so charmed with the beauty of the situation, that he determined to take up his residence here, and solicited a grant of the place from De Monts, whose jurisdiction as Lieutenant General of the territory of Acadia, extended from the 40th to the 46th degree of north latitude. Having obtained his request he named the place Port-Royal. They do not however appear to have made any settlement here at that time, but sailed to St. John, and from thence to St. Croix, where they spent the winter. Finding that place unsuitable for settling they returned during the summer of 1605, to Annapolis (Port-Royal) and began to erect their public buildings, &c. In the following September, De Monts and Pontrincourt returned to France, and on the 27th July, 1606 (the year of the inscription) they arrived again at this place. In the preceding summer, they had effected nothing beyond a secure shelter against the inclemency of the weather, but immediately on his return, we are informed that Pontrincourt took possession of the property granted to him, and cleared a piece of ground for winter grain. I have every reason to believe that the spot where the stone was found, was the very field which Pontrincourt cleared; and that in fact it was placed there by him to commemorate the first cultivation of Acadia, and to record the date of his own possession. This conjecture is founded on a passage in the Journal of Lescarbot, a French lawyer, who visited the colony that year, 1606; and to whom we are indebted for a very minute and authentic account of the expedition. He was an eye witness of what he relates, and his narrative is always mentioned with great respect by French historians. Charlevoix says of him, vol. 1, p. 119, – 'On y voit un Auteur exact, & judicieux, un Homme, qui a des vûes, & quit eût été aussi capable d'établir une Colonie, que d'en écrire l'Histoire.'[4] Lescarbot in describing the versatility of the climate, says, 'The weather was so mild, and the river so open in January 1606–7, that they went in an open boat on a Sunday, after divine service, upon the river, and enjoyed the serenity of the weather, diverting themselves with music; and in the same month went two leagues to see their corn-field, and dined cheerfully in the sunshine.'[5] Now this place is exactly two leagues from Annapolis, and it is very remarkable that in the ancient French maps, there is depicted, nearly opposite to this place, which had been cleared by the express advice of Lescarbot, a small island which has long since been washed away by the violence of the tide, and at present forms a sand bar visible at low water, which island, in consequence of their frequent visits to this place was called by Pontrincourt after his friend 'Lescarbot Isle.' This suggestion is strengthened by the appearance of the stone, for, it would seem, from having no name engraved upon it, that it was designed to perpetuate a date, rather than to mark the grave of an individual. Indeed we are told by Lescarbot that only four died that winter, and, as this clearing was made the preceding autumn, and they had to go two leagues by water to it, it is probable they were buried near the fort, where their sepulture could be more conveniently and decently performed. In short, if they died as related in the winter, the date would not correspond with the fact, for taking the commencement of this winter, that remarkable season to be the first day of January, the death of these people must have occurred in the early part of 1607.

Independent of the time and distance corresponding with the statements of Lescarbot, the choice of the place for the settlement and future residence of Pontrincourt, may also be accounted for, from the extreme beauty of the situation, from the good anchorage opposite to it, and from its commanding the narrow channel of the river between it and Goat Island.

When you reflect that this inscription was made 221 years ago, only three years after the death of Queen Elizabeth, just 14 years before the settlement of the New England states, and that it is unquestionably the oldest European inscription to be found on the continent of North America, you will think this investigation well worth pursuing. This is the most plausible conjecture I can found upon it; if you can find a better one,

Candidus imperti, si non hoc utere mecum.[6]

On visiting the ground where the stone was discovered, I was led to examine the remains of an old fortification in its immediate vicinity, known by the name of the Scotch Fort. I had heard of these ruins before, but owing to the obscurity of that part of our history connected with the ill-directed enterprises of Sir William Alexander, I had referred them to a much later date, and supposed them to have been entrenchments thrown up by the New England troops, commanded by Col. March and Col. Appleton, who were sent to capture this place in 1707. But on a personal examination I was soon convinced of my error. From the size of the embankments and the labour expended upon them they appear to have been designed for a permanent fortification; and it has often been observed that erections composed of earth, though they suffer in common with every other work of man from the effects of age and accident, exhibit their original form much longer than those of brick and stone. – I refer you, for the comparative duration of these materials to a very ingenious letter, written by the late Reverend Jacob Bayley to Doctor Belknapp, dated 10th April 1795, and the remarks on that communication by the Rev. John Birkland of Boston, both of which are preserved in the 4th vol. of the 1st series of the collections of the Massachusetts Historical Society.[7] In Champlain part 2d, page 267, you will find the following allusion to this Fort: 'les Anglois, qui n'y auoient esté que sur nos brisées, s'estans emparez depuis dix à douze ans les lieux les plus signalez, mesme enleué deux habitations, sçauoir celle du Port Royal où estoit Poitrincourt, où ils sont habituez de present.'[8] To explain this passage it is necessary to observe that the river of Annapolis forms three separate basins, one between Digby and Goat Island, another between that and Annapolis, and a third between that place and the Upper Narrows. The oldest map of this harbour ever drawn was made by Lescarbot, which is still extant, from which it is evident that Port Royal was the name given to the basin lying between Annapolis and Goat Island, and not to the town. For the title of the plan is 'Figure du Port Royal in la Novelle France;' and though the fort is marked out, yet the name of Port Royal is not attached to it. Thence it appears that the harbour gave the name to the town, and not the town to the harbour. Therefore the two places which he mentions at Port Royal, are the two settlements on the harbour of that name, to-wit, Annapolis (Port Royal) and the Scotch Fort. The traditionary name of this fort is also confirmed by a passage in the memorial delivered to the French court in 1753, by Governor Shirley and Wm. Mildmay, commissioners appointed under the Treaty of Utrecht to settle the boundary line. The part to which I allude is as follows, 'It is remarkable that there remain to this very day, the ruins of a fort built about that time, (1627) at the entrance into the basin which preserves the name of the "Scotch Fort".' It was within the limits of this old fortification that the other stone was found. It is a common tho' unhewn stone, and bears the following inscription,

LEBEL
1649

which is in excellent preservation, and perfectly legible. This stone, though dated 43 years later than the other, is nevertheless, when in connection with our early history, quite a piece of antiquity; having been engraved just 100 years before the building of Halifax. The Scotch Fort, together with those on the River St. John, were conveyed by Sir William Alexander to Charles Etienne La Tour; and it appears from the commission of the Sueur Charnisay of 1647, and the latter commission which La Tour obtained from the court of France in 1651, that they continued in the possession of the French until 1654, when Major Sedgewick, by order of Oliver Cromwell, captured the forts of St. John River, Pentagoit and Port Royal, after which period it does not appear to have ever been inhabited. It is probable therefore that some one of La Tour's garrison in the old Scotch Fort, perhaps the officer commanding there, having died, was buried near this stone, and his name LEBEL inscribed upon it, as well as the year of his decease, 1649. In this respect, they are clearly distinguishable, the first merely containing a date, the letters of which are unusually large, the latter both the name and the date in letters such as are in ordinary use on tomb-stones. I am rather inclined to suppose this inscription monumental, and not the amusement of a soldier's idle hour, as several stones of a similar description, but of much more recent date, have been found in the old French settlements on the eastern side of the Basin of Minas with names engraved upon them in the same manner, and have always been regarded as tomb-stones.

There is another engraved stone in the same neighbourhood, where these two were found; and I made application to the owner of the farm where it is, to point it out to me; but the removal of the others having given rise to many extraordinary reports that people had been digging for, and had found hidden treasures, and that the dates would be held to have some connection with the quit rents,[9] he affected to have forgotten the spot where he had seen it; and it is not improbable that it will be subjected to a blast of powder, either to ascertain whether there is not a quantity of gold hidden within it, or to destroy an aged witness which has been called, after the repose of two centuries, to rise from the dead to bear testimony to the justice of this antiquated and odious tax. The oldest English inscription I have met with in this province, was on a tomb-stone in the graveyard of this place, dated 1718. I went to look at it this morning to copy it for you, but alas! this 'frail memorial' had crumbled to pieces, and will no longer protect the spot, it was meant to guard from the sexton. The next in point of time is the following,

> Here lyeth ye body of
> Bathia D^{o}uglass wife
> to Samuel D^{o}uglass who
> departed this life Octr.
> 1st 1720 in ye 37 year of
> her age

Pub.: the *Novascotian*, 27 September 1827: 320, col. c; 321, cols a and b

1 George Renny Young (1802–53), editor of the *Novascotian*, received the letter but was not the original addressee. Haliburton is the probable author of this letter, although it is unsigned.
2 See the *Historical ... Account*, vol. 2, 156–7.
3 Champlain and De Monts made landfall at Cape LaHave (Lunenburg County) on 8 May 1604. 'Rossignol' was the early name for Liverpool, not Port Royal. Haliburton is in error here.
4 The French of the *Novascotian* is corrupt, so I have adopted the version found in P. De Charlevoix, *Histoire et description generale de la Nouvelle France*, 6 vols (Paris 1744) I, iii, 186. Compare the English version: 'We are indebted to this advocate [Mark Lescarbot] for the best memoirs we possess of what passed before his eyes, and for a history of French Florida. We there behold an exact and judicious writer, a man with views of his own, and who would have been as capable of founding a colony as of writing its history' (Rev. P.F.X. Charlevoix, *History and General Description of New France*, trans. John Gilmary Shea [New York 1866] I, iii; 257–8).
5 The full passage can be found in Marc Lescarbot's *Nova Francia: A Description of Acadia, 1606*, trans. P. Erondelle, (New York and London 1928) Book I, Chapter XVI, 121.
6 Horace, *Epistles*, I, VI, 68: 'If you can mend these precepts do: / If not, what serves for me may serve for you.'
7 'Observations and Conjectures on the Antiquities of America, By the Rev. Jacob Bailey, of Annapolis-Royal, in Nova-Scotia,' dated 'Annapolis-Royal, April 10, 1795,' included

in *Collections of the Massachusetts Historical Society, for the Year 1795*, First Series (1795; Boston 1835) 4, 100–5

8 I have adopted the French of *The Works of Samuel de Champlain*, ed. H.P. Biggar (Toronto: Champlain Society 1936) 147. Compare the English version in *The Works of Samuel de Champlain* (Toronto: Champlain Society 1936) VI, Part 2, Book III, Chapter VII, 147: 'The English ... having only followed in our tracks. Within the last ten or twelve years they had thus seized upon the most prominent places, and even taken from us two settlements, namely that of Port Royal, where Poutrincourt was established ...'

9 An order in council was made for the collection of quit rents from 1 January 1827 after a lapse of many years. They amounted to two shillings per one hundred acres and one farthing an acre.

---

26 To John A. Barry[1]

Annapolis [Royal]
20 Oct 1828.

My dear sir

When I had the pleasure to see you in town, you were so good as to say that you would on your return from Shelburne reply to the queries formerly given you respecting said county –

I am now at work at the acct of your county, and shall be much obligd to you for an acct of the *rivers ports* & *settlements* within it, including *present* state of Shelburne as I have the former from Mr Robertson[2] –

If you can favor me with it please to begin at the Clyde and take them in order round the coast, omitting the most inconsiderable except by name – I should suppose they would not furnish matter for more than 3 or 4 pages of print (exclusive of the early history of Shelburne)[3] –

An early answer, if convenient to you would, confer an additional obligation upon me –

Yours always
T C Haliburton

Desbrisay Museum MS

1 John A. Barry (c. 1790–1872), dry-goods merchant and MLA for Shelburne Township, 1827–30, during which period he was a controversial figure in provincial politics
2 Alexander Robertson (1784–1851) is listed in the preface to the *Historical ... Account*, vol. 1; viii. He was born in Perthshire, Scotland and emigrated to Nova Scotia in 1801.
3 *Historical ... Account*, vol. 2; 177–99, part of Chapter 2, section IV. The section occupied more space than he anticipated.

27 To the Lieutenant-Governor

Ann[a]p[o]lis [Royal]
11th. May 1829

Sir –

During the sessions of the legislature a petition was presented to the assembly for a sum of money to effect an alteration in the post road in Wilmot so as to avoid two hills called 'Hicks's Hills,'[1] to which petition was appended a plan of the alteration –

I did not at the time think it necessary to apply for a special grant for this purpose, having county money sufficient to effect it, & therefore in conjunction with the other county member[2] placed two sums one of 70 & another of 80 on that line of road with the intention to cover the expence of this alteration –

The plan tho drawn by a competent person[3] I am not altogether satisfied with, as such alterations should only be undertaken after a most careful & effectual survey and am therefore desirous that an order should issue, if agreeable to his Excellency,[4] to three persons to examine the grounds & report upon the same to his excellency – If upon that report he should approve of the alteration, the ordinary steps will be taken to effect this desirable object – The damages will be *nominal* the only expence being in the removal of fence –

I shall therefore be obliged to you, if you will have the goodness to state this to his Excellency & to request he will be pleased, if he approves of the measure, to enable me to accomplish it by issuing such order –

The most competent persons are James Parker (the road commissioner) Francis Smith, and James Hall[5] –

If you will be kind enough to enclose to me a letter to these persons I will see that it is properly executed –

Charles Glode the Indian has just called upon me to know if any steps can be taken to procure for him the condemned bedding at Annapolis which he wanted last winter –

          I have the honor to be
          Your obt svt.
          Tho. C. Haliburton

PANS MS

1 Bridgetown was formerly called 'Hicks's Ferry.'
2 W.H. Roach
3 Probably John Elder, i.e., John Harris, surveyor, MLA for the Township of Annapolis, 1811–18
4 Sir Peregrine Maitland (1777–1854), lieutenant-governor of Nova Scotia, 1828–32
5 James Parker was the third son of Abigail Parker, who settled in Granville and later in Wilmot, Nova Scotia (Calnek, 561); Francis Smith, 'was some years Deputy Sheriff and was a candidate for the shrievalty in 1821, well supported' (Calnek, 603); James Hall (1764–1846), was appointed JP in 1807, although his appointment was challenged 'on account of his alleged democratic principles and because he was a "Newlight" [i.e., a seceder from old Congregationalism]' (Calnek, 519).

28 To G.K. Nichols

[Annapolis Royal]
22d Jun[e] 1829

My dear Nichols –

If you can oblige Davies by waiting upon him a little while, I should be very glad, he is endeavouring to make arrangement for the payt. of all his debts, and if you can consistently wait, as he is an obligeing good fellow I shall take it as a favor –

Do for Gods sake get Judge Wiswall to settle that affair of Hoyts –

Yours
Tho C Haliburton

PANS MS *Pub.*: Chittick, 48, one line only

29 To G.K. Nichols

[Annapolis Royal, 1829][1]

My dear Nichols –

I send you the draft of the sketch for county of Annapolis[2] for your perusal & our friend the Judge – I should be glad if you two would spend a morning over it correct its errors & add what has been omitted – *Particularly Digby The Neck Brier Island Sissiboo River* and other matters connected – I beseech you not to fail me & to return it if possible by first mail, if not next Monday, certainly the Monday following – I call it the poorest report I have – Let your accompanying remarks be free and without reserve, I have no pride of authorship, and dont care how much it is cut to pieces – Only send the original back unaltered, for it is all I have and let

remarks accompany, it by letters A B.C.D – referring to corresponding letters on other paper – I entreat you not to disappoint me –
The mackerel fishery I have in another place[3]

> With great regard
> Yours ever
> T.C. Haliburton –

Will you have execution of these – & bil setled & kindly return of this paper –
    Let Mr. Bonnell[4] frank it to me,
Can I do any thing for you in Halifax [?]

PANS MS *Pub.*: *Report of the P.A.N.S.* (1946), Appendix C, 48

1 The letter is docketed '1829.'
2 *Historical ... Account*, vol. 2; section 4, 152–77
3 *Historical ... Account*, vol. 2; 91 and 170
4 W.F. Bonnell was deputy postmaster at Digby.

2
The Young Judge, 1829–1837

In February 1830, Haliburton moved his family back to Windsor and devoted himself to his new position as an Inferior Court judge. A group of letters, written to his superiors during the early years of his judgeship, from 1830 to 1834, have survived at the PANS. A consistent theme of these letters is that holders of public office must sacrifice – and be seen to sacrifice – their own acquisitive motives to the good of the community; that sheriffs, magistrates, and other public servants not upholding the public good should be dismissed. Stern (but humane) is the character that he reveals in these letters, his humanity showing itself whenever he was asked to reconsider a case that involved human suffering.

Judges presided over court sessions and undertook special commissions. They also presided over the General Sessions of the Peace, when the construction of roads and bridges, vital to communication between one part of the province and another, were often the subject of discussion. In 1835 and 1836, Haliburton was president of a joint-stock company created to finance the building of a bridge across the Avon River at Windsor. Haliburton had not been in Windsor during the first abortive attempts to bridge the Avon River in 1829. Although the new attempt experienced setbacks (both human and financial), the end result was the bridge that had long been needed in the area.[1]

Haliburton's central position in the community of Windsor is well illustrated by his presidency of the local Board of Health. The cholera scare, from 1832 to 1834, resulted in local boards of health being formed around the province, controlled by a central board in Halifax. The needs of Windsor – a town of 'comers and goers,' – and its surrounding areas were of a specific nature. The central board issued packages of blankets and other items to be used by the local communities in time of crisis. But at

Photograph, by Edw. Graham, of Wolfville, NS, of an oil portrait of
Haliburton, *c.* 1831, by William Valentine of Halifax

'Clifton,' the residence of Judge Haliburton at Windsor, NS, by W.H. Bartlett, 1842

Windsor, the local board, headed by Haliburton, bought a boat and stationed it at the mouth of the Minas Basin (Parrsboro), ready to quarantine any ships coming from New York, where cholera had already broken out.

Haliburton worked hard in his early years as a judge, as is clear from a claim for remuneration for extra services that he sent to the provincial secretary in 1834. When he submitted this claim, he had just returned from a visit to his Aunt Abigail in Boston.[2] The visit could well have been a crucial one as far as his literary ambitions were concerned. When he returned, he started to organize the building of Clifton, the retreat in which he would bring up his large family (five girls and three boys), enjoy the remaining years with his wife, Louisa, find solace from the rigours of the judicial circuit, and eventually write most of the works that would win him international fame. Considerable gaps still exist in our knowledge of the genesis of *The Clockmaker*, the first twenty-one episodes of which were published in the *Novascotian* from September 1835 to February 1836. Joseph Howe issued the book with the addition of twelve chapters on 4 January 1837.[3]

1 In late October, one of the spans of the bridge collapsed, injuring several men.
2 The *Novascotian*, 7 August 1833
3 See Bruce Nesbitt, 'The First *Clockmakers*,' *Thomas Chandler Haliburton Symposium*, ed. Frank M. Tierney (Ottawa: University of Ottawa Press 1985) 93–102.

---

30 To William Hill[1]   Windsor 14th. January 1829[2]

Sir –

At the last General Sessions of the Peace for the county of Hants, held in Windsor in the present month of January,[3] it was resolved by the said court that his honor the President[4] should be solicited to offer a reward for the discovery of the persons concerned in the murder of Thomas M Rudolph or to [?][5] as should give such evidence as to lead to their conviction which said T.M Rudolph was murdered near Rainy Cove in the Township of Kempt in the county of Hants in December last.[6]

I have therefore to request you will be pleased to communicate the said resolution of the court to his honor the Prest.[7] for his consideration.

>   I have the honor to be
>   Your obt.
>   Tho. C. Haliburton

To William Hill Esq.
Dy. Secy.

PANS copy

1 (1787–1848), provincial secretary until 1832; solicitor-general, 1832; puisne judge of the Supreme Court, 1833
2 My text is taken from a typescript copy in the RG 1 collection at PANS. The originals (according to archivists) were removed and destroyed because of mould. The typed transcripts were made under the guidance of Dr D.C. Harvey and are a literal transcription. The date, however, is an error. The murder of Thomas Rudolph occurred on 6 December 1829. Probably, the MS did read '29' and Haliburton had not yet adjusted to the new year.
3 The Inferior Court of Common Pleas and General Sessions of the Peace were held at Windsor on the first Tuesday in January.
4 The president of the council was Michael Wallace (1747–1831), MLA for Halifax County from 1785 to 1803; provincial treasurer, 1797; member, HM Council, from 1803 to his

death; administrator of the government in 1818, 1825, 1828, and from 21 October 1829 to 30 May 1830.
5 Hiatus in copy. Several words indecipherable to original copyist.
6 Mr Rudolph had left Windsor to 'serve some papers upon T. Halliburtons tenants at Kempt and was murdered – it is thought by some of the tenants – he was thrown into a Brook and lay there for a week although diligent searches had been made for miles around the spot where his hat & Pocket Book were found – ' (Harry King to Halli Fraser, 20 December 1829 [PAC, King-Stewart Family Papers, MG 24, 1, 182, vol. 1, file 2, 214]).
7 President

31 To William Hill   Windsor, 9th. April 1830

Sir,

In reply to your letter of the 5th. instant I have to state to you for the information of his honor the President that I have summoned a special sessions to enquire into the charges respecting the custody of the persons charged with the murder of Thomas M Rudolph; and that it appears that Mr Cochran the Sheriff[1] and his jailor[2] were both absent in Douglas,[3] and that the wife of Wilcox and his sister in law were the only persons to be found in the jail beside the prisoners – that a son of Mr. Cochran had been left there but was absent during the day at school and that neither of the prisoners were in irons.

I immediately ordered the prisoners to be put in irons and as information has been received of a conspiracy having been formed by a body of armed men to liberate the prisoners I have ordered a guard to be placed at night in the jail and directed that Mrs Wilcox be dismissed.

I am also informed that last night while the guard were on duty two men came to the jail between 12 and one oclock, in apparent ignorance of these precautions to obtain access to the prisoners, and that Mr. Cochran who has since returned has refused obedience to the order for the dismissal of Mrs Wilcox, and I have reason to suppose that he will remove the irons placed on the prisoners in his absence.

I feel it my duty to report to his honor the President that the whole conduct of Mr. Cochran from the period of the arrest of the prisoners until this date as respects their custody has been irregular and disgraceful. Card playing, drinking, and other abominable excesses have been permitted to the prisoners in jail, debtors have been put into the same room with these felons and there has been such gross negligence in their custody, that Mr. Cochran lies under the suspicions of either being accessory to a plan for their escape, or willing to [?][4] at it. Great scandal has been given to this community and I feel it incumbent upon me to recommend to his honor the immediate removal of Mr. Cochran from office and the appointment of a new sheriff, in which recommendation Mr. Justice Wilkins[5] desires me to say he fully concurs. Should a new sheriff be appointed, the jailor and his domestics, if resolved to do their duty, would be equal to the custody of the prisoners though the house should be attacked by their friends, but without the cordial concurrence of the Sheriff (which Mr. Cochran has never afforded the magistrates) a guard must be maintained until the sitting of the court at a great expence, as no doubt rests[6] that an attempt will be made for their rescue.

As I shall leave Windsor on Saturday for the circuit,[7] if you should have any further communication to make be pleased to address it to Joseph Sentell Esquire[8] the chairman of the committee appointed to enquire into these matters[9] & to communicate his Honors orders to the Sheriff.

> I have the honor to be
> Your most obt servt.
> Tho C Haliburton

William Hill Esq
Secty etc. etc.

PANS copy

1 Terrance Cochran, high sheriff of Hants County
2 Mr Wilcox, the jailer at Windsor
3 Haliburton described Douglas as one of the finest townships in the province in his *Historical ... Account*, vol. 2, 112–13.
4 Hiatus in copy. Left blank by copyist
5 Lewis M. Wilkins (1768–1848), MLA for Lunenburg County, 1799–1817; Supreme Court judge, 1816–48
6 The context suggests this word should be 'remains.'
7 The Inferior Court of Common Pleas met at Lunenburg on the second Tuesday in April, and at Liverpool on the fourth Tuesday in April.
8 JP at Windsor
9 Michael Wallace appointed Joseph Sentell and Benjamin Shillito to investigate the conduct of the high sheriff of Hants County (see PANS, RG 1, vol. 236, doc. 107).

32 To William Hill   Windsor 20th June 1830 –

Sir –

I have the honor to acknowledge the receipt of your letter of the 10th. inst. enclosing a petition of Mr. Francis Pyke,[1] and conveying to me his Excellency's desire that I should enquire into the complaints it contains & report thereon –

I have accordingly instituted enquiries into the same, and beg leave to report as follows –

The petition of Dr. Pyke contains two charges – 1st that a maniac was landed at Windsor from Parrsboro, and that application was made to Messrs. Dewolf[2] & Wright[3] – two Justices of the Peace and also to the [magistrate ?] for his security & relief, who neglected their duty and [?][4] wander at large in consequence of which he was frozen to death 2y That Joseph Sentell and P. Wright – esquires two Justices of the Peace refused to grant a warrant for the apprehension of a person who had murdered a man by the name of Cochran –

With respect to the first it appears that a maniac was landed as stated in the petition, late in the autumn of 1827, and that the overseers of the poor (in consequence of an opinion of a professional man of some eminence[5] that they could not legally support a transient pauper,) had declined their aid, it was arranged on a consultation of magistrates that he should be apprehended and committed to jail until further measures should be adopted for his custody and support, – but that in the mean time & before their [decision was carried into effect][6] the lunatic escaped from the village and perished from the inclemency of the season –

It would not be difficult on this statement of facts to ground a general charge of unfeeling neglect upon the magistrates and the overseers of the poor, or even to reflect upon the humanity of the people of Windsor, but it is not so easy at this distance of time to ascertain whether there has actually been any culpable neglect, and still less so to fasten such an accusation upon any particular person – From all I can learn, I am inclined to think it one of those unfortunate events, of which it may be said that it might have been prevented, if such a calamity had been anticipated, and on which it is easier to *impute* than to *justify* a charge against the parties concerned – I am the more inclined to adopt this opinion as I find that the subject has been [before] the Grand Jury in January 1828, and that their presentment on the subject contains nothing more than an insinuation of neglect –

With respect to the second charge – it appears to be altogether unfounded, and that the magistrates so far from being remiss, were extremely active and zealous in endeavouring to apprehend the criminal alluded to in Dr Pykes petition –

I have not called upon Dr Pyke to substantiate his charges, because it does not appear to me that these facts can be varied, and also because it seems to be the general impression, that for several weeks past he has been affected with partial derangement, which tho not so palpable as to cause him to be pronounced mad, is yet sufficient to pervert his understanding – all which is humbly submitted –

> I have the honor to be
> Your obt sert
> T.C. Haliburton

[William Hill Esq.]

PANS MS

1 The petition is dated 4 June 1830, and concerns an incident in late December 1828, when a James Ratchford of Parrsboro sent an 'idiot' or 'maniac,' 'lashed with most unnecessary rigor,' in a small schooner to Windsor. According to Pyke, the magistrates at Windsor, Patrick Wright and Benjamin DeWolfe, refused to give the order to convey the man to Halifax 'in security according to the statute.' The fugitive wandered out of the village and was found frozen to death next morning.
2 Benjamin DeWolfe was one of the leading merchants at Windsor. He was MLA for Windsor, 1824–36.
3 Patrick Wright, high sheriff of Hants County, 1823–6, formerly a lieutenant in the Royal Navy
4 MS indecipherable
5 Unidentified
6 The manuscript is faded from mould. The text is from an earlier typescript version.

---

33 To William Hill   Windsor 15 No[vembe]r 1830.

Sir

I have the honor to acknowledge the receipt of your letter enclosing a special commission of Oyer & terminer[1] to be executed at Horton[2] and have now to report for his Excellency's information that under the authority thereof a court was held at Horton on Tuesday and Wednesday the

9th. & 10th. of November, when a bill of indictment having been found against 'Michael McCormick' for grand larceny, he was tried and convicted and has been sentenced as follows:

> 'To be removed at such time as his Excellency the Lieutent. Governor shall appoint, to the Bridewell[3] at Halifax, there to be confined at hard labor for the space of two years.'

You will have the goodness to observe that his Excellency's commands are necessary before he can be removed, or the sentence carried into execution.

> I have the honor
> To be
> Your obedient
> Tho. C. Haliburton

Wm. Hill Esqr.
Pro. Sec.
etc. etc.
Halifax

PANS copy

1 The most comprehensive of the commissions granted to judges on circuit, directing them to hold courts for the trial of offences
2 Harry King accompanied Haliburton. He wrote to his fiancée, Halli Fraser of Halifax, that the case was one of theft of more than £50 (Harry King to Halli Fraser, 6 November 1830, PAC, MG 24, 1, 182, vol. 2, file 3, 775–6, 779–80).
3 Bridewell was established in 1815 as a 'house of correction' in a building formerly used as a poorhouse (Raddall, 155).

---

34 To William Hill

[Windsor]
20th. Novr. 1830

Sir

In the year 1824 a law of the province was passed entitled 'An Act to make Provision for the Equal Administration of Justice in the Province of Nova Scotia'[1] by which the Leut Governor was authorised to appoint professional men to preside in the Courts of Common Pleas –

As their appointment virtually superceded the gentlemen who then filled those situations, it was deemed just that it should not deprive them of the fees to which they were entitled, and which they were in the habit of receiving – A clause was accordingly introduced into the law which directed that the fees of the First Justice, should not be payable to the judges appointed under the act, but to the former judges[2] –

In the district in which I preside, one or two of the former incumbents have died and the fees have devolved to me as their successor –

In appropriating however these fees to myself, I am under the necessity of taxing the bills containing them, and altho I entertain no doubt of my right to enact & receive them, yet I am aware that the 6th. clause of that act is not worded with as much precision and clearness as it might be –

Exceedingly averse from putting any construction upon a law in which I am personally interested, and desirous to avoid deciding for myself I must request you to have the goodness to lay this communication before his Excellency the Leut. Governor and to request that he will be pleased to call for the opinion of the law officers of the Crown in this province on the following question –

'Is the First Justice of the Courts of Common Pleas appointed under the Act 4 & 5, Geo 4th. C 38 entitled to the fees of office, on the death of him who presided as First Justice, before the passing of said act' –

>I have the honor to be
>With great respect
>Your obt
>Tho. C. Haliburton

William Hill Esquire
Pro. Secry
&c &c &c –

PANS MS

1 The act became law on 6 March 1824.
2 The sixth clause in the 1824 act reads: '*And be it further enacted,* That no Fees whatever, other than the travelling Fees hereinbefore mentioned, shall be payable or paid to any Judge so appointed, under this act, but that the Fees heretofore payable to those Judges of the said Courts, who now act as First-Justices thereof, shall continue payable, and be paid to them, so long as they shall attend the said Courts, and that no person so appointed under this Act, shall practice as an Attorney, Solicitor or Proctor, in any Court of Law or Equity within the Province, nor shall he hold any other place, appointment or situation, of profit, under Government ...' *Statutes at Large* (Halifax 1827) 3: 198–9.

35 To William Hill

[Windsor]
[c. 6 December 1830][1]

Mr. Fielding having been sent to me by Mr. Sentell during the investigation of the affair alluded to in Mr. Fieldings memorial,[2] he has requested me to certify thereon my opinion – I beg leave therefore to state for his Excellency's information that Mr Fielding since his arrival with his family in this place has given great cause of dissatisfaction[3] – He has kept a riotous and disorderly house – There have been constant complaints of father against son and son against father, repeated assaults, and several charges of one against the other for robbery – That by their drunkenness their house and goods have been exposed to the depredations of others also – I have reason to believe that every exertion has been made use of by Mr. Sentell and Mr Wright to trace out the robbery mentioned by Fielding, altho they have not been successful, and that the complaint is utterly without foundation –

And further I have great pleasure in stating to his Excellency that the two gentlemen complained against, are unquestionably the most zealous, active, and useful magistrates within the whole of my district, and that at Windsor the greatest part of the labour and fatigue of the police duty devolves upon them and is performed in a manner most satisfactory to the public, and creditable to themselves –

Tho. C. Haliburton

PANS MS

1 Haliburton wrote this as a codicil to a letter addressed to William Hill from Joseph Sentell and Patrick Wright, the two magistrates who were the target of William Fielding's complaints.
2 Fielding complains in the petition that his store had been broken into and £300 worth of goods stolen. The theft had occurred when Mr Fielding was away. Upon his return, Mr Fielding concluded that the authorities had been neglectful of their duties (PANS, RG 1, vol. 236, no. 98, 20 November 1830).
3 Haliburton concurred with the view of the magistrates who had maintained that the Fielding family had laid themselves open to theft by their disordered mode of living (see PANS, RG 1, vol. 236, no. 96).

36 To Sir Rupert D. George[1]

private
Windsor 20th Jny 1831

Dear sir –

On my return to Windsor I referred to the letter written by Millar to Mr. James,[2] and find that it contains the following paragraph – 'His Excellency was pleased to express himself most favorably and *wished me* to obtain the request of the magistrates in the county in favor of the prayer of the petition which he handed to me *for the purpose of forwarding*' –

It is owing to the perversion of his Excely words that he has been put to the pain of a second refusal, for wishes thus conveyed amount to commands, and no doubt they thought they were doing an agreeable thing to his Excellency – The clergy & one or two others,[3] could otherwise never have forgotten the indecorum of a second application – I send you the extract, to apprise you of the fact for your own knowledge, in future interviews with him, for I conceive written communications to Millar, far preferable to verbal ones – You may recollect a former instance[4] in which his hearing or memory failed him, relative to expressions used in court by S. Fairbanks[5] relative to yourself, which Fairbanks explained at your request before me in open court, and in which explanation every one present, who had heard the previous words, perfectly coincided –

He has always been what I call factious and troublesome, (but what he calls independent & perhaps thinks so) and it appears to me his object has been to ascertain whether he could obtain this womans release *without* my report, or *against* it, and if he had succeeded, I should ever after have had great trouble from him –

Your most obt.
Th C Haliburton

Sir Rupert D. George
&c.&c.

PANS MS

1 (1796–1856), provincial secretary and registrar of Grants, Patents and Records. He was also clerk of the Executive Council.
2 Garret Millar (1770–1840), JP, of Lunenburg County, and Mr James, the custodian of the jail. Haliburton disliked Millar but regarded Mr James as a respectable custodian.
3 Both the clergymen at Lunenburg signed the petition.
4 Haliburton's father had had a similar experience with Garret Millar in 1825 (see PANS, RG 1, vol. 232, docs 29, 30, 43, 47, and 93).
5 Samuel P. Fairbanks (1795–1882)

37 To Sir Rupert D. George   Windsor 9th March 1831

Sir –

In June 1829 a man by the name of James Gormley was tried before Judge Stewart at Annapolis, found guilty of manslaughter and sentenced to an imprisonment of seven years in the work house at Halifax[1] –

As I conducted his defence, his wife has thrice come thro to Windsor to prevail upon me to intercede for a remission of the remainder of his sentence, under the conviction that no one knows so much of her husband as myself and the strange delusion that 'a word from me' as she calls it is all that is wanting to obtain his discharge – I have in vain endeavoured to undeceive her in this particular, and to assure her that any communication from me to say the least of it, would be indelicate – But altho I cannot think any thing can justify a judge of one court to interfere at all with subjects not connected with his own proceedings, I have found it altogether impossible to resist any longer her distracted and affectionate supplications – I have therefore taken the liberty of enclosing the certificates she has produced to you *personally* (for I cannot bring myself to make any communication to his Excellency on the subject) and if you think proper to forward her own and her husbands petition to his Excellency, to state the case for your own information –

Gormly was a pensioned non commissioned officer of the artillery residing at Dalhousie[2] in the county of Annapolis – He was a man of good character frugal and industrious habits, and at the time of the unfortunate affair that brought him to the work house was possessed of the most *cultivated farm*, the *best buildings* and the *largest stock* in the settlement – He generally abstained wholly from liquor but owing to a wound in his head received either in service or by accident I forget which whenever he did take ardent spirits, it had the effect of rendering him quarrelsome & violent and in one of those fits of intoxication in a scuffle with one of his old associates the fatal affair happened for which he is now suffering punishment – It should not be concealed that had it not been for this infirmity he must have suffered death – The verdict and sentence were both unexceptionable, as may well be supposed, when Judge Stewart presided, he cannot possibly have any thing to complain of, altho his previous good character may perhaps form some ground for hope that a remission of some part of his sentence may be granted to him as the same indulgence has been sometimes extended to others – The enclosed certificates of character are signed by most respectable people, and the document is as good of the kind as could be procured in the place – Last autumn I went to see Gormley to reconcile him to his abode and to convince him of my inability to aid him in the way he desired, and I was then informed by the keeper that his conduct had been altogether uniformly decent and orderly since he had been there, and I make no doubt if he should obtain such remission that he will be found as deserving of it as any other to whom it may have been heretofore granted – After his sentence, his pension was stopped, which has thrown his family (a most deserving and decent one) into great distress, which is perhaps one of the strongest points of his petition –

I must apologise for the liberty I have take in thus troubling you, but really these journeys from Annapolis[3] which this poor woman has made (two of which were on foot) are so distressing to witness, that I shall rely on the same feeling in you to excuse, that has induced me to trespass on you –

>I remain
>Your most obt
>Th C Haliburton

Sir Rupert D. George –
&c &c –

PANS MS

1 Judge Wiswall presided at the trial with Judge Stewart. In his letter to the lieutenant-governor, dated 25 March 1831, Wiswall regretted that he could not recommend that Gormley be released (PANS, RG 1, vol. 238, doc. 96).
2 James Gormley was the subject of a petition (dated 17 June 1829) from the inhabitants of Dalhousie. The document contains thirty-four signatures (PANS, RG 1, vol. 248, doc. 198) and maintains that Gormley 'has been a most Quarrelsome & Blood thirsty man.' Gormley, however, was pardoned (PANS, RG 1, Series 'GP,' vol. 1, no. 53, 'Pardon of James Gormley').
3 Approximately eighty-four miles

38 To Garret Millar   Windsor 1st. December 1831

Sir

I have the honor to acknowledge the receipt of your letter of the 28 ulto enclosing a petition[1] of Mrs Corcum praying for her release from imprisonment under a sentence of the court passed upon her in October last –

I assure you that I feel the greatest compassion for the sufferings of the unfortunate woman, and the destitution and distress of her husband and children – Consulting my own feelings and guided by them alone, I should not hesitate (if called upon by the Governor for my opinion) to give the certificate she requires, but this is not the first painful instance in which I have found, that persons placed in a judicial situation must sometimes make their pity give place to sterner feelings of necessity and duty – Her offence is one of so serious a nature, that public justice requires an atonement – If it is viewed as an assault, we find it of so atrocious a kind that it almost involved a murder[2] – and if it is regarded as an attempt to take the life of a public officer in the discharge of his duty, the obvious consequence of impunity is the subversion of the administration of justice and of the peace and good order of society –

There have been several instances of the kind, of late, in my district and inadequate punishments seem to invite a repetition – This offence was committed with a full knowledge of all the consequences resulting from it, she must therefore attribute her misfortunes to her own ungovernable passions and vindictive temper, and not to the cruelty of the law, or the severity of her judges – Under these circumstances it is with the greatest regret I feel myself bound to say that considering her case as not possessing any claims upon his Excellency's clemency, I cannot at present with any propriety recommend it for its exercise – Should the Sherriff however at our next sittings in April report favorably of her conduct and behaviour in jail we may then perhaps consider whether sufficient punishment may not have been inflicted for personal correction or public example –

Her pregnancy (if not simulated for the purpose of exciting compassion) is a subject that ought to be provided for, and I therefore gave orders to the Sherriff[3] at the time, and shall now renew the same that in the event of her being confined in jail she should be tenderly and kindly used, and that she should not want for any of those comforts required by women in that condition –

I may add however in the event of similar applications hereafter that if I had felt myself authorised to have reported favorably in this case I could not have added my recommendation in the manner required –

I have always abstained from obtruding my advice or recommendations unasked, considering it both more decorous and more regular, to wait until the party seeking relief presents his petition to the governor, who, if he thinks the case requires any opinion from me will call upon me for a report –

To cause me to deviate from this plan would require stronger, much stronger circumstances than any presented in the case of Mrs Corcum –

>I have the honor to be be
>Your obt sert
>Tho. C. Haliburton

PANS MS

1 There were two petitions.
2 See the next letter for Haliburton's account of the case.
3 John H. Kaulbach (1758–1833), high sheriff of Lunenburg County

---

39 To Sir Rupert D. George

Windsor
8th Decr. 1831

Sir –

I have the honor to acknowledge the receipt of your letter of the 5th. inst. enclosing a petition of Mrs. Corcum (presented at the request of Mr. Garret Millar, and conveying his Excellency's commands that I should report thereon – I beg leave therefore to state for his Excellency's information, that that petition had been previously sent to me by Mr. Millar with a request that I would add to it my recommendation – This I was under the necessity of declining, for reasons stated to him in my letter, a copy of which I now enclose and to which I beg leave to refer you[1] –

After receiving that letter (which I think ought to have satisfied any man having *no other object in view* than the relief of the prisoner) I cannot but express both my surprise and regret that he should persist in attempting to force this release upon me – To refuse applications of this sort, is at all times extremely painful but to compel a second refusal inflicts additional pain and throws an unnecessary odium on the person doing so – Much as I feel for this poor woman, I am sorry to say, that as there is no one mitigating feature in her case I cannot recommend her discharge – It is therefore I assure you, with no little pain, that I feel myself compelled by this course to appear as the only obstacle to her release –

She was indicted 'for an assault upon the Sherriff, while in *the discharge of his duty*, with an intent to *take his life*' – It is not perhaps necessary to trouble you with all the particulars of the case, but I should state, that tho the sherriff escaped with his life it was only by one of those uncommon accidents, by which providence sometimes interferes to defeat the purposes of the murderer – He was attacked by Mrs Corcum and her son, the former armed with a pitch fork, and the latter with an axe – While endeavouring to evade the blows of the son, Mrs Corcum made a furious thrust at him with the pitch-fork, which he most fortunately received on his uplifted arm *between the prongs,* but the blow was so violent, and the parties so close, that it forced this arm against the body, and drove both points thro his clothes to his ribs – On his Examination he swore most positively that he had no doubt of her intention to kill him, and that the blow must inevitably have caused instant death, had its violence not have been intercepted in the extraordinary manner just described –

I have been given to understand by the magistrates, that she is a woman of notoriously bad character, and that her husbands reputation is if possible still worse – The Court of Sessions, on the day on which she was brought up was uncommonly full (only one or two justices being absent) and their sentence, (for it was not mine alone) was one years imprisonment in jail – As far as I can recall the fact to my mind *they were unanimous,* but most certainly it had their very general concurrence, and I cannot recollect one dissenting opinion – That they still retain the same view of it may be inferred from the fact, that their very respectable custos Mr. James, and every magistrate for the township of Lunenburg has declined to sign her petition –

I hope you will pardon this prolixity, but Mr. Millar's pertinacity has placed me in a most painful situation – Should any accident happen to this woman (to which however from her poverty she would be as liable at home as in jail) as the responsible head of the court, having twice declined (nay thrice for I refused her husband at Lunenburg)[2] to approve of her discharge, I am not insensible that I should receive the epithets of cruel and unrelenting – Driven to this extreme I must either advise a measure altogether destructive of the safety of public officers, and of the peace of that community, or incur the hazard (in the event of accident to her) of sustaining the accusation from some people of having sacrificed her to the dictates of a cold prudence, or an unfeeling heart –

Every individual in a community has a right (and the exercise of that right is highly creditable) to procure if possible the release of unfortunate prisoners, but I think I have reason to complain, that Mr. Millar in his zeal, has forgotten that he is a judge of that court that condemned her, *and as such* that something is due to the feelings and opinions of his colleagues, and something also to the propriety & decorum of public duties –

> I have the honor to be
> Your obt. servt
> Tho. C. Haliburton

To Sir Rupert D. George Bart.
Pro. Secty &. &.

PANS MS

1 Haliburton's letter of 1 December 1831, above. The copy that Haliburton enclosed differs verbally from the version printed above, although it is essentially the same letter (PANS, RG 1, vol. 237, doc. 63, 'Copy,' 31 November 1831).
2 The first petition is dated 24 October 1831. It pleads for Mrs Corkum on the grounds that she is pregnant and in danger of her health if she remains confined to prison (PANS, RG 1, vol. 237, doc. 64). The second petition, dated 22 December 1831, is from Henry Corkum, on behalf of his wife, Elizabeth. Even the sheriff, Mr Kaulbach, the victim in the original case, signed the second petition. The third occasion on which Haliburton was approached is probably the second petition, which was delivered to him at Lunenburg on the second Tuesday in October.

---

40 Sir Rupert D. George   Windsor 13th. January 1832

Sir –

I have the honor to acknowledge the receipt of your letter of the 12th. inst. enclosing a petition of Willm Kilfoil[1] with his Excellencys commands that I should report thereon – I have therefore the honor to state for his Excellency's information that Kilfoil was a servant of one Wm Fielding a shopkeeper at Windsor and was charged with having robbed him while in his employ of several articles of merchandise – The goods were found in his possession and he was convicted on undeniable testimony, and not on loose circumstantial evidence as stated in his petition, and that when brought up for judgement he admitted the theft, and attempted to extenuate the offence on the ground of intoxication and the persuasions of an accomplice – As Mr. Fielding had been several times robbed, and no trace of the perpetrator could be discovered, it was thought necessary to impose the punishment of two years imprisonment, for the purpose of effectually checking the increase of that species of crime, in a place so exposed as Windsor must necessarily be, from possessing no police, and being a thoroughfare between the provinces of New Brunswick and N Scotia –

The objects of all punishment, are personal correction and public example, and in this case perhaps both have been already amply attained –

The circumstance which appears to me to have most weight in his favor, is not mentioned in his petition, but he should not on that account, lose its benefit – Mr Fielding and his wife were people of considerable property, both in money and merchandise, and were not only careless but often intoxicated, and the exposure of so many articles, and the facilities so often afforded for their clandestine removal were too much for most men, who perhaps had been previously honest rather from the absence of strong temptation, than any rectitude of principle – Under these circumstances public example at Windsor has been satisfied by the sentence, *the execution of which the people do not witness*, and the remission of the remainder of his term (considering that he has already undergone eleven months imprisonment) may perhaps operate favorably on his future conduct –

Should this view of the case meet his Excellencys approbation, I beg leave to suggest, that his discharge should be granted, on the express condition *of his not returning to Windsor* for the reason above stated –

>All which is humbly submitted
>I have the honor to be
>Your obt. servant
>Tho C Haliburton

Sir Rupert D. George
Pro Secty &c &c.

PANS MS

1 He was accused of stealing 'a piece of linen' and sentenced by Haliburton to two years in the house of correction. At the time of writing his petition for clemency, Kilfoil had served eleven months of his sentence. A note from the commissioners of the house of correction, appended to the petition, recommends it be accepted.

---

41 To Sir Rupert D. George   Windsor 28th. January 1832

Sir –

The Revd Mr Cochran of Lunenburg[1] called upon me a few days ago, and stated his opinion, that the health of Mrs Corcum was suffering from her confinement in jail – I requested him to communicate this information in writing, which he did in the enclosed letter, to which I beg leave to refer you[2] – Punishment follows convicted crime as a matter of course, and the only agitation of mind a prisoner suffers is in the first instance, as to the nature and extent of the sentence; – but in this case this unfortunate woman has been kept in a state of constant excitement, by promises of relief, given by those who had no power of fulfillment, and who by inflicting the bitterness of disappointment have unhappily increased her punishment, and added most painfully to the responsibility of others[3] –

The mere inconvenience of Mr Corcum & his family in being deprived of the society and labor of his wife, or the additional plea of the pregnancy of Mrs Corcum, did not in themselves offer sufficient grounds, why so atrocious an assault as that committed by her, should not be punished, particularly as the mode selected was the mildest that could be adopted for a female, restricting her to the precincts of a jail –

If however her health is actually suffering (a fact which coming from so respectable a quarter can not be doubted) I cannot consistently, either with reference to the views of the court or the dictates of humanity, any longer decline to recommend her discharge to the consideration of his Excellency the Lt. Governor –

Should his Excellency concur in this view, may I beg the favor of you, instead of taking the trouble to write to me in reply, to address a note to H. Kaulback Esqr Sherriff of Lunenburg,[4] thro the post office at Halifax, to that effect, by which much time will be saved –

> I have the honor to be
> Your most obt. servt
> Tho. C. Haliburton

P.S. I have had from the commencement of the applications in this womans behalf, all my fears awakened, and I can assure I have suffered myself more anxiety and distress of mind, than I can well express, –
I do not know whether I have rendered myself quite intelligible as to the distinction between the first and present application, but I hope his Excellency will approve of the course I have adopted throughout[5] –
Sir Rupert D. George
Pro. Secty.

PANS MS

1 Rev. James C. Cochran (1798–1880), Anglican rector of St John's, Lunenburg, second son of Dr William Cochran (1757–1833)
2 Cochran's letter asks Haliburton to reconsider his decision (PANS, RG 1, vol. 237, doc. 53).
3 Haliburton alludes to Garret Millar's endeavours on behalf of Mrs Corkum.
4 Sheriff Kaulbach was at the centre of the incident that led to Mrs Corkum's incarceration. He was attacked by her with a pitchfork while engaged in the discharge of his duty.
5 The provincial secretary, in a letter dated 10 December 1831, accepted Haliburton's report on the case and conveyed the lieutenant-governor's approval of Haliburton's handling of the matter (PANS, RG 1, vol. 148, 102–3).

---

42 To Sir Rupert D. George   Windsor 12th. June 1832

Sir –

At the last meeting of the General Sessions of the Peace for the County of Kings[1] the following resolution of the legislature was submitted for the consideration of the court –

'Resolved that the sum of £1,150 be granted and paid to the inhabitants of King's County and others in addition to the sum of 750 pounds heretofore granted whenever a good and sufficient brdge shall have been built and completed across the Cornwallis River at such site as shall be selected by the Magistrates and Grand Jury of Kings County and approved of by his Excellency the Lt. Governor and according to such plan and under such securities for durability as the Govr. & Council shall approve' –

This vote having been taken into consideration it was unanimously agreed by the justices and Grand Jury, (in which such of the representatives as were present concurred) that it was highly expedient to have a survey, plan, specific estimates & practical directions from a competent engineer, or from some person having experience in the erection of wooden bridges over rivers subject to floating ice and the usual effects of frost[2] – Having unfortunately made two unsuccessful attempts to erect a bridge over the Cornwallis River from not having taken this precaution the justices and Grand Jury have requested me to submit this their opinion to his Excellency the Leut. Governor, and to beg the favor of his Excellency to employ some suitable person from the eastern part of the United States for that purpose[3] –

The resolution requiring the selection of the site to be made by the court, the justices and Grand Jury have directed me further to state their readiness to reassemble at any time during the summer, for the purpose of meeting and consulting with such engineer –

All which I have the honor to communicate to you for His Excellencys information –

> I have the honor to be
> With great respect
> Your obt. sevt.
> Tho. C. Haliburton

Sir Rupert D. George
Pro Sect &c –
Halifax

PANS MS

1 The Inferior Court of Common Pleas and General Sessions of the Peace met in Kentville on the third Tuesday in May.
2 The bridge was completed in 1835 (see PANS, RG 5, Series GP, vol. 8, no. 67).
3 Unidentified

---

43 To Samuel Fales[1]

[Windsor]
15th June, 1832.

My dear sir –

I received your letter by the [mail?][2] with the enclosures, and regret very much your intention of visiting Saratoga[3] instead of Nova Scotia. As our little flock will be added to this summer[4] I shall defer my visit to Boston until last of May next year before which time I will have the sitting of the court altered, and I then hope to have the pleasure of escorting you down to this province. Tell Mrs. Fales we have wonderful mineral springs here,[5] and faith quite as strong as the waters, and that for people who can sometimes fancy themselves sick (I don't mean to insinuate) why they will make them fancy themselves well, quite as much as any Republican spring in the world –

I delivered your message to Georgina,[6] respecting Miss Parker and her six little step children[7] – Ready made articles are sometimes convenient but suit the taste not so well as those made to order.

Wishing you an agreeable summer,

> Yours try.
> Thos. C. Haliburton

Pub.: DeCoursey Fales, *The Fales Family of Bristol, Rhode Island* (1919) 98–9

1 (1775–1848), shopkeeper, dry-goods merchant, and president of the Union Bank, Boston (1844–6). He was a successful businessman. In 1801 he married Haliburton's Aunt Abigail. See *Fales Family*, 80.
2 The printed version reads 'Mark.' 'Mail' is more appropriate in the context.
3 Famous for its more than one hundred natural mineral springs
4 Arthur Lawrence, Haliburton's youngest child and third son, was born on 26 September 1832, at Windsor.
5 'The Medicinal Spring, in Wilmot, Nova Scotia, is acquiring great notoriety and celebrity, for the cures effected by it ... ' the *Novascotian*, 22 June 1831: 194, col. b. Mineral springs were also located at 'Spa Springs' near Windsor.
6 Georgianna Haliburton (1803–88), Haliburton's cousin
7 Unidentified

44 To Sir Rupert D. George Windsor 24th. July 1832

Sir –

The Central Board having communicated to the Board of Health at Windsor, that the correspondence between them had been laid before his Excellency the Leut. Governor; – At a period like the present[1] when their time is occupied by matters of deep importance, the board have thought it advisable at once to anticipate any enquiries on this subject and to state to his Excellency the reasons that induced the board to return a letter of the secretary of the Central Board –

I am desired respectfully to state for his Excellencys information that the board deemed that letter highly objectionable both in tenor and tone, and such as ought not to have been addressed to persons, who are not *stipendiary officers*, but *voluntary agents*, encountering a most painful responsibility, and a most laborious and difficult duty, under embarrassments of no ordinary kind, arising from a law most difficult of construction, and from resources both limited and doubtful –

Thus situated the board conceived that a correspondence commenced in this manner, would probably be conducted with continued mortification, and could alone terminate in those painful results which inevitably flow from an absence or disregard of the courtesies that regulate the intercourse of gentlemen – At a loss to know whether such a letter emanated from the Central Board, or was the spontaneous production of their secretary the board thought it best, to return it to the person from whom it came, and altho painful after what had passed, renewed their correspondence, on account of the importance of their duties, with the central board without any allusion to what had taken place –

The board further desire me respectfully to observe that this is a subject in which feeling and not principle is concerned and on which it is difficult for others than those interested to judge, but they could not fail to remark what must be obvious to all, that in his official communications that officer, who from his station, has alone the right to use the language of dictation, in such correspondences, has never on any occasion conveyed an order of government to the humblest individual in terms and manner similar to that of the central board –

The central board have however by a resolution, communicated to the boards, that they perceive offence has been given, but that such offence was wholly unintentional, on their part, and is the subject of regret –

With this avowal the board are perfectly satisfied, and convinced that similar occasion will not be given, are willing to unite their efforts with the Central Board, for the purposes for which they were organised purposes that unhappily demand unremitting toil, and undivided attention –

The board have desired me further to express their deep concern that his Excellency should have been troubled with the matter, and to apologize to you for a communication, which from its reference to personal matters, must be far from agreeable –

I have the honor to be
Your most obt. sevt.
Thos. C Haliburton

Sir Rupert D George Bart.
&c. &c. &c.

PANS MS

1 Raddall vividly describes the cholera scare of the eighteen-thirties (176–7). The cause of cholera – contaminated water – was not known in the nineteenth century.

---

45 To Sir Rupert D. George   Windsor 28th January 1834

Sir –

I have the honor to enclose for the consideration of his Honor the President,[1] a report of extra services performed by me, at different times, under special commissions by order of the local government –

These commissions have been rendered necessary at Liverpool from the number of the prisoners, and the insecurity of the jail; and in the other instances to relieve the counties from the expence attending the support of the accused, for so long a period as intervenes between the usual sittings of the Supreme Court[2] –

The business which has thus devolved upon me is both the most responsible and most painful a Judge has to perform, but I have not felt myself justified, either on that account, or its not appertaining to my office to decline its performance, when the public service required it should be done –

I should add however, that the labor and anxiety of those trials, the extension of the Terms & the expences incidental thereto, is all for which I feel myself entitled to remuneration, as it has always been so managed, by holding these special courts during the same weeks the other courts in which I preside were held, that it has not been necessary to travel to those Counties for that sole purpose –

>I have the honor to be
>Your most obt servt.
>Th. C. Haliburton

To
Sir Rupert D. George Bart
Pro.Secty.
&c &c

1834
Hants County
January Term 1831

1.
Special Com –

Rex v. William Kilfoil	} – – Larceny
Rex *Michl. McDermot*	} receiving stolen goods

2
Special Com.

    Rex
      v.
Thomas McCormack

King's County

} Larceny

3d
Special Com.

    Rex
      v.
William Chambers.

Queens County
Ap 1832.

} Larceny

    Rex
      v.
William White
Eleanor Roberts

} Receiving stolen goods.

4th.
Special Com

    Rex.
Michael Graham
Samuel Davies

April 1833
Queen's County

} Larceny.

    Rex
      v.
William ONeale

} – do

    Rex.
      v.
1st Sylvester Jennings

} – do

    Rex
2d – Sylvester Jennings

} – do

    Rex
      v.
John Davies

} – do

    Rex
      v.
Martin Huskins

} – do

5th. *Special Com*

King's County

1st   Rex
    v.   } Arson
John Lawson

Rex   } Prisoner discharged.
    v.   Arson
John Lawson

I have not the indictments by me from which to state their offences, in some instances they were burglary, breaking into stores and other statutable offences, and this report of evidence & other causes were corrected of the minor offences – The period of service has been 4 years –

Th C Haliburton

PANS MS

1 Simon Bradstreet Robie (1770–1858). The request for extra remuneration was referred to a three-man committee of the House of Assembly who recommended that Haliburton be paid £65.
2 The Supreme Court usually met at Liverpool on the first Tuesday in July (i.e., once a year).

---

46 To Thomas N. Jeffrey[1]   Windsor, 6th July, 1834

Sir,

The magistrates of the county of Hants, availing themselves of the opportunity afforded them, by being assembled in General Session, have by a *unanimous* vote of their body, requested me to express to you, on your retirement from office, the high sense they entertain of the very able, zealous, and impartial manner you have conducted the government of the province.

They desire to assure you that they have great satisfaction in thus bearing testimony in a body, in favor of an administration distinguished alike for a firm support of the prerogatives of the Crown, and for a proper regard for the rights of the people.

The regret they feel at your retirement from an office, the duties of which you have discharged with so much honor to yourself and satisfaction to the public, is diminished by the knowledge that you still remain in the province, and that on a similar occasion the same ability and the same zeal will be at the disposal of His Majesty.

In thus complying with the vote of the General Sessions, permit me to add that I have great pleasure in being the medium of a communication, so much in accordance with my own feelings.

I have the honor to be, with great respect, your most obedient servant, (Signed) Tho. C. Haliburton, President.

To the Honorable T.N. Jeffery, late Administrator of the Government, &c.

Pub.: *Hants and King's County Gazette*, 21 July 1834

1 Thomas N. Jeffrey (1782–1847) was appointed collector of customs at Halifax. Jeffrey's estate, Lakelands, was just inside the boundary of Hants County, approximately three miles from Mount Uniacke, the estate of Richard John Uniacke.

47 To T.W. James[1]   Lunenburg 16th. Octr. 1835

Sir –

I have just received the enclosed letter[2] from the magistrates of Lunenburg, which I beg leave to forward to his Excellency the Leut. Governor,[3] and to recommend to his favorable notice –

> I have the honor to be
> Your obt servt.
> Tho C Haliburton

Thos. W. James Esqr
Acg. Pro. Secty

PANS MS

1 Thomas W. James, deputy provincial secretary in 1835
2 The enclosure is missing.
3 Sir Colin Campbell (1776–1847), lieutenant-governor of Nova Scotia, 1834–40

48 To W.H. Chipman[1]   12th. Nvr. 1835

Sir –

You will have the goodness to see that the fees now due & accruing to the judges be regularly paid in up to date –

> Tho C Haliburton

Mr Chipman
Prothy –

PANS MS

1 William Henry Chipman (1807–1870), merchant, landowner, later MP and deputy protonotary of King's County

---

49 To Joseph Howe[1]

[Windsor]
[15 November 1835]

Dear Howe,

I have just returned from western court, where I believe your letter went, for I did not receive it till several days after date.[2] I see by the papers there will be a new election.[3] What do you do? There is not much fun in two of them two years running. It is rather awkward I think. I can't help repeating what I have said before. I do think you won't advance your own interests or influence by going there. Why does a judge's charge have more influence than an attorney's speech? Because he belongs to *no side*. I fear your paper (always enough on one side of politics) will be thought after your election (for I take that[4] for granted if you offer) a party paper altogether. I fear you will hurt it, and it will hurt you, like a gig that runs over a cow, it kills the animal and breaks the carriage. I say consider well, cypher like Slick,[5] set down the advantages on one side, it will make a deuced[6] small column, and put the disadvantages on the other, and strike a balance.[7] I know nothing so seductive as the request[8] of respectable people to offer a friendly offer to support, a confidence in our talent, a reliance on our power.[9] It is seductive, hard to resist, indeed, but think before you act. I say no more, you will readily[10] see the friend, if I am mistaken in this view,[11] for real friends *only* differ, from us in our favourite projects. If you do offer you have my best wishes, but if you don't I have no fears. Your present career,[12] has no breakers, no quicksands, you have taken the soundings, and know your way, you are an old navigator, tho' you do crack on sail like the devil sometimes, the other voyage, however it may[13] promise, is *after all uncertain*.

If you do start, don't be long,[14] after you make up your mind, in taking the field. I incline to the belief, there will be a general election, from the writs not issuing already. When they do issue, if you do offer, start early, much is lost for want of early canvassing and securing pledges. From what I hear I incline to think that Johnstone[15] will offer, on account of the chair. In all or either case success to you.[16]

Mind the spelling of Slicks nonsense, the dialect is half the wit, the last lost a good deal. Do they stand fair with your folks?

Yours
T.C.H.

Tell Grigor[17] to write to me, a letter about all sorts of things, will you? I have a plan about the railroad I will write to you that will [go?] down yet.[18] After your flustration is over I will write to you about it. Clark[19] was acquitted. I have a long story and a funny one to tell you about it.

Could you borrow Jack Downing?[20] for a few days.

Discontinue advertisement of house.[21]

PAC/Chittick, 393-4 copy

1 (1804-73), politician, author, and journalist
2 Haliburton had just returned from the Inferior Court and Sessions of the Peace held at Kentville on the second Tuesday in November (*Belcher's*, 1835, 65). The opening of the letter is taken from the PAC copy made by Sydenham Howe (PAC MG 30 D 11, vol. 1, Sydenham Howe Correspondence, 12A–B). Howe's copy differs from Chittick in matters of wording and punctuation. I indicate the main differences in wording only.
3 The writ for a general election was issued on 2 November 1836. Howe ran as a candidate for Halifax County. He entered the contest formally on 4 December 1836 and was elected later in the month.
4 PAC reads 'for that I take.'
5 By 15 November, Howe had printed the first eight episodes of *The Clockmaker*.
6 PAC reads 'damn.'
7 PAC reads 'the balance.'
8 PAC reads 'as requests.'
9 PAC has a comma after the first 'offer,' and also reads 'talents' and 'our powers.'
10 PAC reads 'readily, I think see.'
11 PAC reads 'mistaken in this, for.'
12 PAC reads 'present course.'
13 PAC reads 'however to my.'
14 PAC reads 'too long.'
15 Hon. James William Johnstone (1792–1873). He did not offer at this time. Later he had an illustrious political career, becoming premier of Nova Scotia, 1843–7, 1857–60, and 1863–4. He was appointed lieutenant-governor of Nova Scotia in 1873 but died before he was able to take office.
16 From here to the end of the letter exists only in the form of the PAC version.
17 Dr William Grigor (1798–1857), first president of the Medical Society of Nova Scotia
18 In October 1835, Howe started a series of articles in the *Novascotian*, later reprinted in pamphlet form, in which public attention was directed to the practicality and importance of linking Halifax and Windsor by railway.
19 Unidentified. Roger D. Clarke was an auctioneer who advertised regularly in the *Novascotian*.

20 Haliburton might well have been asking to borrow Seba Smith's volume, published in November 1833. It was Seba Smith, not his imitator, Charles Augustus Davis, who made use of the Yankee dialect. See Mary Alice Wyman, *Two American Pioneers, Seba Smith and Elizabeth Oakes Smith* (New York: Columbia University Press 1927) 74.

21 Haliburton was preparing to move into Clifton. The advertisement for Haliburton's house (the old family residence on Water Street in Windsor) first appeared in the *Novascotian*, 17 December 1834, and ran for almost a year, until Haliburton requested its discontinuance in this letter.

---

50 To Robert Parker [Windsor, 1836?]

After a very severe and trying fever, which I had in 1829 at Annapolis, I found a very beneficial change in my constitution. Renewed health brought an increase of appetite and strength. I grew stouter and stronger and have enjoyed better health ever since. About forty years of age is one of the periods that the constitution suffers a sort of fermentation in the blood, like other liquors, which if it passes off quietly is more apt to be beneficial than otherwise,[1] at least such is one of my crotchets, and I think there is something in it. I trust in God you will find it so, and that you may be long spared to your family and friends, and to the province, to which you are so useful in the sphere in which you are placed.[2] I cannot bear to see you write in so sad a strain, and as good spirits contribute more than anything else to convalescence, you must look to the sunny side and cheer up.

Pub.: *Canadian Magazine* 1916: 76

1 The implication of this remark is that the letter is written in 1836 when Haliburton was forty.
2 Parker had succeeded J. Murray Bliss in 1834 as a puisne judge of the Supreme Court of New Brunswick.

---

51 To Sir Colin Campbell Windsor
4th. Ap. 1836

To

His Excellency the Leut. Governor and the Honble His Majesty's Council –
The petition of the Avon Bridge Co[1] humbly sheweth –

That your petitioners have associated themselves for the purpose of erecting a bridge over the Avon River at Windsor, and have entered into a contract for the same –

That the course of travelling thro the western part of the province will by the erection of said bridge, be so far diverted from its present route, as to cause a great increase of that which now passes thro the village of Windsor and consequently require an alteration of the main road in Falmouth –

The main road from Horton to Windsor, by Mount Denson, after passing thro the township of Falmouth terminates at the ferry;[2] it is proposed so far to alter the route, as to connect it with the new bridge, by opening a road from the left bank of the Avon river, to the main road as will appear by the plan hereunto annexed[3] –

Your petitioners humbly pray that your Excellency and your Honble Board, will be pleased to appoint a commissioner to lay out the same pursuant to law, and to report his proceedings thereon for your consideration –

                              And as in duty bound
                              Will ever pray
                              Tho. C. Haliburton Pres. Av.
                              Bridge. Co. for said Co –

PANS MS

1 Notice of the Act of Incorporation was given at a general meeting of the shareholders on 26 October 1835. Tenders were called by 1 February 1836, and the bridge was completed before 1 November 1836.
2 Ferries had been crossing from Falmouth to Windsor since 1765. Service was improved in the eighteen-twenties and did not immediately discontinue with the building of the bridge. See Shand, 65–7.
3 The plan is annexed to the letter.

---

52 To Peter Dawson[1]

Windsor
10th. Ap 1836

The foregoing petition[2] having been presented to the Court [of] General Sessions of the Peace,[3] it was considered that the alteration prayed for, being on the Great Western post road, it would be more a subject of consideration for his Excellency the Leut. Governor and his Majestys

Council, but as it was deemed an object of great public importance it was moved and seconded and accordingly resolved unanimously 'that the President of the Court be requested to transmit the same with the recommendation of the court, for a favorable consideration' –

In conformity to this resolution I have the honor to transmit this petition & plan,[4] and beg leave to add I fully concur in the opinion expressed by the court, of the necessity and great importance of the measure proposed –

Tho. C. Haliburton Pres. Sess.

Peter Dawson Comr.

PANS MS

1 Mr Dawson was appointed commissioner as requested in Haliburton's letter of 4 April 1836 above.
2 Haliburton's note accompanied a petition from Benjamin DeWolfe and others of the village of Windsor, who urged that the road out of Windsor at 'The Old Jail Hill,' and 'The Windmill Hill,' be altered to facilitate travel between Windsor and Halifax.
3 The Court of General Sessions met on the first Tuesday in January.
4 The plan is enclosed with the petition. The proposal was granted 12 May 1836 by the lieutenant-governor (PANS, RG 1, vol. 150, 92).

---

53 To Sir Rupert D. George

Private
[Windsor]
[1836?]

My dear Sir –

I saw by an accidental reference to the late Gazettes,[1] this day, several appointments of magistrates within the mid. division, and as one of them is an uncommonly objectionable one, as regards the man's strong passions, peculiar prejudices, & weak judgt, and will most likely do some extraordinary act very soon that will render it necessary to remove him, I take the liberty of *entreating* you to favor me with the opportunity of being heard on any appt. to the courts in which I preside, and for whose order & decorum I am responsible – This was the invariable practice in times of Sir James & Sir Peregrine and it appears to me of great importance to be adhered to, as it is very hard to rectify a mistake once made – If the cms to swear in have not been sent down, I should like still to be heard against one of these appointments, as it really is one of the most objectionable I have known for many years –

Indeed it would be very adviseable for the com. to swear them in should be sent to me, as it would enable me to give some advice where necessary to the new magistrates –

My dear Sir Rupert – I hope you will excuse the subject of this letter, and as there is not the slightest intention of obtruding advice do not consider it as such –

Yours very truly
Th. C. Haliburton

PANS MS

1 Not located (possibly, the *Halifax Royal Gazette*)

---

54 To T.W. James   Windsor 24th. Nov. 1836

Sir –

I have the honor to acknowledge the receipt of your letter of the 18th. of May last enclosing a petition of Robert Barry a prisoner at Kentville,[1] containing complaints against the Sherriff and other officers of that county, and conveying his Excellencys orders that the same should be enquired into –

Upon enquiry I found there was no such person confined there, but that there had been a man of that name, who was then for the third time, an escaped prisoner, still at large, and it was said a man of very loose character, and of no credibility whatever – As those however were mere assertions (with the exception of his escape) I adjourned the consideration till the next term,[2] to afford time for his recapture and examination –
He has not however been retaken, an investigation therefore cannot under the circumstances, take place at present and I feel myself under the necessity of returning the petition –

All which is humbly submitted
I have the honor to be
Your most obt sevt
Th. C. Haliburton

To T.W. James Esqr
Pro Secty

PANS MS

1 Robert Barry's petition, dated 20 April 1836, complains that the authorities were quick to collect the money he owed, but did not collect the money owed him. As a result, he had been forcibly detained and starved. As a former lieutenant under General Vinson, in the service of 'Canaday,' he did not feel he deserved such treatment (PANS, RG 1, vol. 241, doc. 182).

2 The Inferior Court and General Sessions of the Peace met at Kentville on the second Tuesday in November and the third Tuesday in May.

---

55 To T.W. James   Windsor 24th. November 1836

Sir –

I have the honor to acknowledge the receipt of your letter of the 6th. of April last enclosing a petition of Henry Wilson[1] and other inhabitants of Aylesford to his Excellency the Leut. Governor, complaining of various acts of malversation[2] in office of Thomas Tupper[3] esquire a Justice of the Peace of King's County, and conveying his Excellency's order that the same should be enquired into –

I have now the honor to report on the same as follows – Having directed the parties to the petition and Mr. Tupper to be summoned before the court, the complainants were called upon to prove their allegations, and after a full examination of the evidence, it appeared to the court, that they had failed to substantiate any specific charge against him, and the complaint was accordingly dismissed –

The number however of the petitioners, the readiness with which they attended, and the strong feeling exhibited on the occasion, led the court to conceive, that altho nothing tangible was proved, there must have been on the part of the justice, a want of conciliatory conduct, or too great a readiness to perform those duties, which from their disagreeable nature are rather shrunk from in general, than voluntarily performed, in short an absence of that deportment which attracts respect, and gives weight to the character of a magistrate, and they felt it their duty to express to him this opinion publickly – Beyond this general remark, they did not feel themselves warranted to animadvert – The excited feeling however from whatever cause it originated, did not seem to be wholly allayed and it was hinted there was other evidence, which may yet be adduced – Altho like other judicial investigations when the evidence was closed, it might be considered as terminated, yet so important is the due administration of justice, so essential to the character and integrity of a government, is the deportment of those to whom it is entrusted, that I thought it proper to withhold a report, until the next sitting of the court,[4] intending if the parties come forward again, to give them an opportunity of doing so – The term however has passed over without any such application, and it now becomes due to Mr. Tupper to consider it as closed –

I have therefore humbly to submit the foregoing remarks –

> I have the honor to be
> Your most obt sevt
> Tho.C.Haliburton

To
T W James Esqr
Pro Sectry

PANS MS

1 The petition is dated 25 February 1836 and is signed by Sidney Wilson and approximately one hundred others. The petition notes 'his thirst for money is so great that he will undertake any thing for gain' (PANS, RG 1, vol. 241, doc. 180).
2 'Malversation' is corrupt behaviour in office.
3 There were further complaints in 1842 when Henry Magee of Aylesford petitioned the lieutenant-governor, laying further charges against Tupper (PANS, RG 1, Series 'GP', no. 98; see also no. 108 and no. 109).
4 Haliburton is therefore reporting on the case he heard when the Inferior Court and General Sessions met on the third Tuesday in May at Kentville. They met again at Kentville on the second Tuesday in November.

---

56 To Sir Rupert D. George Windsor 2d Ocr. 1837

During the latter part of the last session of the legislature, after the Committee of Supply had closed, a vote of credit was passed by the Assembly, authorising his Excellency the Lt. Governor, so soon as it could be satisfactorily proved to him, that the sum of one hundred and fifty pounds had been expended by the Avon Bridge Co, on their new route from the bridge, to the post road in Horton, to order a payment of a similar sum to the company[1] –

Instead of the sum contemplated the company has expended three hundred pounds and upwards, and intends to employ a large party of workmen – As vouchers for this expenditure I have annexed an affidavit of Mr Peter Dawson, that he has laid out this increased amount, and also a certificate – from myself as President of the co. that the work has been faithfully expended to our entire satisfaction –

Should these vouchers prove sufficient as I trust they will, to his Excellency, may I beg the favor of you, in the course of the ensuing week, to communicate to me his Excellencys permission to draw on the treasury for the one hundred and fifty pounds contemplated by the vote of the assembly –

I have taken the liberty to mention an early day, as I shall be absent after this week,[2] and no other officer of the co. can sign the draft but myself, and the funds at my disposal for the completion of the work being exhausted –

> I have the honor to be
> Your most obt. sevt
> Tho. C. Haliburton

Sir Rupert D. George Bart
Pro Secty &c –
&c –

I do hereby certify that Peter Dawson has expended under my directions, as President of the Avon Bridge Co, on the new route from Avon Bridge to the Half Way House,[3] on the post road to Horton, a sum exceeding three hundred pounds, being an excess over the amount contemplated by the vote of the Assembly, of one hundred and fifty pounds and upwards – And I do further certify that the said amount has been most judiciously, faithfully, and satisfactorily expended –

> Tho. C. Haliburton –
> Pres Av Bridge Co

PANS MS

1 See *Journals ... of the House of Assembly* (1836), Appendix 57, 1000.
2 The Inferior Court opened at Lunenburg on the second Tuesday in October, followed by the Court at Liverpool on the third Tuesday.
3 Daniel Bishop's or the 'half way house' between the Horton mountains (see the *Novascotian*, 28 December 1836).

3
The Clockmaker and England, 1838–1840

The traditional story of how *The Clockmaker* found its way to Richard Bentley is that it was taken to London and shown to Bentley by Colonel Charles Richard Fox, who had been formerly stationed at Halifax. In 1837, the London publication of *The Clockmaker* involved two other people besides Fox: R.H. Barham, later to achieve fame with his *Ingoldsby Legends*, and Charles D. Archibald, formerly a member of the Nova Scotia House of Assembly, who frequently travelled from England to Nova Scotia and vice-versa. It was on Barham's advice that Bentley published *The Clockmaker*. The lax enforcement of copyright laws enabled Bentley to pirate *The Clockmaker* from Howe's Halifax edition and to present the republication in England to its author as a *fait accompli*.

On 10 January 1838, Haliburton wrote to Richard Bentley complaining of the piracy. He had just received a copy of *The Clockmaker* from Charles Archibald. The sight of an English edition of the book muted Haliburton's tone of complaint and he offered Bentley the Second Series, even before he had received the letter Bentley wrote (on 27 December 1837) to Charles D. Archibald asking Haliburton to write a new work in three volumes and before he had received the piece of plate that Bentley despatched to him in acknowledgment of 'Sam Slick.' Haliburton's initials and name are incorrectly engraved on the plate (now at the Haliburton Museum in Windsor, Nova Scotia), because Bentley was as yet uncertain with whom he was dealing.[1] Bentley's letter was also accompanied by a handsome offer for another work, for which Bentley was willing to pay £250 or £300; a work Bentley hoped would be three volumes, rather than two, and certainly not one volume like the first. Haliburton promptly finished his new work (*The Clockmaker*, Second Series), in one volume, took it to London, and signed the contract with Bentley on 23 August 1838, receiving £300 for the one volume.[2]

After baiting the long line, Bentley must have been surprised at how soon his new author landed at his feet in London. Haliburton sailed for England in April 1838, with Joseph Howe and Charles Fairbanks. He stayed at 202 Piccadilly, London, for most of his visit, moving to 4 Spring Gardens, in February-March 1839. By then, he had established contacts that were to influence his successive visits to England and assure him of a place in fashionable English society. Bentley held a dinner to which he invited some of the wits of the day: R.H. Barham (who had recommended accepting *The Clockmaker*) and the celebrated comic writer Theodore Hook, then at the height of his fame, were among those present.[3]

Richard Harris Barham (1788–1845) had attended St Paul's school with Richard Bentley. Though a cleric, he was also a man of the world: 'Racy, dignified, shrewd and kindhearted ... his right arm partially crippled for life through a coach accident during his schooldays, Barham combined ecclesiastical piety with a genius for the writing of humorous verse.'[4] Barham's *Ingoldsby Legends*, published in *Bentley's Miscellany* from January 1837 onwards, and then, collectively, in 1840, was one of the most popular works of the day. During his visit to England in 1838 and 1839, Haliburton regularly associated with Barham and renewed the acquaintance on a further visit in 1843.

By 8 July 1838, if we can judge by the list of people to whom Haliburton wished presentation copies of the second *Clockmaker* to be sent, his circle of acquaintances included: the Hon. Mrs Caroline Norton, one of the more notorious fashionable figures of the day; Stephen Price, the American actor-manager, and James Haliburton, with whom Haliburton formed an immediate and long-lasting friendship. James Haliburton (1788–1862) was an explorer and Egyptologist, whose father, a successful London builder, had changed the family name from Haliburton to Burton. In 1838, James Haliburton reassumed the Haliburton name. He was, according to the *DNB*, obsessed with his family origins.

In London, Thomas Chandler Haliburton became a member of the Garrick Club, for both Barham and Bentley were members; he was also admitted to the exclusive Athenaeum Club and broadened his acquaintance considerably by associating with its founding members, Decimus Burton (James Haliburton's brother) and John Wilson Croker. Decimus was one of the most successful of Victorian architects: he designed numerous London buildings and many country estates.[5] Decimus lived in Spring Gardens, London, and Haliburton stayed at No. 6, the Burton's home, on all his later visits to England.

Charles Fairbanks, one of Haliburton's fellow travellers from Nova Scotia, kept a journal and commented on how well Haliburton was received by polite society.[6] Surviving letters indicate the nature and extent of Haliburton's social activities. Prominent among his literary friends was Mrs Frances Trollope (1780–1863), already a well-established novelist and writer of travels: 'Mr Bentley was the medium of the introduction which proved to be a very pleasant one,' commented Francis Eleanor Trollope, in her book on her grandmother, in 1895.[7]

When Haliburton met Mrs Trollope she was fifty-eight, a widow and the author of nine books, all published in the previous eight years. One of these, her *Domestic Manners of the Americans* (2 vols; 1832), had won her transatlantic notoriety, being an account of an abortive attempt to establish herself in the new world, in Cincinnati, Ohio. She was a prolific writer. When Haliburton met her, she was preparing a book for Bentley (published as *Widow Barnaby*) and planning another novel of a quite different kind, *Michael Armstrong, The Factory Boy*, which she was researching during the autumn of 1838 by visiting industrial centres in England to witness child labour abuses first-hand. Her son Anthony, later to become the famous novelist, describes her character in his *Autobiography* (2 vols; 1883) as: 'unselfish, affectionate, and most industrious ... with a great capacity for enjoyment and high physical gifts. She was endowed, too, with much creative power, with considerable humour, and a genuine feeling for romance. But she was neither clear-sighted nor accurate; and in her attempts to describe morals, manners, and even facts, was unable to avoid the pitfalls of exaggeration.' Haliburton liked her and was a frequent guest at her table in the autumn of 1838. When he wrote to Bentley in 1839, his enquiries about Mrs Trollope were frequent; 'my friends the Trollopes' is his usual phrase.

Mrs Trollope's family life is of concern here, too, because in 1843 Haliburton wrote to Cecilia, her daughter, and the first letter written to the household is, most likely, addressed to Thomas Adolphus, her eldest son. In 1838, Cecilia was about to be married to John Tilley, a clerk in the post office; and Thomas had just given up his job as a schoolteacher in Birmingham to become his mother's assistant. After finishing her two novels in 1838–9, Mrs Trollope travelled to the Lake District to live at Penrith, where she built a house near her daughter. However, she spent the winter in Paris. In 1841, she travelled to Italy. When Haliburton visited England in 1843, he had to locate Mrs Trollope before he could visit her. She had moved to Devon for the summer to stay with relations.

In November 1838, Haliburton had his portrait painted by Eden Upton Eddis, in order to circulate a print of it among his admirers. During the early weeks of December, Haliburton hastily penned *The Bubbles of*

Canada. Bentley paid him handsomely for the work, which Haliburton wrote in the form of a letter. Addressed to his new friend James Haliburton, it set out to explain the current political situation in Canada, which was attracting daily attention in the British newspapers.

The political situation in the Canadas was about to be transformed by the publication of the Earl of Durham's *Report on the Affairs of British North America* in early February 1839. In London, British North Americans of similar political persuasion to Haliburton felt it their duty to speak out against what they saw as the dangerous tendencies of the Durham *Report*. Scarcely had Haliburton put his pen down after writing *The Bubbles* than he took it up again to send a series of letters to *The Times*, attacking the Durham *Report* under the guise of 'A Colonist.'[8]

John Beverley Robinson, chief justice of Upper Canada, who happened to be in London, also opposed the Durham *Report*, but he chose to make his views known in the back rooms of the Colonial Office. Haliburton made his opposition public and found support among British conservatives. One of them, John Wilson Croker (1780–1857), politician, essayist, and one of the founders of the *Quarterly Review* (1809 et seq.), paid him special attention. Croker was a friend of Decimus Burton's and no 'narrow party man' (according to biographer, Myrom F. Brightfield).[9] Burton and Croker helped to found the Athenaeum Club in order to give 'English writers and political men a common ground of association,'[10] for they had little enthusiasm for the Tory club, the Carlton. Croker published a review of the Durham *Report* and Haliburton's *Reply* in the *Quarterly Review* (March 1839, 457–525), praising Haliburton for exposing the 'most prominent fallacies, both of statement and argument' in the *Report*. Haliburton received a copy of the flattering review essay as he was about to embark on the *Great Western* steamship for Halifax. The article was the final mark of kindness Haliburton received from Croker and his wife; he had also benefited during the last month of his visit (March 1839) from their hospitality.

Haliburton returned to Nova Scotia on 23 March 1839 aboard the *Great Western* steamship. The *Bristol Mirror* (23 March 1839) wished Haliburton had stayed longer, describing him as: 'confessedly one of the wittiest and wisest of Judges ... so powerful an advocate of Conservatism.' The powerful conservative was ecstatic over the new steamship, the greatest British public phenomenon since Waterloo: it was 'the most triumphant voyage ever effected by steam,' he wrote to Croker, and immediately upon his return started work on his next book before his impressions of the voyage faded. This was a series of satirical letters, grouped under the title

The Letter-Bag of the Great Western, or, Life in a Steamer. The *Great Western* was the focus of international attention, and *The Letter-Bag* was designed to take advantage of the considerable public interest in the ship. Bentley printed 3,500 copies as a first edition, the largest initial print run he authorized for many years.[11]

Haliburton's letter of instructions to Bentley concerning *The Letter-Bag*, in November 1839, reveals how disillusioned he was on returning to his judicial duties, to find the House of Assembly wrangling incessantly over the status of the Inferior Court. Haliburton's literary activity from 1838 to 1840 was intense, almost frenzied: it included the Second Series of *The Clockmaker*, *The Bubbles of Canada*, *Reply to the Report of the Earl of Durham*, and *The Letter-Bag of the Great Western*, and was concluded with the Third Series of *The Clockmaker*. The implication of all this activity is that Haliburton was planning an alternative career as a writer and hoping speedily to remove himself from his financial dependence on the provincial purse.

1 BL Add. MS 46,676, f. 26: '– on account of The Clockmaker 1st. ser ... a piece of plate purchased for £31.14.0'
2 BL Add. MS 46,676, f. 26 and BL Add. MS 46,613, f. 120
3 Richard Henry Stoddard, *Personal Reminiscences by Barham, Harness and Hodder* (New York 1875) 37–8, mentions an undated entry in Barham's diary: 'Dined at Bentleys. There were present, Hook, Haliburton, Jerdan, Moran, and my son.'
4 Guy Boas, *The Garrick Club 1831–1947* (London 1948) 24–5
5 See Howard Colvin, *A Biographical Dictionary of British Architects 1600–1840* (London 1978) 170.
6 Chittick, 221–3. The journal has since disappeared.
7 *Frances Trollope: Her Life and Work. From George III to Victoria*, 2 vols (London 1895) 1: 297
8 *The Times*, February 8–16, 1839 (seven letters). See Chittick, 263 et seq.
9 *John Wilson Croker* (Berkeley: University of California Press 1940) 161
10 Ibid.
11 BL Add. MS 46,637, vol. LXXVIII, List, vol. 1, 1829–73

---

57 To Richard Bentley[1]

Windsor Nova Scotia
10th. January [18]38[2]

Sir –

By my friend Charles Archibald Esqr[3] I received a copy of The Clockmaker from you, for which please to accept my thanks – I feel that I have reason to complain of your republishing that work without permission, as you cannot but be aware that it is a British work and not an American and therefore private property, under the protection of the laws[4] –

I am now writing the 2d. series, would you like to have it if so, and supposing it to be equal to the first, what will you give for it, reserving the right (to republish here) –

I sent a copy to my friend John Stephen Esquire,[5] Craigs Court Charing Cross London, but it was lost at Liverpool, may I beg the favor of you to send him a copy with a note saying it is from the author –

>Your obt sert.
>[Th]. C. Haliburton

Harvard MS *Pub.*: ed. W.I. Morse, 54–5

1 Richard Bentley (1794–1871), publisher. See Royal A. Gettmann, *A Victorian Publisher. A Study of the Bentley Papers* (London 1960).
2 Haliburton had written '28' in error.
3 Charles Dickson Archibald (1802–68), lawyer and businessman. See *DCB*, IX.
4 International copyright was not established until 1891. Haliburton felt that his work should come under the 1814 Act of Copyright in England. The act protected the author for twenty-eight years.
5 John Stephen (1771–1850), army agent, of Church Street (formerly Church Lane), Chelsea

58 To Sir Rupert D. George   Windsor, 6th February, 1838.

Sir –

I have the honor to acknowledge the receipt of your letter, requiring me to state if I receive any and what fees, as president of the Court of Sessions or judge of the Inferior Court of Common Pleas.

In reply I beg leave to state that I have not received any fees in either capacity.

>I have the honor to be,
>Your obedient servant
>Thomas C. Haliburton

Sir Rupert D. George, Bart., Provincial Secretary

Pub.: *Journals ... of the House of Assembly* (1838) Appendix 20

59 To Sir Rupert D. George [Windsor?]
15th. March 1838

Sir – By the published debates of the legislature[1] I learn that the judicial establishments of the province have again formed a subject of discussion before that honorable body, with a view to the reduction of the expence at which they are supported, and that these discussions have terminated in a difference of opinion, between the upper and lower [Ho]use, as to the mode in which this reduction is to be effected – To the judges the continual agitation of this subject, cannot but be most painful, but on the present occasion it has assumed a new aspect – The Supreme Court and Common Pleas, tribunals of nearly concurrent jurisdiction, have been brought into contrast, and for the first time they have been tried *by their popularity*.

The proposed transfer of the whole of the business from the latter court, in which the greater portion is transacted, to the other tribunal, has also brought into collision the interests of the country and metropolitan bar, and the one court and the other is alternately lauded or disparaged as they are severally affected by adoption or rejection of this measure – In this stage of the affair the judges of the Supreme Court, in reply to certain queries submitted to them by a committee of the Assembly, have expressed their willingness to undertake, and their ability to perform, the whole business of the Common Pleas, and with a liberality which does them great honor, have not demanded for this increased labor, an increase of salary – So far as I am personally concerned, I feel that under [th]ese circumstances, I cannot consistently with what is due to the public, or to my own honor, withold a tender of my resignation, on such terms as the legislature shall think proper to impose – In accepting the office I have now the honor to hold, I relinquished a seat in the legislature,[2] a local appointment of profit,[3] and a practice at the bar, far exceeding my salary as a judge – Preferring the retirement of private life, to the excitements of politicks, and the study and administration of law, to the active pursuits of a profession I was willing to make the sacrifice, and supposed when I was doing so, that as it was done under the faith of a permanent statute, the arrangement would also be permanent – I have therefore expended a very large sum of money to provide a suitable retreat, for the remainder of my life, a sum so large that I cannot again expect to realise it by sale – Under these circumstances I feel that I am entitled to retire, when my services are no longer necessary, upon full pay – but I waive this right and am willing to relinquish office on any terms that the legislature shall think proper to impose – I feel that my position has been rendered so painful, that I am willing to undergo any privations, and to submit to any pecuniary losses, in preference to a continuance in office – I prefer poverty to degradation – Living in total seclusion and being naturally of unexpensive habits, my wants are few, and I have never hitherto felt the absence of means – It is only now for the first time when wounded feelings dictate a surrender of office, that the want of private resources adequate to the decent support of my family impose the necessity of making that surrender conditional, that every feeling of my mind suggests ought to be unqualified that I feel the unhappiness that arises where independence of mind is not united with an independence of means – I have therefore respectfully to request that you will be pleased to submit to his Excellency the Leut. Governor, this communication, with an application to him on my part, to do me the favor to transmit to the assembly my proposal *to withdraw from office, on any retired allowance they may be pleased to make,* in order that my incumbancy may no longer be a bar to any arrangements they may in their wisdom see fit to make, respecting the judicial establishments of the province –

> I have the honor to be
> Sir your most obt. svt
> Tho C Haliburton – C. Just. Com
> Pleas for Mid Division

Honble
Sir Rupert D. George

PANS MS *Pub.*: *Journals ... of the House of Assembly* (1838) Appendix 64, 154

1 A select committee of the House of Assembly was appointed to examine abolishing the Inferior Court (13 February). The committee reported the opinions of the three Supreme Court judges, who were willing to take on the extra duties of the Inferior Court at no cost to the treasury (*Journals ... of the House of Assembly* 1838, Appendix 39).
2 MLA for Annapolis County, 1826–9
3 Judge of the Probate Court at Annapolis, 1823–9

60 To Robert Parker [Windsor? 24 March 1838][1]

My book has had a prodigious run. In 'Blackwoods Magazine' for November, under the title 'The World We Live In,' you will see a remarkably flattering notice of it[2] ...[3] By the last packet I received a letter from Colonel Fox,[4] informing me that Bentley, the publisher, had at his suggestion presented me with a very elegant piece of plate as a token of the estimation in which my talent is held in the motherland, and concluding by a wish to make my acquaintance if circumstances should take me to England. Shortly afterwards I received another letter from him, containing the key of the box in which he had forwarded the salver, and another from Bentley, offering for another volume. I have another volume ready for the press,[5] which is not so local as the other, and I think better suited for English readers. We are no judges of these things ourselves, but I think it better than the first. I intend, therefore, to go home with it and see it through the press myself, and while abroad will lay up materials for The Clockmaker in England, which, if the work takes, I will write as soon as I return.[6]

Pub.: *Canadian Magazine*, 1916: 76–8

1 The date is supplied by A. Wylie Mahon in the *Canadian Magazine*.
2 'The writer of the volume is evidently a capital fellow. We want such to throw new life even into European literature ... Let him leave Nova Scotia and come to England ... Or, if he must remain on the other side of the Atlantic, can he not give some share of his talents to the illustration of our affairs in Canada?' ('The World We Live In,' *Blackwood's Magazine*, November 1837: 677).
3 Haliburton's ellipses
4 Colonel Charles Richard Fox, aide-de-camp to William IV, husband of Lady Mary FitzClarence (illegitimate daughter of William IV and Mrs Jordan). Haliburton dedicated the Second Series of *The Clockmaker* to Fox.
5 The Second Series of *The Clockmaker*
6 Later published as *The Attaché* (1843–4)

61 To the Judges of the Common Pleas, Magistrates, Gentlemen of the Bar, High Sheriff, and Grand Jury of the County of Lunenburg

[Windsor? 18 April 1838]

Gentlemen –

I thank you for the flattering address you have been pleased to present to me.[1]

It is a source of great satisfaction to me to know that my judicial labours have met the approbation of the public generally, and I beg to assure you that I have felt those labours much lightened by the cordial support and uniform kindness of the bar, magistrates and respective Grand Juries of the County of Lunenburg. My absence from the province though unavoidable, will, I trust, be only of short duration, and should no change take place in the construction of the courts, I shall look forward to a renewal of our official connection with much pleasure, for next to the satisfaction arising from a conscientious discharge of duty, is the feeling derived from a knowledge that the performance has been successful.

Have the honor to be
Gentlemen, with great esteem,
Your most obedient servant,
Thomas C. Haliburton.

Pub.: *Nova Scotia Royal Gazette*, 18 April 1838

1 Members of the legal establishment had sent a letter expressing their high regard for his services.

---

62 To Sir Rupert D. George

[Windsor? *c.* 25 April 1838][1]

Sir –

I have the honor to acknowledge the receipt of a petition signed by Alexander Walker & others inhabitants of Aylesford to his Excellency the Leut. Governor, complaining of the conduct of Thomas Tupper[2] a magistrate, and by his Excellencys command referred to me to institute enquiries upon the subject matter of the same, and report thereon I have now respectfully to submit to his Excellency the following report –

Upon receiving the petition notice was given to the subscribers thereto to reduce their complaints which were of a general nature into specific charges and upon [a] certain day to furnish Mr. Tupper with a copy and file the original in the office of the clerk of the peace, and that on the first day of the ensuing term they should be heard [in] support thereof – At the time appointed the investigation took place – Upon some of the charges, no evidence was offered, upon others the proof failed, while in one or two instances satisfactory explanations were given – In this manner the inquiry proceeded for some time, substantiating no charge of a serious nature, but on the whole leaving a very unfavorable impression against Mr. Tupper, until it was distinctly proved that he had on more occasions than one, delivered writs for the collection of debt to the constable on a Sunday, once carrying them to the house of the constable, and again delivering them at the very door of a place of worship – Upon these facts being proved I felt it my duty to close the investigation and to inform Mr. Tupper that I would proceed no further, feeling perfectly assured that such a gross violation of decency would not and could not be overlooked – It is true that one of the witnesses stated afterwards to me that in one part of his testimony he was in error, but still this remains an uncontroverted fact, and altho Mr. Tupper has presented a petition numerously and respectably signed, certifying to his good character and general fitness for office, I regret to be under the necessity of stating, that after putting the most favorable construction on his motives and conduct, I consider that he is destitute of those qualifications that are essential to a magistrate possessing such extensive judicial powers as he does in this province – Putting aside any specific charges, it would appear that his zeal is vexatious, his demeanour uncourteous, his largesse indecorous, and his standing in the community destitute of that insight influence and respectability which can alone render his motives unquestioned, or his decisions satisfactory to the public –

This is the second public investigation that has taken place upon his conduct pressed against him with great warmth and temper, not by a factious individual, but by nearly a whole community, and altho many of their charges have been unsupported by proof and most exaggerated by prejudice, yet it is evident that he has failed in his estimate of the duties and character of a Justice of the Peace, who can thus agitate a whole community – I am also bound to state the opinion among all the magistrates of the county who were present at the enquiry was unfavorable to him, and while none vindicated his character, several were loud in their reprehension of the general tenor of his conduct–

A third petition[3] has since been presented against him, and I feel satisfied that this will continue to be so, as long as he remains in office – The administration of justice to that county should not be subject to those charges, nor even the suspicions which they eng[ender?] – The judicial duties that are imposed upon a magistrate are not designed to furnish him with the means of support, but to afford protection and peace to his neighbours, and he who misconceives the nature of his office in this particular, is unfit to remain in the commission – Under these circumstances I feel compelled to recommend that his name be omitted from the new one now about to issue –

>All which is respectfully submitted –
>I have the honor to be
>Your mst. obt. svt
>Tho. C. Haliburton

To
Sir Rupt. D. George Bart.
&c.

PANS MS

1 The MS is docketed 'Recd 25th April 1838.'
2 (1774–?)
3 Possibly the one dated 20 March 1838, attached to the report (PANS, RG 1, vol. 243, doc. 39)

---

63 To R.H. Barham [London? *c.* 22 June 1838][1]

Dear sir –

When I had the pleasure of seeing you at Blackwall,[2] you were kind enough to say, if I should make an application for a ticket of admission to the abbey, at the approaching coronation,[3] you would speak to the secretary, to secure me one – As a stranger I am quite ignorant of the forms to be observed upon such occasions, but very desirous of witnessing so unusual and so magnificent a spectacle –

I have therefore presumed upon your kindness to ask the favor of you, to put in a written application for me, in my name, in the usual form –

My Nova Scotian address is 'Chief Justice of the Court of Com. Pleas' –

If I have presumed too far in making this request, I trust you will accept the novelty of the spectacle, and my ignorance of forms as an apology –

> I am dr sir
> Your most obt. servnt
> Tho. C. Haliburton

202 Piccadilly[4]
To
Revd. R.H. Barham
&c &c – .

Chicago Public Library MS [*Ph.*]

1 According to Fairbanks' *Journal*, Haliburton first met Barham on 21 June (Chittick, 222).
2 The taverns at Blackwall were a summer attraction, situated on the bank of the Thames, two and a half miles from London. The Canada Club met at a variety of taverns in Blackwall: Lovegrove's tavern, the West India Tavern, and the Brunswick Tavern.
3 The coronation of Queen Victoria occurred on 28 June 1838. An announcement in the *Morning Chronicle* (16 June 1838, 5), informed the public that admission was by ticket only.
4 Cf. *The Attaché*, Second Series, 2: 129: '... at our lodgings, 202, Piccadilly, (I insert the number, gentle reader, because I recommend Mr. Weeks, of 202, to your particular patronage) ... "Weeks," I said, "is a capital purveyor."' Mr Weeks was the proprietor of a 'Mechanical Museum.'

---

64 To Richard Bentley

[London?]
8th. July 1838

My dear sir –

In the midst of my arrangements yesterday for departure I recieved Col Fox's note respecting the misprints which I forwarded to you – May I beg the favor of you to cancel the incorrect sheets as far as practicable and substitute correct ones –

I will thank you to send to the undermentioned persons a copy in silk binding as the one I have seen of Col. Foxes –

Sir James Kempt[1]   South Audley Street
Lord Glenelg[2] – Colonial Office
C Murdock Esquire[3] – Do
James Haliburton Esqr[4] – 49 Germain Street
Honble. Mrs Norton[5]   Piccadilly
In boards to Captn. Smith[6] 111 Germain Street
to – Stephen Price Esqr[7] *Tavistock Square* –
Garrick Club –

I will thank you to send one also to Carey and Lee[8] of Philadelphia, the copies sent to me for that purpose being too inaccurate for any reprint whatever –

> In haste
> Yours truly
> T C Haliburton

Harvard MS *Pub.*: ed. W.I. Morse, 55–6

1 He lived at 32 South Street, Grosvenor Square (*Robson's London Directory for 1838*, 142).
2 Charles Grant, Lord Glenelg (1778–1866), colonial secretary, 1835–9. He lived at 11 Great George Street, Westminster.
3 Thomas William Clinton Murdoch was an assistant clerk at the Colonial Office.
4 James Burton (1788–1862), explorer, archaeologist, and Egyptologist
5 Caroline Elizabeth Sarah Sheridan (1808–78), granddaughter of Richard Brinsley Sheridan. She was a close personal friend of Lady Mary Fox, wife of Colonel Charles Fox. See Jane Grey Perkins, *The Life of Mrs Norton* (London 1909), 141 and 156.
6 Captain Robert Carmychael Smyth whom Haliburton met on the boat over to England in 1838. See *A Letter from Major Robert Carmychael-Smyth to His Friend the Author of 'The Clockmaker'* (London 1849).
7 Stephen Price (1782–1840), the American theatre manager. Price lived at 12 Tavistock Square. Haliburton addresses the letter to the occupant of 4 Tavistock Square, i.e., Nathan Gould (*Robson's Court Guide* [1838] 73).
8 In 1836, Carey and Lea became Lea and Blanchard upon the retirement of Henry Charles Carey. The firm was continued by William A. Blanchard and Isaac Lea. It became Blanchard and Lea in 1851. According to Fairbanks' *Journal* (Chittick, 222), proof sheets were ready for shipment on July 3.

---

65 To Sir George Grey, Bart[1]

202 Piccadilly [London]
16th. Aug [18]38

Sir –

On referring to my leave of absence, granted by Sir Colin Campbell, I find that it expires in the middle of the winter, at a time when it is unsafe to approach the coast, in such vessels as the Falmouth packets – As there *are no courts to be held* in the interval elapsing between the termination of my leave, and the middle of April, I am induced to apply for an extension of leave of two months, which will enable me to return by the March packet –

I am desired by the Governor of the colony to say that if any reference be necessary to him, he fully approves of the extension herein requested[2] –

>I have the honor to be
>Your most obt
>Servt.
>Tho. C. Haliburton

To
Sir [George?] Grey Bart.
&c &c &c.

PRO MS (Kew Gardens, London)

1 (1799–1852), under-secretary of state for the colonies
2 The reply from the under-secretary was sent on 24 August 1838 and complied with the request (PRO, CO 217/168, f. 222).

---

66 To Thomas Adolphus Trollope

[London?]
19th. Ocr. 1838

My dear sir

I regret that I cannot join your most delightful family circle tomorw at dinner, as I have given up that day to an old friend in a public office,[1] whose duties leave him no other day at his own disposal than Sunday – But I will do myself the pleasure in the evening of paying my respects to Mrs Trolloppe if she is disengaged –

>Yours alwys
>T C Haliburton

Free Library of Philadelphia MS [*Ph.*]

1 Unidentified

Print by M. Gauci from a painting of Haliburton by E.H. Eddis, 1838

67 To Mrs Bates[1]

My dear Mrs Bates –

[London?]
Thursday morng – [8 November 1838][2]

I have just received Mr. Bates' kind invitation for tomorrow evening which I shall be most happy to avail myself of –

Obedient to your commands, I waited upon Mr. Eddis[3] for two hours, and the day after had the pleasure to call upon you to report progress but was not so fortunate as to find you at home, – I am to see him again today at one aclock, after which I will endeavour to find some person to lithograph a copy for you, which I shall hope on my return to town, to find ready for presenting you with –

I have been most anxious to witness the great city spectacle of the Lord Mayors inaugural dinner[4] tomorrow but I am afraid I shall be disappointed unless you will be so kind as to stand my friend[5] upon this occasion –

Please to present my respects to Miss Bates, and believe me with great respect –

Yours always
Tho. C. Haliburton

Harvard MS

1 Unidentified. Possibly the wife of Joshua Bates, 21 Arlington Street, Piccadilly, and East Sheen House, Mortlake, who was a life member of the Royal Literary Fund from 1851
2 The Lord Mayor's inaugural dinner was held on the evening of Friday, 9 November 1838.
3 Eden Upton Eddis was known as 'the father of the Athenaeum Club' (Alexander F. Baillie, *The Oriental Club and Hanover Square* [London 1901]). Mr Eddis drew a portrait of Haliburton that was subsequently lithographed by M. Gauci. See PAC File no. 206–11, Negative no. C–6087.
4 The *Standard*, 10 November 1838, reported that the entertainment was on the usual lavish scale.
5 Probably Charles Fairbanks, judge of the Vice-Admiralty Court. Fairbanks was staying at the same London lodgings as Haliburton and transacting business with the Colonial Office on a daily basis.

---

68 To Richard Bentley [London? c. December 1838][1]

For gods sake stir up those fellows with a long pole, for it keeps me a prisoner here – Did Lockhart[2] get the last pages,? a man that drives so damned hard as Cox,[3] is apt to drop some of his luggage on the road, from behind –

Yours always
T C Haliburton

What says the agent of their almighty superfine everlasting partikilar damned rascals Carey & Lea?[4]

Harvard MS *Pub.*: ed. W.I. Morse, 105

1 This note was likely penned by Haliburton during the writing of *The Bubbles of Canada*, which was completed on 24 December 1838 in London (see Georgianna Haliburton, *A Short Account of the Haliburtons of Windsor Nova Scotia from 1760 to 1865*, MS, 28 February 1873, now at the New England Genealogical Society, Boston).
2 Lockhart is unidentified.
3 Bentley's ledger (BL Add. MS 46,637) lists 9 January as the publication day of *The Bubbles*. The printer is entered simply as 'Cox.' There were several printers of that name in London at the time.
4 Lea and Blanchard of Philadelphia

---

69 To Henry Wood[1]

[London?]
Janry– 20th. 1839–

My dear sir –

I have been so knocked up with tooth acke, I have not been able to write to you, to thank you for your kind attention in the matter of the Clarence,[2] but I beg you to be assured I do not the less appreciate your very considerate and very friendly attention –

I shall be most happy to send the volume alluded to, in your note –

The only difficulty I have is *in the mode*, as I do not publickly avow the authorp. of the wk[3] – If you will allow me to send to do it thro you I shall feel much oblged –

I have a volume for Mrs Wood & an engraving which I am desirous of sending perhaps you will permit me to send these thro you –

Am I to have the pleasure of seeing the ladies in London before I go? If not as my time is fast running out, I will endeavour to go to St. Leonards[4] & take leave of them –

Yours very truly
Tho C Haliburton

Penn. State Univ. MS [*Ph.*]

1 Unidentified. Possibly the Henry Wood who wrote *Change for the American Notes: In Letters from London to New York by an American Lady* (London 1843). Generally attributed to Henry Wood
2 Possibly the London Club, the 'Clarence,' 12 Waterloo Place
3 Although Haliburton published *The Bubbles of Canada* anonymously, it was widely broadcast as being by 'The author of the Clockmaker' and therefore impossible for Haliburton to conceal.
4 St Leonard's-on-Sea, near Hastings. The 1841 census lists Emily Wood, Helen Wood, and Rose Wood (all aged twenty) as the occupants of North Lodge East in the parish of St Mary in the Castle (PRO, HO 107, 1107). Decimus Burton, aged thirty-five, lived at East Ascent, St Leonard's (HO 107, 1107).

70 To Lord Glenelg[1]

202 Piccadilly [London]
6th. Feby 1839

My Lord

Since I last had the honor of seeing your Lordship, I have recieved information from my friends in Nova Scotia that the judicial establishments of the country will again be the subject of agitation this winter, as they have for one or two preceding sessions –

The effect of this is no less injurious to the colony than painful to the judges, and as the withdrawal of some of those officers would enable the legislature to adopt some plan for adjusting this difficult question, I am anxious to renew my offer to your Lordship, if a satisfactory exchange could be made to accept a suitable alternative –

It has occurred to me that the situation lately vacated by Mr Whittle Harvey, and now at the disposal of government[2] might perhaps enable your Lordship, to adjust the conflicting claims of the Assembly and the judges, by providing for me in that manner, and that if your Lordship shall think proper to confer it upon me, altho by no means an agreeable exchange, it would render a service to the colony, by contributing to its peace –

I trust your Lordship will pardon the liberty I have taken in making the suggestion, and have the honor to subscribe

Myself your Lordships
Most obt. servant
Tho. C. Haliburton

To
The Right Honble.
The Lord Glenelg –

PRO MS (Kew Gardens, London)

1 Lord Glenelg was about to relinquish his post as colonial secretary.
2 The job Haliburton solicited was that of registrar of hackney coaches: an office that, Glenelg explained, 'has been given away for some time past.' Glenelg agreed to hand Haliburton's letter to his successor as colonial secretary with a recommendation 'that your wishes for a change in your official situation ... [be] gratified.'

71 To Charles D. Archibald   [London? 9 March 1839?][1]

My dear Archibald

On reflection I am afraid of giving offence to my Canada Club[2] friends, by absenting myself, and will therefore have to give up the opera tonight –

>Yours
>T C Haliburton

Harvard MS

1 The reference to the Canada Club helps to date the letter.
2 The Canada Club, London, established in 1810, existed to promote Canadian business interests amongst Anglo-Canadians. Dinner meetings were held on a quarterly basis and distinguished guests were invited to the meetings. See J.G. Colmer, *The Canada Club (London): Some Notes on Its Origin, Constitution, and Activities* (London 1934) 139 and 156.

72 To Mrs Croker[1]   4 Spring Gardens[2] London
Monday – [c. March 1839]

Dear Mrs Croker

Mr Burton[3] has conveyed to me your kind invitation to go to [?][4] on Saturday next with him and remain there until Monday following –

I am extremly glad the time named falls within the short period yet left to me in this country,[5] and have very great pleasure in accepting your kind hospitality –

From the very hasty note he has sent me, I do not feel quite sure I have the address right, but hope this may reach its destination –

>I am my dear madam
>Yours very truly
>Th. C. Haliburton

Acadia University Library MS

1 The wife of John Wilson Croker
2 *Robson's Court Guide* (1839) lists 'Mrs Palmer,' 'Wm Curry, M.P.,' and 'Jno Rundle, M.P.' as the occupants of 4 Spring Gardens. Haliburton normally stayed at 6 Spring Gardens with the Burtons.
3 Decimus Burton the architect
4 Haliburton's writing is indecipherable. Croker owned a small marine villa at Alverbank, near Gosport.
5 Haliburton was scheduled to leave Bristol on 7 April aboard the *Great Western* steamship.

---

73 To Robert Parker [Windsor, 2 July 1839]

It is the first dispersion of the flock,[1] one of those epochs in a man's life that makes him feel old; the next is – off the scene. Sic transit.[2]

Pub.: Fragment in *Canadian Magazine*, 1916: 76

1 Haliburton's eldest child, Susannah, aged twenty-two, had departed for Scotland. See a letter sent by Lewis Bliss to Henry Bliss, 26 February 1839, which alludes to a Mr Black's returning home to Scotland, and having to look after 'Miss Slick alias Miss Susan Haliburton' (PANS MG 1, vol. 1596, no. 114).
2 So it goes.

---

74 To John Wilson Croker   Windsor Nova Scotia
                                   13th. July 1839

My dear Sir –

I had the pleasure to receive the proof sheets of your most able and triumphant dissection of Lord Durhams report,[1] at the moment of my embarkation at Bristol,[2] and beg of you to accept my best thanks for the same, as well as for other marks of your kindness to me during my residence in England – Our passage on the Great Western tho a tedious one of 22 days was the most triumphant one ever effected by steam, as it was effected against an adverse wind of such intensity as to merit the name of hurricane[3] – I have the pleasure of sending you by this opportunity afforded me by my daughters visit to England a pamphlet of Judge Chipmans of New Brunswick,[4] containing a condensed view of the discussions on the boundary together with a map of the territory which I trust will arrive safe – I do not know whether you feel any interest in the subject,[5] but if you should you will find it a valuable statement, as he knows more about the subject from having been one of the commissioners and residing near the country, than any other man I know of –

Please to present my respects to Mrs. Croker & your circle[6] and believe me my dear sir with great respect

        Your most obt. servt.
        Tho. C. Haliburton

Right: Honble.
J.W. Croker
& & &.

Duke Univ. MS [*Ph.*]

1 *Report on the Affairs of British North America*, 2 vols (London 1839)
2 On the *Great Western* steamship that left Bristol on Saturday, 23 March 1839, with 105 passengers
3 The triumphant nature of this voyage can be appreciated if one realizes that the average sailing time from Liverpool to New York was thirty-six days (twenty-four days on the return journey). The *Great Western* crossed in fifteen days.
4 Ward Chipman (1787–1851), chief justice of New Brunswick, 1834–51, author of *Remarks upon the Disputed Points of Boundary under the Fifth Article of the Treaty of Ghent* (Saint John, NB 1839)
5 Croker did develop an interest and wrote at length about the boundary question in the *Quarterly Review* 67: 501–41. See *The Croker Papers*, ed. Louis T. Jennings, 2 vols (London 1884) 2: 393–5.
6 Croker had a wide circle of friends. At various stages in his life it included George IV, the third Marquis of Hertford, the Duke of Wellington, and Sir Robert Peel.

---

75 To Richard Bentley

Windsor Nova Scotia N.A
20th. Sepr. 1839

My dear sir –

The mail closing earlier than I expected I have just time to say that I have a work ready for transcribing entitled 'The Letter Bag of the Great Western, or Life in a Steamer' By the author of The Sayings & Doings of Saml. Slick &c. –

      Dulce est desippere in Loco[1]

It is a book of fun, altogether, and well calculated to be popular, especially among sea-going people & travellers – It will be some 30 pages short of Clockmaker – It is full of caricature and ought to be embellished, at any rate in a second edition[2] – This will be essential to it, & the more you illustrate it the better – You should have a vignette[3] of the ship (which you will get at their office in London) on cover – & so on –

This work I shall send direct to you without the intervention of a third person – We understand each other too well, you have always acted too liberally and manly a part, for me to commence haggling now – When I send it to you I will name what I consider 'a fair deal' as Sam Slick calls it, and I make no doubt of your meeting my views, & that I shall satisfy you – The book you will recieve by next Halifax packet, which will be in a short month after you recieve this – So you may advertise it if you like, and consider it yours – I shall have it francked to you, in the gov. bag to colonial office – I reserve this side of the water as usual –

Pray remember me kindly to Barham & our other friends & believe me in great haste very truly yours

Th C Haliburton

Harvard MS *Pub.*: ed. W.I. Morse, 57–8

1 'When time allows, / 'Tis sweet the fool to play' (Horace, *Odes*, 4, 12, 28). See *The Works of Horace: The Latin Text with Conington's Translation* (London: George Bell and Sons 1909) 183. Haliburton used it as the epigraph to *The Letter-Bag*.
2 *The Letter-Bag* was published on 3 January 1840.
3 A vignette did appear on the cover.

---

76 To Richard Bentley

Windsor Nova Scotia
25th. Nov. 1839.

My dear Bentley –

Some time since I wrote to you to say I would send you 'The Letter Bag of the Great Western' and have now the pleasure of doing so – It is now the same size as The Clockmaker as far as I can judge, containing 30 articles in all – It is wholly a work of humor, and I think well calculated for popularity, as well on account of the variety in it, as the fun – I have not thought it necessary to use the intervention of any one, or to attempt any bargain making about it –

We understand each other too well for that – you have always been most liberal and manly in your conduct to me, and I have declined entering into any arrangements with any one else, on that account – I think this book both more difficult to write, and better executed than either of the Clockmakers, and have certainly bestowed twice the pains upon it – I think therefore that you will be satisfied to have it classed with them – 500 pounds is your offer for the 3d series the same you will make no difficulty in giving for this, and that sum is both large and liberal, but it will repay you. The bills please to give to Coutts & Co.[1] on my account –

The first letter is a parady on Fanny Kemble & a hoax on her style[2] – The loco foco is a satire on Durhams report[3] – The whole is well calculated for caricature, and I hope you will get it well done in the second edition,[4] as in works of this kind, such things are very attractive –

Get it out soon, that the American edition may not interfere & get to England first. In a fortnight or so after this packet sails, I will send a copy of manuscript to Carey & Lea of Philadelphia – In about a year I hope to see you again, when I will give you a monthly work[5] and on the 1t. April will send you 3d series of Clockmaker – Winter is my time for work, in summer I live with the birds in the open air – in winter with the bears –

I have nothing and see nothing in this damned country, this 'dead sea', would to God I could live in dear old England, which is the only country this side of paradise worth living in – How gets on 'Armstrong the Factory Boy'?[6] I have not heard from my friends the Trollopes since I came out – Please to throw the enclosed letter into the two penny post –

                          Yours truly
                          Th. C. Haliburton

I had nearly forgotten an essential part – the proof sheets – I have begged James Haliburton (whom you met at my lodgings) to overlook them – if he cannot do it for Gods sake be careful, your devils make devlish work certainly, and in a book containing a variety of dialects like this, if greatest care is not taken, it will be ruined, – Besides, my dear friend, it mortifies the author – Do pray do me, the favor, to humor me on this particular, for I am out of reach, – Have some consideration for a man who will be overwhelmed with the sin of swearing, if this goes wrong, for I shall swear most bitterly, if they do this as they did a former one – verbum sat[7] – *Please to send me a copy by January packet under cover to 'Sir Colin Campbell Governor of Nova Scotia' thro Colonial Office –*

Harvard MS *Pub.*: ed. W.I. Morse, 59–61

1 His London banker
2 Fanny Anne Butler (Fanny Kemble) published her *Journal* in 1835. The *Journal* is largely an account of her trip to the USA
3 *The Letter-Bag*, 156–64, is a full-length travesty of the Durham *Report*, in the form of a letter from an investigating Loco Foco of New York (a member of the 'Equal Rights' or Radical section of the Democratic Party, a Democrat) to a sympathizer in Vermont. Chittick felt that it was the 'cleverest piece of sustained political satire Haliburton ever wrote' (298).
4 There was no second edition.
5 The only monthly work of fiction that Haliburton ever wrote was *The Old Judge*, serialized in *Fraser's Magazine*, 1847–8. His next work was *The Attaché*, but he did not publish it in numbers.
6 *Michael Armstrong* (1840), a novel by Frances Trollope (1780–1863). Haliburton did not know that Mrs Trollope had agreed to bring out her novel with Henry Colburn. She had been contracted to write a novel for Bentley, but gave Bentley *The Widow Barnaby*.
7 A word is sufficient.

77 To Samuel Fales

Windsor, Nova Scotia, 19th Dec. 1839

My dear sir –

I have just received from Haliburton[1] a note informing me of the melancholy tidings of the decease of my very kind and very dear aunt,[2] the only sister of my poor father, and the nearest, dearest, and best friend I had. I loved her as a child,[3] and feel her loss proportionately severe, having flattered myself we should have been spared to have met again in the spring, to which I looked forward with much pleasure. I feel that to you and your united and excellent family it is a heavy and irreparable blow, as it is to us all, but amidst this tribulation and affliction it must be a consoling reflection that they have always been so devoted to her, exhibited such filial affection, and proved by their tenderness and care how worthy they were of such an excellent mother. Their conduct towards her has been beyond all praise, and has endeared them still more to me, pray assure them how much I feel for and with them, how much I admire their unremitting, untiring care of her, and what a consolation it is that her virtues have been hereditary.[4] To you I feel it is impossible to offer any consolation while the wound is still fresh and bleeding, beyond the hope we all entertain that she has exchanged a world of care and pain for one of bliss and happiness and the knowledge that you are blessed with a most amiable and charming family, which that you may long live to be happy, as you have reason to be proud of, is the earnest prayer of yours always

Thos. C. Haliburton.

I had intended to have written Haliburton and his sisters but my heart is too full, and I am unequal to the task, when more composed I will do so.

Pub.: DeCoursey Fales, *The Fales Family of Bristol, Rhode Island* (1919) 97–8

1 Haliburton Fales (1815–69), son of Samuel and Abigail Fales
2 Abigail, Haliburton's aunt. She died on 29 November 1839 and was buried in Mt Auburn Cemetery, Boston.
3 Thomas Chandler Haliburton was only five years old when his Aunt Abigail married Samuel Fales. His acquaintance with her sprang from the many return visits that the family made to Nova Scotia. The most recent visit had been in 1829, following the death of Haliburton's father.
4 Abigail's children were Lucy Ann, Samuel Bradford, Susanna Maria, Eliza Ann, and Haliburton.

78 To Richard Bentley

Windsor Nova Scotia N A
19th. Decr. 1839

My dear sir –

By the last packet I sent you 'The Letter Bag of the Great Western' – I cannot bring myself to doubt that it will have arrived safe, long ere this will reach you, but as I send *this day* a copy of mss. to Lea & Blanchard[1] of Philadelphia, should any accident happen to your package, it is just possible the American edition might come out first, – I therefore used such parts of the drafts as were fit, & had the other parts transcribed, and now send you a duplicate – As the chances are all in favor of your getting the first, I will not repeat what I then wrote till I hear from you –

The third series of The Clockmaker is on the stocks & will be launched in the spring – In a year I hope to see you, and will outline the monthly work we talked of –

I believe you are aware that ten years ago I published a History of Nova Scotia in 2 vols, somebody I dont know who has reprinted it in London,[2] which I am sorry for as it is now an old work – I am loudly called upon here for a new edition that shall bring the statistics down to the present day, and I should like to do it, if it would cover expences – If you can find it worth while to give 250 pound for this service,[3] the book itself I will say nothing about, as my object is utility to the country, and not money – Let me know immediately and I will go to work at it – It is said to be the best colonial history, by every review of it,[4] that has appeared, and was as perfect at the time as I could make it, but our civil divisions are all altered since,[5] and so have our statistics materially changed – It cannot have a great circulation in England nor would it be worth your while to pay for the work, but if revised in the way I have spoken of might suit your views, and mine – All I require is the expence of revision and correction – Let me know soon, as we have a new census[6] now, and it is a favorable time –

How does Mrs Trollopes Factory Boy take? I have not seen it –

In haste yours truly
Th C Haliburton

P.S. I hope you have had every care taken in revising proofs of Letter Bag –

Harvard MS *Pub.*: ed. W.I. Morse, 61–2

1 Haliburton is now aware of the change in name of Lea and Blanchard.
2 Later he discovered it was a bookseller's trick of placing a new titlepage on old copies of the *Historical ... Account* (1829).
3 He made a similar appeal to the provincial purse on 18 November 1840.
4 Chittick, 145, mentions how 'cordial' the American reviews of the *Historical ... Account* were.
5 Halifax was divided into three counties, Halifax, Colchester, and Pictou (19 February 1835); Cape Breton was divided into the three counties of Cape Breton, Richmond, and Juste au Corps; Annapolis County became Digby and Annapolis County (27 March 1840), and on the same date parts of Colchester and Cumberland County, formerly annexed to King's County, were separated from it.
6 The census of 1838

4
A Literary Career, 1840–1856

In 1829, when Haliburton accepted a position on the bench, he left a lucrative legal practice and a life of active politics. He thought the position would be permanent so he built 'Clifton' which was completed in 1836. Two years later he realized that his days as an Inferior Court judge were numbered. The House of Assembly was bent upon a revision of the judicial system. He realized also that he lacked sufficient private means to enable him to retire without a pension, so his offer of resignation or retirement to the provincial government was on condition that an allowance would be forthcoming. As a direct result of the unsettled state of the judiciary, he sought (unsuccessfully), while in England, the position of registrar of hackney coaches. On his return, even though he was feted by his Halifax friends, his function as an Inferior Court judge was soon to end.

Perhaps as a consequence of this state of affairs, his energy for literary projects increased. In late 1840, Haliburton wrote separate letters to Richard Bentley and Provincial Secretary Sir Rupert D. George, attempting to arouse interest in a revision of the *Historical ... Account* (1829). But neither party showed much enthusiasm. In the flow of inventive spirits that followed completion of the Third Series of *The Clockmaker* in September 1840, Haliburton told Bentley of his plans to write: *The Attaché* (which would necessitate another visit to England); *The English in America* ('Colonies & Colonists in North America ... constitutional, historical, & political,' for which Henry Colburn had offered him £600); and *The Old Judge* ('another volume of Sketches of American Life *by Sam* ... Colonists and Colonies is a more popular form for the work heretofore engaged, a more readable thing, less formal & dry and more sketchy than history ...' [1 December 1840]).

His professional insecurities were resolved when he was offered a place on the bench of the Supreme Court of Nova Scotia after the House of Assembly finally abolished the Inferior Court. The man who appointed him on 29 March 1841 was Lucius Bentinck Carey (1803–84), the tenth Viscount Falkland, lieutenant-governor of Nova Scotia (1841–5), with whom Haliburton sustained a friendly correspondence long after Falkland left Nova Scotia and was posted to India as governor of Bombay. In 1851, Haliburton dedicated *The English in America* to Lord Falkland. Haliburton renewed his friendship with the Falklands in 1857, when Richard Bentley sought to publish Lady Falkland's journal of life in India, *Chow-Chow*, and Haliburton acted as an intermediary.

In March 1838, Haliburton proudly wrote to tell his old school friend Robert Parker about the reception his book had received in the 'motherland.' Parker was a puisne judge of the Supreme Court of New Brunswick from 1834 to 1865, a post that he held until he was appointed chief justice shortly before his death in 1865. Haliburton regarded him, of all his 'early and later friends,' as the one to whom his heart turned 'so warmly and affectionately.' Yet they had markedly different natures: Parker was a 'devout Anglican ... President for many years of the New Brunswick branch of the Auxiliary Bible Society and an avid supporter of the temperance movement in the province' (*DCB*). Haliburton loved a drink, a cigar, and the Victorian pleasures of the dinner table.

Haliburton faced his years on the Supreme Court bench without his wife, Louisa, at his side. She died suddenly on 29 November 1841, and her death cast a cloud over these years: 'The truth is that a desolate heart, blasted hopes, and a dreary future have taught me that we have little to expect here ...' he confessed to Robert Parker. Writing was the only antidote to gloom that Haliburton knew. When *The Attaché* was finished, Haliburton decided to take the new work to London himself and embarked for England on 18 May 1843, staying with the Burtons at 6 Spring Gardens, London. To celebrate Haliburton's return to England, Bentley commissioned a special essay on Haliburton for *Bentley's Miscellany* XIV: 81–94, 'Notions of Sam Slick [With a Portrait of the Author].' It was as flattering a puff for *The Attaché* as Haliburton could have wished.

Once more in London, Haliburton renewed his friendship with R.H. Barham at the Garrick Club – where he was admitted as a 'visiting member' – and with Mrs Trollope. He declared himself willing to travel the length and breadth of the kingdom to shake hands with her once more. But time was short. Haliburton was scheduled to return home on 3 September. And the Colonial Office threatened to withhold half his pay as a judge for the period of his absence from Nova Scotia, a decision that he appealed successfully, in late August, to Lord Stanley, the colonial secretary. Yet, as he confessed to Mrs Trollope: 'I have not enjoyed the visit as I did my last, my spirits are not the same, and when alone I suffer a good deal of depression ...' (3 August 1843).

When Louisa died, Haliburton's family of eight children – five daughters and three sons – ranged in age from his nine-year-old youngest son, Arthur, to his twenty-four-year-old eldest daughter, Susannah. One by one, over the next ten years, the daughters married. His eldest son, Thomas, a young man of precocious musical talents, died in a Massachusetts lunatic asylum in November 1847. The event is shrouded in mystery. His second son, Robert Grant, qualified as a lawyer, became secretary to the Great Exhibition of 1862 (the Nova Scotia exhibit), and developed his scholarly interests in science, anthropology, and history. Arthur, his youngest child, entered the army commissariat and rose to the top of his profession, eventually becoming under-secretary of state for war, for which achievement he was created Baron Windsor – recognition on a scale that had eluded his father.[1]

In the eighteen-forties, with his children in various stages of development, Haliburton travelled the province as a circuit judge (he estimated one year that he was away from home for 120 days). He developed his estate at Clifton, now a frequent stopping place for North American travellers, a number of whom (besides W.H. Bartlett, the engraver), penned portraits of the experience.[2] Here he continued to write. The literary output of the decade included two series of *The Attaché or Sam Slick in England*, 1843 and 1844, followed, almost immediately, by *The Old Judge*.

In 1843 and 1844, Haliburton made tentative arrangements with George Nickisson, the editor of *Fraser's Magazine*, to publish *The Old Judge* in numbers, rather than collectively. Haliburton despatched the first part, 'The Lone House,' prior to 22 April 1846, on which date he received proofs from Nickisson. The first instalment was published in the May 1846 issue of *Fraser's Magazine*. However, the illness of his fellow judge, Lewis Wilkins, increased the work load of all the other Supreme Court judges and delayed Haliburton's new book. In November 1846, he sent the remainder of *The Old Judge* to Nickisson in monthly instalments. Publication continued in *Fraser's Magazine* for February 1847 and was completed in the December issue of that year. Haliburton planned to visit England in August 1845, hoping to travel with Lord Falkland (who had resigned), but the illness of Judge Wilkins prevented him from leaving. Haliburton's next visit to England was not until 1853, at the conclusion of a new burst of literary activity.

Although the immediate remedy for his depression of spirits was work, later in the decade Haliburton's interest in formal religion increased. In 1845, he donated the land upon which a new Anglican Church in Windsor was built.[3] In 1848, four of his children were confirmed by the bishop during his annual tour of the Nova Scotia dioceses, an occurrence that brought him into conflict with the Rev. Alfred Gilpin, the local minister, who objected to the lack of preparation of candidates for confirmation. Haliburton's temperate approach to religious matters is revealed in his reply to Gilpin's charges.

Haliburton's role as a Victorian father is evident in his concern that his daughter Laura not marry a local man, John Cunningham, whose prospects were uncertain. Laura later married William Cunard, second son of Samuel Cunard, in 1851, and the marriage was of much greater benefit to her and to Haliburton. Laura, whose artistic talents won her Royal Academy recognition, became a gracious hostess, mistress of Orleans House, Twickenham (and of another home in the south of France), and enjoyed the best that nineteenth-century English and French society could offer.[4] She died in Nice, France, in 1910. Haliburton's influence on his other daughters' marriages might well have been similar: Susannah married a widower, a man well placed in the judicial establishment of New Brunswick and ten years older than herself; Emma married John Bainbridge-Smith, a mathematics professor at King's College, Windsor; Amelia married Edwin Gilpin of Annapolis Royal; and Augusta married an English friend of Haliburton's, a businessman, by the name of Alexander Fowden Haliburton, and lived comfortably in fashionable Torquay where she became a pillar of the local community. Haliburton enjoyed visiting her there in the eighteen-sixties. Augusta was the last daughter to marry, and her wedding in September 1854 tolled the knell for Haliburton's life at Clifton.

Publication of *The English in America* (1851) marked the completion of the last of the projects Haliburton had outlined to Bentley at the beginning of the eighteen-forties. In addition to those projects, Haliburton contracted with Henry Colburn to compile two collections of American humour. Haliburton fulfilled this further obligation by 12 May 1852, although the second of the two collections, *The Americans at Home*, was not published until 1854. In May 1851, he had been pleasantly surprised to receive a letter from Richard Bentley desiring to renew their lapsed friendship. Haliburton agreed that it had been a small matter that had kept them apart and immediately offered Bentley his new work, *Sam Slick's Wise Saws*. Bentley's business was not in the best of health (although Haliburton did not know this). Bentley could offer Haliburton only £150, claiming that markets for fiction were depressed. Haliburton turned, reluctantly, to

Hurst and Blackett, successors to Henry Colburn, and let them publish his continuation of Sam Slick.

Even though the structure and format was very much as before, the book's singularity and style won readers. In 1853, Haliburton travelled to England to oversee its publication. William Jerdan wrote a flattering review of it in the *Literary Gazette*, and Haliburton renewed friendships now more than ten years old, staying once more with the Burtons at 6 Spring Gardens.

He attended the Royal Agricultural Show at Gloucester in July, and in a speech at the dinner, Haliburton confessed he had not been so happy for ten years.[5] One reason for this new-found happiness was the attendance at the agricultural ball of a forty-four-year-old widow, Sarah Harriet Williams, in the company of her friends, Mr and Mrs Watkins. Haliburton signed the preface to the Second Edition of *Sam Slick's Wise Saws*, in August 1853, at Sarah Harriet's home in Eaton Mascott, Shropshire, a month after the visit to Gloucester.

That Haliburton had been thinking about remarriage is evident from a letter to the unidentified 'Miss Guthmin' in 1851, where his view of English women corresponds to his other rosy views of English life. Until 1853, he had no one particular in mind. The visit of 1853 changed this, and when he left Nova Scotia in August 1856, he married Sarah Harriet Williams at St George's Church, Hanover Square, London.[6] They rented Gordon House, a Thames-side villa at Isleworth, and embarked upon a new life.

1 See J.B. Atlay, *Lord Haliburton: A Memoir of His Public Service* (London 1909).
2 For example, James S. Buckingham, *Canada, Nova Scotia, New Brunswick, and Other British Provinces in North America with a Plan of National Colonization* (London and Paris 1843) 386, and Sir James E. Alexander, *L'Acadie: or, Seven Years' Explorations in British America*, 2 vols (London 1849) 2: 229–30
3 See *The Gateway to the Valley* (Windsor 1977) 26.
4 See Kay Grant, *Samuel Cunard: Pioneer of the Atlantic Steamship* (London 1967) 148.
5 See *The Times*, 15 July 1853, 8, col. c.
6 30 September 1856. See the *Shrewsbury Chronicle*, 10 October 1856, 4, col. b.

---

79 To Richard Bentley   Windsor Nova Scotia 7th. May 1840

My dear sir –

I had the pleasure to receive your letter of February last and am much obliged by the handsome & liberal manner in which you received 'The Letter Bag' and beg of you to accept my best thanks for the same –

The 3d. series of The Clockmaker is written, and remains only for revision and fair copy, for which I fear I can not find time till June, so that you will receive it about middle of July – I have been rather fortunate in this work, for it has cost me less trouble, and is far better than its predecessors, combining more humor & more sense in it than the other series – you need have no apprehension about this, it will *take* for you for there is much taking matter in it – If you desire to select any article of it for your Miscellany 'Trading in Bed' or 'Great Unknown' would do better than others for that work especially the former – Whenever you desire to commence advertising, you need not be afraid to incur expence in doing so, as this work will repay you all such outlays – Next packet I will send you a table of contents, which I would insert in some of the advertisements –

Will you read over my last letters, particularly the one that went with duplicate 'of Letter Bag' – you have not replied to them –

Your books never came to hand, did you send them thro colonial office or by British Queen?[1] If by latter China would do as well – With kind regards many thanks, & best wishes yours always Tho. C. Haliburton

University of Illinois MS [*Ph.*]

1 The *British Queen* was the largest ship in the world when launched on the 24 May 1838 by the British and American Steam Navigation Company. It was capable of carrying 280 passengers, but not capable of delivering mail to Halifax, as it called at New York!

---

80 To Richard Bentley

Windsor Nova Scotia 1st. Sepr. 1840

My dear sir

I have the pleasure to send you the 3d series of The Clockmaker – It is the best of the set, and will bear advertising well and if the public are not tired of Sam Slick will be more generally popular than its predecessors –

You did not do me justice in The Letter Bag – It was written for illustration, and I took it for granted a sense of your own interest would have induced you to have done so – What would the Comic Latin Grammar[1] and such works be without their illustrations? Works of *mere* fun, require this aid, or the fun tires, they become wearisome like a man who always laughs – I was mortified to find you had not done so, or rather to hear so, for I have not seen it – With respect to the double entendres[2] I have wholly ommitted them in this work – If you wish it when you are ready, I will revise the 2 first Slicks, and The Letter Bag also, and make some additions to the latter for you so, as to remove any objections of that nature – I mean this of course *gratuitously* –

This work having a substratum of sense running thro it, and a moral to each article may not require illustration so much, but depend upon it, it would repay you well Some of those to the Sam Slick [volume are] capital and quite in keeping with the book

Playing at Cards	If you wish to insert
Trading in Bed	any one in your Miscellany,
Too Knowing by Half	you had better perhaps
Behind the Scenes	select from those mentioned
The Unburied One	in the margin[3]

If you will have the goodness to look at the last article [in] The Attaché, you will see a notice in it that seems to announce an English work under that tittle that is, Sam, as an Attaché to the American legation – I shall not begin this work till I hear from you, whether the public have had enough of Yankee character – I proposed it as a work in numbers –

I find that there was *no* English edition of the History of Nova Scotia published, that it was a trick of a bookseller here to dispose of the remaining copies by giving a new tittle page – I am sorry you declined it, because I do not wish to publish with Colburne,[4] but as the work must either be republished or superceded by some one else I shall have to do it – At the same time that this will be revising another work in two volumes 'Colonies & Colonists in North America'[5] will probably be written, but this also I presume for similar reasons, is out of your line – Before I communicate with him I should like to hear again from you – He made me several specific, and some very liberal general offers in writing before I left London, but I told him you had treated me liberally, and I had no reason to be dissatisfied, that where this was the case I did not feel at liberty, to publish with any one else – [Un]less you decline it yourself I will not do so now [?] I said before, you have been always most liberal and manly in all your transactions with me, – I have derived great satisfaction in publishing with you –

'Colonies & Colonists' will be constitutional, historical, & political – Colobourns offer was for any work on America in 2 Vols – 600 pounds –

I enclose a letter to Mr. Haliburton[6] to beg the favor of him to look over proof sheets – If he cannot *pray have pains taken with it* – Every succeding edition of Slick has been *more anglicised* than the last – *Pray have pains taken in this particular.*

I flatter myself that this work will give you much satisfaction – I wrote it easily, and have taken great pains in touching it since – It has more than 250 new Americanisms[7] in it – Perhaps Horace Twiss[8] will again do the pretty for it in The Times – No 18 & 19 will give texts to work on –

I have not sent a copy to Lea and Blanc[hard] because I did not know whether you would publish it now or later in the season and I was afraid to hamper you – Please to hold it back a while for them & send them a copy in time, as on the last occasion they acted with much more liberality and seem disposed to continue so – As you have an agreement for this work in writing it is not necessary to make a new assignment as that will convey the property – Have the goodness to give the bills to *Coutts & Co* on my account – When you see Mr. Barham please to present my kind regards to him & believe me my dear sir

With every good wish
[Th.C.] Haliburton

Harvard MS *Pub.*: ed. W.I. Morse, 62–5

1 Percival Leigh, *The Comic Latin Grammar*, with illustrations by John Leech, was published by Bentley on 28 November 1839.
2 Some critics of *The Letter-Bag* disliked Haliburton's excessive use of double entendres.
3 Bentley selected 'The Duke of Kent's Lodge,' 'Too Knowing by Half,' 'Behind the Scenes,' and 'Facing a Woman' for inclusion in his *Miscellany* 8 (1840).
4 Henry Colburn (d. 1855), publisher, and former partner (1830–2) of Richard Bentley
5 *The English in America*, published by Colburn and Co in 1851
6 James Haliburton
7 Public interest in Americanisms resulted in James Russell Bartlett's *Dictionary of Americanisms* (1848).
8 Horace Twiss (1787–1849), wit and politician. See *DNB*.

---

81 To Sir Rupert D. George   Windsor Novr. 18th 1840

Sir –

I have had it in contemplation for some time past to prepare a new and revised edition of my History of Nova Scotia, and have been in communication with Mr. Bentley the publisher on the subject, who informs me that a pirated edition having made its appearance in London during the last year, another would issue at some pecuniary loss – In the former work which was printed at Halifax, there are numerous errors of the press, and some important omissions, while the statistical tables now eleven years old, require a complete revision – The civil divisions of the province have been materially changed, and some considerable modifications in the constitution effected, since that time, which render the first volume imperfect, and the second not only inaccurate, but almost useless – I am very desirous, after having incurred so much trouble and so great an expence in compiling that history to render it as perfect and as useful as possible, but as I am unable to make such another pecuniary sacrifice I have no alternative but to abandon the object or solicit his Excellency to permit some portion of the cost to be borne by the casual revenue.[1]

For this purpose a sum of two hundred and fifty pounds would be requisite – May I beg the favor of you to submit this request to his Excellency for his consideration – The former work to insure its usefulness bore no reference to local politicks, it is my intention should I be enabled to complete the revision, to pursue the same [course] again –

> I have the honor to be
> Your obedient servant
> Tho. C. Haliburton

To
Sir Rup. D. George
Pro. Secty.
&c. &c

PANS MS

[1] The Legislature had made grants to John George Marshall to work on his volume of *Provincial Laws*, so Haliburton's request was not without a precedent.

82 To Richard Bentley   Windsor Nova Scotia 1 Decr. 1840.

My dear sir –

I received your letter of the 17th. of Ocr. by mail, but not the copy of the book, which you mention as intending to forward, which I the more regret as I am unable to point out the inaccuracies, or make any remark on it that might be useful in a new edition[1] – When you reprint the work have the kindness to mention in the tittle page and its advertisement that it is *a second* edition, as you must be aware how beneficial this is, both to the book and to the author – I will send you the History when done, but it is too soon to advertise it yet as a revision of such a work is very laborious, and slow work, and requires scrupulous accuracy in every thing contained in it – The Attaché is a new name and character for Sam Slick whom I wish to take to court as Stephensons[2] confidential man, under no other name could I get a Yankee Clockmaker into society, and this appointment for him obviates all the difficulty I have had in placing him among gentlemen, without violating either probability or the usages of life – To complete this work would I think require me to visit England – I have done nothing to it yet, because I wish to know from you 1st, *how such a work would take* 2d – *whether the public will bear more of this sort of thing* and 3d which you would advise – *numbers* or *an entire work* – on these heads advise me early – It is a work as I before observed that will require time – In the mean time I could give you another volume of Sketches of American Life *by Sam*, somewhat similar to The Clockmaker but under a new name for The Clockmaker must be now closed, – *How would it do?* Colonists & Colonies is a more popular form for the work heretofore engaged, a more readable thing, less formal & dry and more sketchy than history[3] – On these matters pray give me your opinion at length –

The article in The Times newspaper signed 'Sam Slick' on the state of Europe[4] was not by me, and I am surprised to hear from my friends that you could think so – I am glad however it occurred because it enables me to say to you that I never have *used the name* otherwise than in those books, and *never will* without informing you, – If then it be appended to such things again, either likely to injure you or me, contradict it as not genuine – I never write for newspapers, the last thing was the Durham affair,[5] and I never wish to publish but with you – Notwithstanding the very sage advice I received, from a rival friend of yours, to be wary of you & the prophecy that we could not long remain upon terms, I am satisfied that we shall continue as we have begun, and can only say you must treat others very different from what you do me, or you have been greatly slandered, for I have great pleasure in acknowledging the very handsome manner in which you have always treated *me* –

The only complaint I have is, that you are a bad correspondent & that you do not answer fully material queries – Pray remember me kindly to Mr Barham, & believe me yours always Tho. C. Haliburton

address
Windsor Nova Scotia
N.A.
Halifax Steamer

Harvard MS *Pub.*: ed. W.I. Morse, 65–7

1 The Third Series of *The Clockmaker* was published on 30 October 1840.
2 Andrew Stephenson (1784–1857), American minister to Great Britain, 1836–41
3 The idea of this work sounds very much like *The Old Judge* (1849).
4 A correspondent, signing himself 'Sam Slick,' wrote to the editor of the London *Times*, 24 September 1840, on the 'War Question.'
5 Published in *The Times*, 18–26 February 1839, seven letters 'By a Colonist,' later reprinted as *A Reply to the Earl of Durham*

---

83 To De Witt Power[1]

Windsor Nova Scotia
14th. Decr. 1841

Dear sir

I have the pleasure to acknowledge the receipt of your letter of the 15th. of November, and would most cheerfully aid you in your reserches if I possessed the information you desire – I have in vain endeavoured to recal to my mind the name of 'Power' among my acquaintances in England – The only one I can recollect was the gentleman who unfortunately perished in the President[2] – Indeed I am inclined to think the family from whom you derived your information, have been rather misinformed or have mistaken me for some other person – I have not the pleasure of knowing any family in Rhode Island nor have I ever been there – It is possible they mean Chief Justice Halliburton,[3] who if I recollect aright told me he was a native of that place, or that his father Dr Haliburton formerly resided there[4] – Tho our name is the same we are not related – When I see him I will mention your enquiry to him, and if he has the information you seek will transmit it to you –

The only person I know that would be likely to assist you to what you want is a Mr. Sumner[5] a lawyer of Boston whom I repeatedly met in London, three years ago – On those occasions it was in circles not usually accessible to strangers, and from what I saw and knew of him, I should think he had a more extensive acquaintance in England than any American gentleman has enjoyed for many years past – I have now only to express my regret that I cannot give you any more satisfactory answer –

> I am dr sir
> Your obt servt
> Tho. C. Haliburton

To De Witt C Power Esqr.

Historical Soc. of Pennsylvania MS [*Ph.*]

1 De Witt C. Power was a member of the Harvard faculty in 1841.
2 The *President* was lost in 1841. It was the *Great Western*'s partner on the Atlantic route.
3 Sir Brenton Halliburton (1775–1860), chief justice of Nova Scotia, 1833–60
4 Sir Brenton's father, John Halliburton (1725–1808)
5 Charles Sumner (1811–74), US senator and notable advocate of the emancipation of slaves. At the age of twenty-six, Sumner spent two years in Europe, during which time Haliburton met him.

---

84 To A. Deuchar[1]

Windsor
11th. Ap. 1842

Dear sir –

In reply to your letter I have to say that in the autumn I shall be very glad to place my family under your charge, & will make a class for you, but that until then there are reasons[2] which will prevent their having the benefit of your instructions –

> Yours in haste
> Tho. C. Haliburton

Historical Soc. of Pennsylvania MS [*Ph.*]

1 Alexander Deuchar wrote two letters to the Colonial Office about Canadian matters in 1838, when he was empowered to act on behalf of the heirs of Viscount Canada. His address was then 73 George Street, Edinburgh (PRO CO 217, 168). Haliburton addresses his letter to the 'Halifax Hotel/Halifax.'
2 The reasons possibly relate to the death of Louisa Haliburton in November 1841.

85 To Richard Bentley

[Windsor]
Saturday [1842]

My dear sir –

I have just noticed with more astonishment than I can well express an advertisement in the Quarterly R.[1] of 'Slick in England' a work of which not 5 pages are written, which may never be written, and if written may not please me sufficiently to publish – All this you have heard over and over again, and therefore I cant tell you how much hurt I feel at your announcing this work at this time without saying a word to me on the subject – I can only say that I do not now feel inclined to write it, and if you will do me the favor to forget any projects I have talked to you about, relative to works that I might hereafter write, I shall feel very much obliged to you –

Yours very truly
Th C Haliburton

Harvard MS *Pub.*: ed. W.I. Morse, 67

1 Possibly a loose-leaf insertion in the magazine. I have found no reference to the advertisment in the magazine itself. *The Attaché* was published on 1 July 1843 (Bentley's ledger, BL Add. MS 46,637, vol. 1, 1829–73).

---

86 To L. Mariotti[1]

[Windsor]
Thursday [1842?]

Judge Haliburton requests the honor of Mr Marriotti's company at dinner tomorrow at 6 o'clock –

Harvard MS

1 Antonio Carlo Napoleone Gallenga (pseud. L. Mariotti; 1810–95). Mariotti lived in Windsor during the winter of 1842 and reminisced about his experiences in *Episodes of My Second Life*, 2 vols (London 1884) 2: 114–35. Mariotti was briefly professor of modern languages, history and literature at King's College in Windsor.

87 To Richard Bentley

Windsor Nova Scotia 3d. Jany [18]43

My dear Bentley –

I received your letter and the parcel of books accompanying it, for the latter of which I am much obliged – As respects the subject of your letter I shall comply with it & release you from your undertaking –

With respect to the work of humor I shall bring it with me in the spring, when I revisit London – It is needless however to make arrangements before hand, as you may perhaps produce a *miscariage* again – I never saw the 3d series of The Clockmaker[1] till the other day when Ld Falkland lent it to me (your copy having been stolen out of the steamer) – I never saw anything so bad as the illustrations – any thing half so abominable – I send you his note, to shew you I am not singular in this opinion – Enclosed are two little things of Mr McDougalls[2] for your Miscellany – Please insert them – Yours trly

Tho. C. Haliburton

Harvard MS *Pub.*: ed. W.I. Morse, 67–8

1 It was published on 30 October 1840
2 Alexander McDougall (1804–55), lawyer, MLA for Sydney County, 1836–40; member, Legislative Council, 1844–55, and Executive Council, 1848–54. The two poems were, 'On a Member of the House of Assembly, not remarkable for his veracity' (four lines) and some comic verse entitled 'Lines to Ellen.' They were published in *Bentley's Miscellany* 13 (1843).

88 To Major Henderson[1]

[Windsor] 15th. Jany [18]43 –

My dear sir

I shall have great pleasure in dining with you on Saturday next –

I am sorry I cannot aid you either with divorces or mottoes, the turn of my mind being rather for the ludicrous –

I could furnish some absurd combinations, but they would suit [H–B's?]

purpose better than yours, as they would be inappropriate to your object –

>Yours very truly
>Tho. C. Haliburton

Major Henderson

NY Univ. – Fales Library MS

1 John Alexander Henderson (d. 1858), a major in the Rifle Brigade. See *The Rifle Brigade Century: An Alphabetical List of the Officers of the Rifle Brigade (the Prince Consort's Own) (Regular Battalions) from 1800 to 1905*, compiled by Colonel Gerald Edmund Boyle (London 1905) 82–3.

---

89 To Richard Bentley

[Windsor]
1st. Mar 43

My dear sir –

Will you put the proper address on the enclosed for me – I shall leave this for England on the 18th. of May, and bring my new work 'The Attache or Sam Slick in England' with me – How long ought it to be advertised?
  How long will it take to get it thro the press?
  How much delay will illustrations make?
  Write me by return of Steamer – It is a work well calculated for popularity and the illustration of English topics, by Yankee anecdotes, or Yankee topics in juxta position, has a very droll effect – I promise myself a good reception for it,[1] and I want to see it thro the press myself –

>Yours trly
>T C Haliburton

Harvard MS *Pub.*: ed. W.I. Morse, 68

1 While the First Series of *The Attaché* did not fail, the Second Series did. Bentley wrote to Haliburton informing him that although the work was 'favourably noticed by the press,' the 'paucity of matter' affected sales. Bentley recorded 'a loss' on the venture.

90 To Messrs Lea and Blanchard

Halifax 18th. May 43

Gentlemen –

I embark this day for England – I carry with me mss. of 1st. series of The Attaché or Sam Slick in England – Do you wish a proof copy? If so write to me at *No 6 – Spring Garden London,*[1] and let me know what you are willing to give for it, that I may know whether it is worth your or my while to arrange for it –

The work is of that kind, I should think, as to be popular in U States –

Yours
Tho. C. Haliburton

Mesrs Lea & Blanchard –

An original print (with authors concurrence) I conceive exempt from colonial post exclusive and it might so appear 'Published by the authors directions, simultaneously with London edition' –

Historical Soc. of Pennsylvania MS [*Ph.*]

1 In 1841, 6 Spring Gardens was occupied by William Burton, aged fifty-five, merchant. In 1851, his son Decimus Burton, the architect, brother of James Haliburton, is listed as the occupier (1841 and 1851 Census, PRO, London).

91 To Richard Bentley

[London? 27 June 1843][1]

My dear sir –

I have read the article for the magazine[2] – With the exception that I fear I do not deserve the laudation of the author, I must say I think it a remarkably well written article – If there were time to add a word or two about the Revd. Mr Hopewell, who is rather a prominent character in all the books and will be still more so in the forthcoming one, it would make it more complete[3] – There were things to be said too wise and too deep for Sam, these I have given as the talk of an aged – gentleman – a scholar and divine – 'in wit a man simplicity a child'[4] wise in constitutional law – in natural & moral philosophy of great kindness and goodness of heart – but simple in his manners, and utterly ignorant of what Sam knows so well – wordly knowledge –

If there were time a small addition here might render the sketch more perfect, but as I have said before, as it is, it is a remarkably well written article –

Yours
T.C.H.

Harvard MS *Pub.*: ed. W.I. Morse, 69

1 The letter is postmarked 'JU 27 1843.'
2 'Notions of Sam Slick [With a Portrait of the Author],' *Bentley's Miscellany* 14 (1843) 81–94
3 Haliburton's advice on Mr Hopewell was followed: 'in his sketch of the Rev. Mr. Hopewell ... Mr. Halliburton has taken a higher flight than any he has yet attempted, and tasked his powers of thought to the utmost. Nothing can be loftier, more humane, or more replete with philosophic wisdom ...' Ibid. 92
4 Alexander Pope, 'Epitaph on Gay': 'Of manners gentle, of affections mild/In wit a man, simplicity a child.'

---

92 To Major Henderson [London? *c.* 18 May 1843]

My dear sir,

I did not receive your parcel of prints in time to thank you for the same before I left Halifax – I now return them with our united acknowledgements for the amusement they have afforded us –

I should be most happy to dine either with the *minor major* or the *major & his minors*, but am '*in these premisses*' under the *conclusion* to leave town in the morning – Q.E.D.

I am sorry I cannot assist in '*cup-ping*' the General –

Yours truly
Tho. C. Haliburton
'*Half pay* judge'[1]

To Major Henderson
In *full pay* of Rifles

NY Univ. – Fales Library MS

1 Haliburton successfully negotiated his exemption from receiving only half his pay during his absence abroad.

93 To R.H. Barham

6 Spring Gardens [London] 7th. July 1843

My dear sir –

I received your kind note informing me of the committee of the Garric having done me the honor to elect me as visiting member of their club[1] –

For this as well as all other acts of kindness I have received from your, pray accept my most sincere thanks –

At the close of the next week I propose leaving London, previous to my going away I want much to see you, would you do me the favor to mention any day and hour, you are likely to be at the Garric and I will be there to meet between 10 and 6 aclock –

                Yours always
                Tho C Haliburton

Revd R Barham –
I have written to the secretary Mr Winston[2] a letter acknowledging the admission and thanking him for it –

Harvard MS

1 Barham was the author of a posthumously published account of the Garrick Club, *The Garrick Club Notices of One Hundred and Thirty-Five of Its Former Members* (Privately printed 1896). The club was founded in 1831 as a 'society in which actors and men of education and refinement might meet on equal and independent terms' (Barham, *The Garrick Club*, vi).
2 James Winston (?1778–1848) was one of the founders of the Garrick Club. He was part proprietor of the Haymarket Theatre (Guy Boas, *The Garrick Club 1831–1947* [London 1948] 10).

94 To Cecilia Tilley[1]

Edgworth near Cirencester[2]
July 18th/[18]43

My dear madam –

I have the pleasure to acknowledge the receipt of your very kind note of the 4th inst, and shall hope to have the gratification of thanking you personally. As soon as I reached London I enquired of Bentley whether Mrs Trollope was then at Penryth and was told in so positive a manner as to preclude all further enquiries that about a month since she had gone to the continent, that I abandoned all hope of seeing her.[3]

I am delighted to find she is still in England, and whatever part that is I must see her. Shall you be so kind my dear madam, as to send me her address to 'No. 6 – Spring Gardens London' and at the same time say when she will return to Penryth. If it shall be so, that she returns to the latter place, before I go to N. Scotia (which will be on 3 September) I shall be certain, please God, to have the gratification of seeing you both together again. Of Mrs Trollope's uniform and great kindness to me, during the whole of my late sojourn in London,[4] I entertain and ever shall a most grateful and affectionate remembrance. I shall be most happy to go to any part of the kingdom to have an opportunity of again shaking hands with her, and renewing my acquaintance with a friend whom I respect so much and love so well as I do your excellent mother. When you write to her pray do me the favor of remembering me in the kindest terms to her, and say I only await her address to write to her, and an engagement or two I have made to pass off when I shall hurry off to see her, before I again cross the water. My time is so limited here, I fear I shall have to go to Edinburgh by water, as it is a visit for a particular object which will require only two days sojourn there. If my time (for my days here are numbered) shall hold out, I shall most gladly proceed to by Penryth for the gratification of seeing you again. Please to present my respects to Mr Tilley[5] (whom I have had the pleasure of seeing at Baker St.) and believe me, my dear Madam, Yours always,

Tho C Haliburton

Professor Raymond M. Bennett copy

1 Mrs Trollope's daughter, Cecilia (1816–49)
2 The home of Edmund Hopkinson (1787–1869), Haliburton's friend, and James Haliburton's brother-in-law. In dedicating the First Series of *The Attaché* (1843) to Edmund Hopkinson, Haliburton wrote: 'I have spent so many agreeable hours at Edgeworth.'
3 Mrs Trollope spent the summer at Exeter and left for the continent in October.
4 In 1838–9, when Mrs Trollope lived at 20 York Street
5 John Tilley was post office surveyor for the Lake District. He married Cecilia Trollope on 11 February 1839.

95 To Mrs Frances Trollope

London 6 Sprng gardens
3d Aug [18]43

My dear Mrs Trollope –

On my return to London from the country I found your very kind note and lose no time in assuring you of the great gratification it has given me, to be assured that we can meet once more – My leave of absence was only for three months, and I am obliged to embark again for Nova Scotia on the 3d of September – If I can get thro my business at the Colonial Office in time I will go down to Devonshire[1] before the 17th. inst, if not I will arrange matters so as to be positively in London on the 25th. and hope to be able indeed to accomplish both – If you come to London what will be your address? Because as it will be close upon the heels of my embarkation, I should like to call upon you as soon as you will be able to give me the gratification of an interview – I am much grieved to hear that your health requires nursing, and that your fears as well as your comfort have been so materialy interfered with by indisposition, – I trust in God that the change of air which you propose, will accomplish a perfect restoration – My last three or 4 days are devoted to an excursion to the lakes, during which I promise myself the pleasure of renewing my acquaintance with Mrs Tilly[2] –

I am sorry to say I have not enjoyed this visit as I did my last, my spirits are not the same, and when alone I suffer a good deal of depression, but I am much benefitted and hope to return with a better tone of nerves – I shall move heaven and earth to leave this, if possible on the 12th. or 13th. – At all events please God at one or other of the days you have mentioned I shall have the pleasure to shake you by the hand, and assure you the attachment of yours alwy

Thos. C. Haliburton

UCLA MS [*Ph.*]. *Pub.*: Frances Eleanor Trollope, *Frances Trollope: Her Life and Work* (London 1895) 1: 297–8

---

1 See Frances Eleanor Trollope, *Frances Trollope: Her Life and Work*, 2 vols (London 1895) 2: 28.
2 Mrs Trollope's daughter, Cecilia

96 To Lord Stanley[1]

London, 6, Spring Gardens,
21st August 1843.

My Lord,

Previously to my leaving Nova Scotia I was furnished by direction of Lord Falkland with an extract of a despatch of Your Lordship desiring that in future no leave of absence should be given to a judge without his being given distinctly to understand that one half of his salary would be withheld during his absence.

Without remarking upon the extreme hardship of the application of such a rule to officers not only poorly paid but so severely worked as the judges of Nova Scotia, but for whom no retiring pension is provided, and who are thus deprived in sickness and other unavoidable cases from recruiting their strength or attending to their own private affairs, I beg leave respectfully to call your Lordships attention to its total inapplicability to my own case.

1st, I receive my salary under the provisions of a colonial law, which contains no such restriction, and which I presume if it had been thought expedient in Nova Scotia would have been added to it. As I find it necessary to resort to Europe for the education of my sons[2] I should have hesitated to accept the situation I now hold at its present inadequate salary[3] had the law contained such a clause. It has therefore all the effect of an ex post facto law passed *in this country* relative to the internal affairs of a colony.

2nd, I must suppose that your Lordship meant by the word *absence*, absence *from duty*, and not absence *from the province*. The public service has not been postponed to my convenience, but I have been put to the greatest personal inconvenience and no inconsiderable expense to accommodate myself to the exigencies of the public; as I have performed my spring circuit before I left the province.[4] As soon as I shall return, I must embark for Cape-Breton and hold five courts this autumn. I have therefore not been able to select my own time, but have been compelled to take the only period I could be spared, which unfortunately was the most inconvenient portion of the whole year, to myself. As the courts are now constituted the circuits are indispensible duties for of the five judges,[5] four only are able to travel the circuits, one of them from indisposition being unable to undergo the fatigue of distant journeys at inclement seasons of the year.[6] As there are four circuits therefore, no leave can be granted that shall extend over a circuit without closing all the courts in that circuit. This I have not asked, because it ought not to be granted, but I have been subjected as I before observed to the greatest possible inconvenience and considerable expense. Between these two circuits (from neither of which I shall be absent) is a term at Halifax in July, at which juries do not attend, where very little business is done, and which from the inconvenient season of the year at which it is held will probably be abolished this winter.[7] There are four judges left to hold this short and almost nominal term in my absence, at which the law has not made the attendance of all or any number of judges indispensible.

I have thus, my Lord, had to restrict my request for leave of absence to four months, in order to avoid neglecting any essential duty. One of these months must necessarily be spent at sea, and the three remaining ones have proved so insufficient for transacting my business that I am compelled to leave it unfinished. Independent of the right, my Lord, which I conceive I have established to an exemption from the rule, I think, when I state that in addition to all other official duties I was absent from home last year one hundred and twenty days on the business of the courts, your Lordship will consider such great labor performed in the worst state of the roads, in the worst state of the year entitled to a favorable consideration.

Under these circumstances, I submit this application with the utmost confidence, because I feel that the severe and stringent application of the rule to a case like mine was never contemplated by your Lordship. It was doubtless designed to guard the public service, by preventing the unnecessary absence of public officers from their duty, but your Lordship never could have intended that the highest officers of a colony should be deprived of that occasional opportunity for relaxation from labor or attention to urgent private affairs, which is granted to the humblest clerk of every public department in this country.[8]

            I have &c.
            (Signed) Thos Haliburton

PANS copy

1 Edward George Geoffrey Smith Stanley, fourteenth Earl of Derby (1799–1869), colonial secretary during Sir Robert Peel's administration, 1841–4
2 Haliburton mentions in *The Attaché*, First Series, 1: 241, obtaining passports to visit Germany, 'where I had a son in school.'

3 See letter of 21 July 1848, below, where Haliburton gives a full account of his arrangement with the government of Nova Scotia.
4 The April–May sittings of the Supreme Court in 1843 in Halifax, King's, Queen's, Lunenburg, Shelburne, Yarmouth, and Cape Breton counties
5 Chief Justice Brenton Halliburton, assistant judges Lewis M. Wilkins, William Hill, William Bowers Bliss, and Thomas Chandler Haliburton
6 Haliburton refers to Lewis Wilkins, who was seventy-five years old and in poor health.
7 An act to postpone the next ensuing sitting of the Supreme Court at Halifax and on the Western Circuit was passed on 29 March 1844.
8 James Stephens replied on behalf of Lord Stanley on 6 September 1843. His lordship did not insist on enforcing the letter of the law in this case, as Haliburton's absence did not interfere with the performance of his duties.

---

97 To Richard Bentley

Windsor N[o]va Scotia
1st. Ap [18]44

My dear sir

I have completed the 2d and *last* series of The Attache or Sam Slick in England – I have added four chapters to it, to increase both the bulk & the variety of it –

I am well satisfied with the work and hope it will prove equally so to you – I set out on the circuit in a week, and as it has to be revised and fair copied, will not be able to send it before June, when I will put the manuscript under Lord Falklands cover to the Colonial Secretary who will send it to you – I write thus early that you may as the time approaches advertise – When you do call it the *last* series, and you may add '*Which will complete the Sayings & Doings of Mr Slick*' so as to shew there is to be an end of these papers[1] – Do ... to ...[2]

Yours alwys
Th. C. Haliburton

Harvard MS *Pub.*: ed. W.I. Morse, 70

1 *The Attaché*, Second Series, was published on 21 October 1844.
2 Hiatuses in ms

98 To Robert Parker [Windsor 3 June 1844][1]

The truth is that a desolate heart, blasted hopes, and a dreary future have taught me that we have little to expect here, and that though the form and mode of affliction may vary, come it must in some shape or another, and that none of us can hope for exemption from a lot common to all. I enter into your experience most fully and feel for you most sincerely[2] ...[3] I keep busy. I have to do so. If I am not occupied I become gloomy. I have another book written in two volumes. I think it my best decidedly. It is a second and last series of The Attache, and terminates my clockmaking. Whether I shall hereafter write again I know not.

Pub.: *Canadian Magazine*, 1916: 78

1 The date is supplied by A. Wylie Mahon.
2 Besides the early deaths of several children, Haliburton had recently (November 1841) experienced the death of his wife, Louisa.
3 Mahon's ellipses

99 To Richard Bentley Halifax Nova Scotia 18th Sepr. [18]44

My dear Bentley –

I send you by this steamer the msst. of the second and last series of The Attaché – It was drafted as long ago as February but ill health has prevented me revising and completing it until lately – It contains 7 more articles than the preceding series altho I do not think now that it is done I have carried out my intention of enlarging it much – It is however a little larger, and of course contains more variety –

I think it will sustain the reputation and I hope increase it, of the entire work – you will find it contains many *extractible* and *taking passages* –

The first volume must terminate at the end of No 18–[1] [And?]the second will commence with No 19 The Pleasures of Hope – As this is a large package I have given it to Mr. Cunard[2] who undertakes to forward it to steam agents – Should there be any delay in the delivery please to cause inquiry to be made at their office in town or at McEwens their agents in Liverpool,[3] and as I am anxious to ascertain its safe arrival will you do me the favor to let me know as soon as it reaches you

The bills please to give to Coutts & Co. as usual.

Enclosed is a note for Millar[4] – I do not know his address, will you be so good as to put on the address and throw it into the post office –

I will thank you to send me by first steamer after its publication two copies, in a parcel addressed to me, and cover that parcel (so addressed) in another cover to *Honble* Saml Cunard Esqr Halifax, and send this to their agent the McEwens – at Liverpool –

–Here is an end of Saml. Slick –

My good wishes for you both, and so I bid you for the *present* farewell –

Tho. C. Haliburton

What do you think of the work promised in the last chapter 'Sketches of Colonial Life'[5] –

Harvard MS *Pub.*: ed. W.I. Morse, 71–2

1 'The Horse Stealer'
2 Sir Samuel Cunard (1787–1865), merchant, shipowner, and entrepreneur
3 David and Charles MacIver, who managed the operations of the Cunard fleet at Liverpool. Haliburton mistakes the name.
4 Unidentified. Possibly either J.F. Miller, the bookseller, or J. Millar, author of *Voyages*, published by Bentley (BL Add. MS 46,640 f. 193).
5 *The Old Judge*

100 To Richard Bentley   Windsor Nova Scotia 2d Decr 1844

My dear sir –

By the steamer of the 19th of Sepr. I sent you the mss of the last series of The Attaché thro a private conveyance, and by the mail addressed a letter to you requesting the favor of you to relieve my anxiety by acknowledging its receipt –

By the boat of the 3d of October, I hoped to have heard, by that of 18th I felt certain of a letter, by that of the 3d of November, after all allowances for delay I felt confident of a reply but alas there was none – The steamer of the 15th. arrived as usual with no news, and to my amazement that of the 3d of December also brought additional disappointment – During all this period I have been in great perplexity to know whether it had ever reached you, and finally came to the conclusion that it had miscarried – A day or two ago a friend sent me a Literary Gazette[1] containing an extract from it which is the first intimation I have received of its safe arrival, – I have written this day for a copy to the States, which I hope to receive in a fortnight – Why I should have been subjected to such supercilious indifference I do not know – I am not conscious of having given you any cause of offence, and if I have unintentionally done so, no man would be more ready than myself to make amends to a person with whom I have had not only no misunderstanding whatever, but for whom I have always felt and expressed a great personal regard – I can only say I feel very much hurt at such an unaccountable procedure[2] –

>With every good wish
>I am yours
>Th. C. Haliburton

Richd Bentley Esqr

Harvard MS *Pub.*: ed. W.I. Morse, 72–3

1 *The Literary Gazette*, 2 November 1844, contained extracts and a favourable review of the Second Series of *The Attaché*.
2 Bentley's reply, dated 31 December 1844, is printed in full by W.H. Bond, 73–4: 'I was out of town when the M.S. arrived, and also when the work was published. Thus the announcement of the arrival was entirely overlooked.'

---

101 To the Earl of Aberdeen[1]

Windsor Nova Scotia
N.A.
My Lord, 16 Dec. 1844

I have taken the liberty to address your Lordship on a subject of much interest to the bench the bar and the clergy of the Church of England in this and the adjoining province of New Brunswick – There is now and has been for half a century a college at Windsor N.S.[2] which for thirty years was presided over by Dr Charles Porter[3] of Oxford with a zeal ability and efficiency above all praise – During this long period of colonial rule he educated nearly all the judges eminent lawyers and with some few exceptions all the clergy-men of both provinces – He is now living in retirement in the parish of St Thomas Exeter England with a broken constitution a large family and small means. We all feel greatly attached to him and have often deplored the want of patronage here that some provision might be made for the sons of a man whose whole life has been devoted to the improvement of the children of others – He is too far advanced in years and too infirm to be the object of reward himself, but he has a son resident in Halifax N.S. Mr Michael Wallace Porter 25 years of age, of the most unexceptionable character and conduct, well known and respected by us all who is now unprovided for – If it should happen to be in your Lordships power to confer upon him a consulate *anywhere*, for which he is well qualified, or indeed any other piece of patronage, it would be a most acceptable and gratifying act of kindness to the numerous class of persons in these provinces to whom I have before alluded, and indeed to every graduate wherever situated by all of whom Dr Porter is held in the highest veneration and respect. – Had this young gentleman been a relation or companion or ordinary friend of mine, I should not have had the presumption to address your Lordship – I do so now with the utmost reluctance because I feel most sensibly that it is a great liberty, but as I am activated by considerations of a public nature as much as by a lively feeling of gratitude to a person to whom I am indebted myself for any little reputation I may have acquired as an author I will trust to your Lordships kindness to pardon my intrusion on account of the motive – I avail myself of the opportunity to pay my respects to your Lordship whom I had the honor and pleasure to meet when in London a few years ago at Lord De Greys.[4]

> I have the honor to be
> Your Lordships most obedient
> Tho. C. Haliburton

To the Right Honble
The Earl Aberdeen.[5]

BL Add. MS 43,243 f. 96

1 George Hamilton Gordon, fourth Earl of Aberdeen (1784–1860), statesman
2 Founded in 1789
3 Charles Porter (1778–1864), professor of divinity, mathematics, and Hebrew, as well as president of King's College, 1806–36
4 Thomas Philip De Grey, Earl De Grey (1781–1859), first lord of the Admiralty, 1834–5, lord lieutenant of Ireland, 1841–4, and the first president of the Institution of British Architects
5 In his reply, the Earl of Aberdeen said he was unable to accede to Haliburton's request (BL Add. MS 43,243).

102 To Richard Bentley

Windsor, Nova Scotia,
31 Jany [18]45

My dear sir

I received your letter by the last steamer, and must express myself greatly astonished that your long continued silence has at last been broken merely to tell me that you have withheld 250 pounds of the stipulated price of the 2d series of The Attache – You say it is fifty pages short of the 1st. series, but give me no means of judging, having never sent me a copy of the work – A correspondence carried on in this manner, is not likely soon to end, I have therefore sent your agreement to Mr Burton[1] 6 Spring Garden whom I have requested to see that justice is done to me –

[?][2]
Tho C Haliburton

Harvard MS *Pub*: ed. W.I. Morse, 75

1 Possibly Septimus Burton, of 10 Lincoln's Inn, London, brother of James and Decimus
2 Ms damaged

103 To George Haliburton, Snr[1]

Windsor 26th Jany [18]46
Nova Scotia

My dear George –

I send you some manuscript musick of Toms[2] – Will you be so good as to dispose of it to some of the people who publish these things, and forward by the sailing packet to Halifax a few sheets of each to us – If as his name 'is unknown to fame'[3] they are not saleable (beautiful as they really are) then give them to some publisher, that his name may be brought forward and ask him to send a few copies –

You will see by the papers I have had Alfred appt. Sherriff of Sydney[4] – Have the goodness to drop me a line in reply –

Yours truly
Tho. C. Haliburton

Boston Public Library MS [*Ph.*]

1 George Mordaunt Haliburton (1777–1861), Haliburton's uncle, who removed to Boston in 1831
2 Thomas, Haliburton's eldest son (1821–47)
3 Thomas Gray, 'Elegy in a Country Churchyard,' line 118: 'A youth to fortune and to fame unknown.' (From The Epitaph.)
4 George Mordaunt's son Alfred Fales, baptized at Windsor, 29 May 1820, d. 1906, aged eighty-six. He was a lawyer at Sydney with his brother, John Gustavus Peoples Haliburton.

---

104 To Lewis Cist[1]

'I am Sam Slick says I, at least what is left of me'
Tho. C. Haliburton

                Windsor, Nova Scotia,
                1t. Aug 1846

Sir –

I have the pleasure to acknowldge the receipt of your letter of the 10th. May last inclosing one for Mr. Slick and requesting me to use my influence with him to send you his autograph –

Mr. Slick, is a good natured man, and like all his countrymen whom I have ever had the pleasure to know, remarkably obliging to strangers, and he sat down immediately and wrote for me, at the top of the page what may serve your purpose –

I send it to you not that I think it worth having, but because I think a request that has caused some trouble to prefer when it can be complied with so easily should not be refused –

                I am sir
                Your obt sert.
                Th. C. Haliburton

To
L.J. Cist Esquire –

NYPL: Ford Collection MS [*Ph.*] *Pub.*: Chittick, 342–3

1 Lewis Cist, bank clerk, poet, essayist, and noted collector of autographs

105 To George W. Nickisson[1]

Windsor Nova Scotia N A
Novr 15th. 1846

My dear sir

I have the pleasure to acknowledge the receipt of your letter of the 22d of April last enclosing a proof of 'The Lone House' a portion of my new work entitled 'The Old Judge' and should have replied to it long since had I not been in hopes of revisiting England with our late Governor Lord Falkland in august last and having the pleasure of a personal interview with you – But the same cause which has hitherto deprived me of leisure for any continued literary effort, or for leaving the province (the old age and infirmities of one of my brother judges) still exists – I find it will therefore be more convenient for me to publish my work in monthly numbers than collectively, and if you still continue of the same opinion as when I last saw you I shall be happy to furnish you with them for your magazine,[2] sending you the 2d No by the steamer of the 1t. of January, so as to appear in February and thenceforward periodically until the work shall be completed – As some time has elapsed since we conversed on the subject I have not a very distinct recollection as to the arrangement beyond that it was satisfactory and that the copyright was reserved – I shall feel obliged to you therefore for the particulars and an answer by the return steamer of the 1t. Decr. next –

Yours very truly
Tho. C. Haliburton

G. W. Nickisson Esqr

Univ. of Virginia Library MS [*Ph.*]

1 George Nickisson, editor of *Fraser's Magazine* from 1841 or 1842 to 1847
2 'The Lone House' appeared in May 1846, 33: 505–14. The second instalment, 'The Tombstones,' did not appear until February 1847, 35: 141–7. The remaining instalments continued monthly until December 1847

106 To Richard Bentley

Windsor Nova Scotia 1st. February [18]47 –

My dear sir –

I should like to see a new edition of The Clockmaker issued in a cheaper form for general circulation and also The Attache either to make one united work in two volumes, or seperate works in one volume each or in some such way[1] – As the property is vested in you of course this cannot be done without your consent or cooperation – If the plan suits your views I should be glad to hear from you on the subject – To give it a new and attractive form each part (that now forms a volume or separate work) ought to have original prefaces, and the whole be elucidated with rather copious notes, some of which would be curious – If it were practicable some good illustrations would amazingly improve it – If such a plan meet your views, you can name what you think suitable for the additional labor of putting it in this new and improved form, and as it will take some time to do it properly I will take it in hand and work at it as opportunity offers –

Yours very truly
Tho. C. Haliburton

Richd Bentley Eqr

Harvard MS *Pub.*: ed. W.I. Morse, 76

1 Bentley reissued *The Clockmaker* in his 'Cabinet Library' the following year, 1848. Bentley reissued *The Attaché* in 1851. In 1853, Bentley published *The Clockmaker*, *The Attaché*, and *The Letter-Bag* as the first three volumes in his 'Parlour Bookcase.'

107 Sir John Beverley Robinson[1]

Windsor, Nova Scotia,
14*th September* 1847.

My dear Chief-Justice, –

I received your note with very great pleasure.

It would afford me infinite gratification to have an opportunity of renewing my acquaintance with you, either here, in Canada, or in dear old

England. There are many subjects which I should delight in talking over with you, in most of which I believe we fully agree.

These are, however, all too prolix for the limits of a note, which only enables me to assure you of my very great respect and regard. – I am, my dear sir, yours always,

Th. Haliburton.

Pub.: C.W. Robinson, *Life of Sir John Beverley Robinson* (London 1904) 368

1 Sir John Beverley Robinson (1791–1863), chief justice of Upper Canada, 1829–62

108 To Rev. Joseph Hart Clinch[1]   Halifax 17th. Decr. 1847

My dear friend

Your letter has been forwarded on to me at this place, just as I am leaving for Windsor, and in time to procure a draft for the amount you were so good as to disburse on my account and to enable me to enclose it in the English mail for Boston – Pray accept my most grateful – most heartfelt thanks and believe me dear Clinch I can never forget your kindness[2] – a thousand thanks and blessings –

Yours always
Th.C.Haliburton

Maine Historical Society MS [*Ph.*]

1 Rev. Joseph Hart Clinch was the minister of St Matthew's Church, Boston. He was related by marriage to the Cunningham family of Windsor.
2 Possibly kindnesses consequent upon the death of Haliburton's son Tom, on 3 November 1847

109 To John Cunningham[1]   Windsor 8th. Ap 1848

My dear John –

I have just received a letter from Lord Falkland enclosing one from Mr Trefnel[2] announcing his regret that he cannot include your name in the list of appointments in consequence of the urgency of previous claims –

Altho I have never had any conversation with you on the subject of an understanding existing between you and Laura,[3] I have not been either inattentive or unanxious about it, and so long as any reasonable hope existed of a prospect of settling in life in a manner conducive to your mutual happiness I neither could or would offer any objection to her union with a family I so sincerely regard and respect as yours or with one for whom I entertain so great a personal affection as yourself –

I confess however I do not see the way clear for a suitable provision for you both – My own means are unfortunately not only limited, but my expences are equal to all my income – I cannot make her such a provision as she ought to have nor are your prospects equal to supply that deficiency until my death, when she could alone have the distributive share of my property – I do not under these circumstances think a further continuance of any understanding on this subject conducive to the happiness of either party, and therefore with great pain and distress of mind feel compelled so to inform you – Grievous as this communication will doubtless be to you, years hence you will recognise in it only the duty of a parent to my own child and the affection of a friend to you – In the haste in which this is written to prevent a painful interview, if I have not expressed myself as kindly as I ought, pray attribute it to my agitation – For I feel for you and towards you every k[indness] and good wish – I think it not [?] you may [think?] I might have said this befo[re] – perhaps so – but I hoped while there was hope of some settlement in life adequate to your station[4] and the inevitable expences of settlement in life and now feel as her father – your friend – & the friend of your family that what I say is for your future welfare, as it is my plain duty –

I am dear John yours very truly and affectionately

Th. C. Haliburton

Maine Historical Society MS [*Ph.*]

1 John Cunningham (d. 1851) was the youngest child of Richard Cunningham (d. 1830) and his second wife, Sarah Apthorp Morton (1782–1844). See Gwendolyn Shand, 'The Cunninghams of Hants County,' ts, PANS.
2 Unidentified
3 Laura Charlotte, Haliburton's third daughter, who married Samuel Cunard's second son, William, in 1851
4 In 1849, Perez clarified the legal control he had over the estate, purchasing from his two sisters, Charlotte Griselda Eastwicke and Sarah Frances Wentworth, and his younger brother, John, their shares in the estate.

110 To Joseph Howe   Halifax, 21 July 1848.

Sir,

I have the honour to request that you will be pleased to lay before his Excellency the Lieutenant Governor[1] and his Executive Council the following statement of facts and the claim grounded thereon for their consideration.

In the year one thousand eight hundred and forty, an act of the legislature was passed abolishing the several Courts of Common Pleas in this province and providing pensions for the judges, while at the same time it authorised the appointment of an additional justice of the Supreme Court at a salary of seven hundred pounds currency per annum. At that time I had presided in the Courts of Common Pleas and General Sessions of the Peace for the middle division of Nova Scotia for a period of about twelve years and became entitled under the provisions of the before mentioned act of the legislature to a pension of three hundred pounds.

It was then my intention to have retired into private life and left the province when I received a letter from Lord Falkland, then Governor of Nova Scotia, offering to me the situation of additional judge created by the act. Although I was very reluctant to be burdensome to the country, I could not but feel the inadequacy of the provision for such onerous duties as would naturally arise from the new situation and also the invidious distinction of salary thus established between the additional judge and his brethren on the bench, which amounted to one hundred and twelve pounds ten shillings a year. Nor could I reconcile to myself the peculiar anomaly of my position considering the pension of three hundred pounds as the just reward of past services. I was called upon to relinquish it or suffer it to merge in the salary, which in effect was asking me to perform the duties for four hundred pounds when others received eight hundred and twelve pounds ten shillings per annum or more than one half. I therefore felt myself compelled to decline the offer when I was assured that if I would consent to be a party to effecting a saving of three hundred pounds a year to this province and give the public the benefit of my services and long experience as a judge, I should positively be advanced to the receipt of the full salary of eight hundred and twelve pounds ten shillings per annum on the demise of any one of the then senior incumbents; an event which the very advanced age and dangerous illness of the late Mr Justice Wilkins appeared at that time as likely to occur at a very short period.

On this express condition and on this only I accepted the appointment and surrendered my pension. Although several years have elapsed since this occurrence took place I feel satisfied that the distinct understanding which was then come to between the government and myself on this subject must be still fresh in your recollection who was then a *leading* member of the administration and naturally desirous of effecting so great a pecuniary saving to the province.

Having been thus drawn from the retirement of private life and a literary leisure infinitely more productive than any judicial salary paid in this colony, I have fulfilled my part of the engagement by devoting eight years of severe labour to the public. During this period a saving has been effected to the country of two thousand four hundred pounds by the cessation of my annuity, while for the same term I have received nine hundred pounds less than the senior judges, and if to this be added the accumulated loss of my pension, which was peculiarly my own, three thousand three hundred less than my brethren on the bench.

I have therefore to request that my salary may now be placed according to promise on the same footing as that of the Mr Justice Wilkins whose demise entitles me to receive six hundred pounds per annum from the provincial treasury and two hundred and twelve pounds ten shillings from the casual revenue. It may not be amiss perhaps to observe that whatever questions have arisen on the construction of the inchoate act of the legislature passed in the year one thousand eight hundred and forty four relative to the civil list they do not in any manner apply to this case which was discussed and settled four years previously, and further, that this application involves no additional charge on the casual revenue, being merely for the substitution of the name of one judge for that of another deceased leaving the gross amount unaltered. Had I sought the situation I now hold and were this demand a common application for an increase of pay I am free to admit that it would be very reasonable to reply that having accepted office at a fixed salary I have now no right to complain of its inadequacy. This however is not the case. The appointment was unsolicited by me and so strongly did this invidious distinction above alluded to press upon my mind that when provisionally made I did not as is usual in such cases apply to the colonial minister of the day Lord John Russell,[2] for its confirmation. I felt that as a pensioner I could not well decline the office and for the reasons assigned I could not ask that which I neither desired nor approved. When tendered to me it was expressly accepted upon these terms. For their fulfilment I now confidently rely upon the honour and good faith of the government to which I alone appeal waiving all considerations of what is due to an old and faithful public officer whose judicial services extend over a period of twenty years. In conclusion, permit me to observe that I now only seek that justice which in my official capacity I am daily called upon to mete out to others in the ordinary transactions of life between contracting parties.[3]

> I have the honor to be
> Your obt. servt.
> Th. C. Haliburton

Honble. Joseph Howe
Pro. Secty.

PANS copy (signed by Haliburton)

1 Sir John Harvey, lieutenant-governor, 1846–52
2 Lord John Russell (1792–1878), statesman, colonial secretary, 1839–41
3 Only what follows is in Haliburton's hand.

---

111 To Messrs Lea and Blanchard

Windsor Nova Scotia
20th. Feby [18]49

Gentlemen –

As you have had heretofore the republication of my works in the U States, I think it due to you to address myself to you now in preference to any other persons – I have alwys reserved the right and intended to exercise it of having a colonial edition of them[1] – As they have now accumulated to several volumes I am now desirous of having them re-appear in a uniform edition – Namely 1st. 2d – 3d series of The Clockmaker which appeared in single volumes – 1st. & 2d series of The Attaché which appeared in 2 vol. each and the 'Old Judge' just published in 2 volumes – 9 volumes of the English edn. which might well be produced in 3 volumes –

The English books have been so expensive that all beyond the 1t. vol of The Clockmaker is but little known in the colonies where there is a very extended field for their circulation – The 3 Clockmakers it appears to me, may well be produced in one volume – the 4 vols. of Attache in one – & the 2 vols of Old Judge in one – and the arrangement so made that subsequent works can appear in uniformity with them so as to be had singly or together to suit the taste or the means of purchasers – Having a claim to the priority from our previous intercourse do you feel inclined to undertake their republication? If so what are you disposed to offer me for my colonial right – The work will require a preface from me and also a revision of the proofs of those volumes that were not published under my own inspection – As regards my late work 'The Old Judge' a great fraud has been practised upon me & the American public by a publishing house in New York 'Stringer & Townshend'[2] who have reprinted 7 or 8 numbers that appeared in Frasers Magazine and put them forward as the entire work, of which they scarcly form a third –

The latter work I hope to see faithfully republished – in all respects but the errors of the London press which are most numerous –

Have the goodness to let me know by return steamer whether you are disposed to this re-publication & to the supply of the colonial demand, and what you are disposed to offer for the *exclusive* colonial right (excepting English copies) and the *precedence* of the American market – If your offer meets my views I shall be glad as I would rather it emanated from you, and shall correspond with no one else on the subject – Further particulars relative to revision – preface – or prefaces – &c can be entered into hereafter –

> I am gentlemen
> Your obt
> Th. C. Haliburton

Messrs. Lea & Blanchard –
It is needful to say that an American republication, instead of a colonial one revised, will not save the duty –

Haverford College Library MS [*Ph.*]

1 A combined edition of *The Attaché* issued from the presses in Philadelphia in 1849, but no complete edition of Haliburton's works.
2 The first London edition of *The Old Judge* was published by Henry Colburn in two volumes.

---

112 To Rev. Alfred Gilpin[1]   Liverpool[2] 27th. Ap.1849

My dear sir –

Your letter of the 12th. inst. followed me to this place and I now avail myself of the first leisure moment at my disposal to answer it – I have a very great repugnance to enter into any such correspondence as your letter invites, and invariably decline being a party to communications that have a personal bearing – In this instance as you think you have some right to an explanation I will give it, but I hope you will excuse me for saying, that I cannot further pursue the subject –

In reply to your first enquiry who the person is that was confirmed by the Bishop[3] at Windsor without having been previously baptised by a clergyman of the Church of England, if my memory serves me she is a daughter of a man of the name of Holman who lives near the Chapel of Ease[4] –

The dissatisfaction felt at the manner in which the candidates for confirmation were received, without having been previously visited or assembled, examined instructed or prepared by you, I believe to have been general, and as four instances occurred in my own house,[5] I think it better to furnish you with my own name, than involve others in an unpleasant reminiscence – With respect to your second enquiry as to the names of those poor persons who feel themselves neglected in your parochial visitation the answer is obvious – The whole number of parishioners belonging to our church is very small, and altho the proportion of the poor is unhappily too large yet the total aggregate is not so great as to render the parochial visitation a matter of any great difficulty or labor – It is easy to put it out of the power of any one to complain by exercise of more zeal, and this course will be found to be infinately more beneficial than a vain attempt to justify or explain the past – as I stated at the meeting, it seemed perfectly unaccountable to the congregation, and had a most pernicious appearance in the eyes of dissenters, that you should persist in not availing yourself of the aid of any and every clergyman in your parish, who was not pre-occupied on the Sunday, and was willing to assist in the services – The disgust felt at this procedure (it is a strong word but exactly expresses my feelings) was so great as to call for that expression of feeling at the vestry meeting – While this course is perservered in, it is impossible to say that the best has been done for the parish that can be done, that you cannot be in two places at once, which different conduct would enable you to effect, by yourself and your assistant brethren or that the remote stations receive that supervision they ought – With respect to the termination of chanting which formed such an attractive and interesting part of the service, I make no remark beyond a general expression of regret – It is a subject upon which I do not feel called upon to enter – But the manner in which it was done, without notice to the ladies who had so kindly undertaken the task, without thanks for their services, and without any reason assigned is calculated to work lasting inconvenience for who will submit himself or permit his family to be treated discourteously or disrespectfully – Can it be wondered at that the church which was so rapidly filling, and recommending itself to the esteem and affection of the people, should have again become empty, more so indeed than ever from the effect of its short but bright contrast – People have seen what it might become from what it has been, and naturally ask themselves – what is the cause of all this change? You have put the question to me 'Who are discontented?' – I cannot reply for others, but so far as I can answer I say – every body but the rector –

Having now answered your letter fully & frankly, I beg to take leave of the subject altogether as I do not wish to have any further discussion or correspondence on the subject – It is foreign from my nature and my habits, and if I have spoken plainly now it is to obviate explanation hereafter, and you will have the goodness to remember, it has been done wholly at your own request –

The concluding part of your letter astonished me beyond measure wherein you express your regret 'that a want of cordiality & good feeling should subsist between us' – I am so utterly unconscious of ever feeling any thing of the kind towards you individually that I cannot conceive to what you allude, or what you mean – In our personal intercourse, now that you mention it, it has once or twice occurred to me that you were more distant than usual, but then I attributed it to your natural reserve and it passed out of my mind for ever, your avowal of it now fills me with astonishment –

It is however a matter of taste, and I have no observation to make upon it, but a regret that you should harbour such a feeling for offences never given or if given never intended –

I hope you will not take amiss my repeating that this letter must close this correspondence – I am dear sir

Yours very truly
Th. C. Haliburton

Revd. Alfred Gilpin

PANS MS

1 Rev. Alfred Gilpin (1795–1886), rector at Windsor. See PANS, Gilpin Papers, 1812–56, MG 1, vol. 329, no. 38, folder 4, a letter sent, Windsor, 4 November 1856, which gives an account of Gilpin's life.

2 The Inferior Court of Common Pleas for Queen's County met at Liverpool on the fourth Tuesday in April. Haliburton had already been away a week attending the court at Lunenburg (on the second Tuesday in April).
3 Bishop John Inglis (1777–1850), the third bishop of Nova Scotia
4 The church was 'St Matthew's Chapel of Ease' built on Gray Street in Windsor in 1845. Haliburton donated the land for the church to be built. See *Gateway to the Valley* (Windsor: Nova Scotia 1977) 26.
5 Possibly his four youngest children

113 To ——?   Windsor 19 May 1849

I certify that I have been absent from home thirty five days in attendance upon shore circuit of the Supreme Court this spring –

Th C. Haliburton

35 guineas £49 16 8

PANS MS

114 To Lady Falkland[1]   Clifton Windsor Nova Scotia
19th. Decr. 1849

My dear Lady [Falkland?] –

I have taken the liberty to send two brace of our partridges to you, enclosed in a box to a friend who will undertake to deliver them – They are equally unlike English partridge or pheasant and resemble rather the Scottish grouse – I hope they may arrive safe, and in a condition that is presentable – I heard from Lord Falkland as late as the 29th. of September – Altho he says he is well and the climate agrees with him the tone of his letter sounds dull to me which may perhaps be attributed to the fact of the colera having visited his establishment and killed two of his servants, and two of his guard, a circumstance well calculated to depress ones spirits – He is looking forward to the arrival of Lucius[2] to spend the Christmas, I hope his appearance will not disappoint him –

I am sure you will be grieved to hear that our political condition in British N. America is very critical –

The policy pursued by Lord Elgin[3] has so alienated the affections of the British portion of the population, that it is impossible to conceal from ones-self the fact that we are now in a state of chrisolis – What we shall expand into when we assume wings of our own I know not – but independence on the one hand, and absorpsion with the great republic on the other, at present are the only painful alternatives, unless the home government change their policy – It is a very distressing thing for a resident to contemplate, for these states of transition are always [feverish?] and generally dangerous – Great men become the prey of both parties – I am delighted to find by the papers that the colera has nearly disappeared from England, where its ravages appear to have been in some instances quite frightful – Strange to say last year was a season of unusual drought with us and the woods were on fire on every side, the fumigation was so great tho the colera was in Canada and the neighbouring states Nova Scotia wholly escaped, another remarkable illustration of the theory that it is wholly atmospheric.[4]

Please to give Lord [?][5] my regards and compliments, and believe me, my dear Lady [Falkland?][6] very truly & gratefully

Yours always
Th. C. Haliburton

Right Honble.
Lady Falkland –

National Library of Scotland MS [*Ph.*]

1 Amelia FitzClarence, Lady Falkland, the illegitimate daughter of William IV and Mrs Jordan the actress. Lady Falkland died in 1858, shortly after the publication of her *Journals*.
2 Lucius William (1831–71), the only son
3 James Bruce, eighth Earl of Elgin and twelfth Earl of Kincardine (1811–63), diplomatist; governor-general of Canada, 1847–54. Lord Elgin was making a 'progress' through Upper Canada and being received with great respect.
4 Cholera was caused by contaminated water.
5 MS heavily overscored
6 MS heavily overscored

115 To Rev. E. Hawkins[1]

Windsor, Nova Scotia,
14 January [18]51.

Revd. & dear sir,

When I had the pleasure of seeing you at this place, I happened accidentally to mention that there was a farm here belonging to the Society P.G.[2] but your surprise at hearing it lead me to suppose that I must have been under a mistake. The term 'Bishop's Farm,' for by such name it is known, might easily mean a farm belonging to the Bishop personally, or to the see generally. I have instituted enquiries as you will see by the enclosed note[3] and find I was right. It is the property of the society *generally*, and not limited to *particular* uses. It is worth one thousand pounds currency. Whether it was purchased with funds of the society in the hands of the then Bishop, (Charles Inglis)[4] or a donation from him does not appear, but the former supposition is more consistent with the conveyances. As the title deeds are not forthcoming, by our law the record is made evidence of them, and if you desire a copy I will send one to you. I should think however the minute of Cunningham[5] would be sufficient to file among your muniments.

I find further that the tenant always paid rent to the grantor (C Inglis), his successor Stanser, & lately to our deceased Bishop,[6] and that there is no attempt either to overhold or dispute title.

I fear there will be some difficulty in providing the salary for a Bishop. It is much to be regretted the vacancy was allowed to occur before provision had been made for such a contingency, for already the want of an efficient head to direct and influence measures is sensibly felt. Of our own clergy none have the requisite weight and influence unless it be the Arch-deacon, and he is of a school now rapidly passing away.[7]

Zeal, energy, moderation, and orthodoxy are easier extolled than found, and their union is of rare occurrence. Unless the choice be judicious we would far better under the care of the adjoining Bishops Medley & Feild.[8] I have a work in hand (which I hope to finish by April, though the research is great & the labor much more than I expected) – 'The English in America'.

> I hope you will approve of it.
> Yours very truly,
> Th. C. Haliburton

Revd. E. Hawkins.
Mr. Smith[9] desires me to remember him to you.

PAC copy

1 Rev. Ernest Hawkins (1802–1868), secretary of the Society for the Propagation of the Gospel, 1843–64. See *DNB*.
2 The Society for the Propagation of the Gospel. The society was the missionary arm of the Anglican Church.
3 The copy is a letter from 'Percy' (i.e., 'Perez') Cunningham to Haliburton, dated Windsor, 14 January 1851.
4 Rev. Charles Inglis, (1733–1816), first bishop of Nova Scotia

5 Perez Cunningham
6 Rev. Robert Stanser (1760–1829) succeeded Charles Inglis as bishop of Nova Scotia in 1816. Ill health forced him to live in England, where he eventually resigned his bishopric. He was succeeded by Rev. John Inglis.
7 Rev. Robert Willis, archdeacon (1785–1865)
8 Rev. John Medley (1804–92), first bishop of Fredericton and second metropolitan bishop of Eastern Canada; Rev. Edward Feild (1801–77), bishop of Newfoundland. Hibbert Binney, aged thirty, was appointed bishop in London in 1851.
9 Possibly one of the following: Richard Smith (1784–1870), MLA for Hants County, 1827–30; Benjamin Smith (1786–1873), MLA for Hants County, 1836–47, 1851–5; or Bennett Smith (1808–86), MLA for Hants County, 1858–9

---

116 To Richard Bentley

Windsor Nova Scotia 11th May [18]51 –

My dear sir

I have just this moment received your note[1] & have barely time to save the mail by return steamer for England – It has given me very great pleasure I assure you – I not only entertain towards you all those sentiments you have expressed, but the additional one of a very grateful remembrance of your personal kindness and hospitalities to me on many occasions in London, and I may add also your liberality in matters of business –

The misunderstanding which occurred between us never could have happened if we had seen the light of each others countenances – a few minutes talk would have set all to rights –

I am very much pleased to find that all has passed from your mind as it long since has from mine, and much regret that there ever should have been an interval of interruption –

In great haste
I am my dear sir
Yours very truly
Th. C. Haliburton

Rich. Bentley Eqr.

Harvard MS *Pub*.: ed. W.I. Morse, 77–8

1 Bentley's note is entered into his *Letterbook*, 'May 27th 1851': 'With respect to the differences which took place, now long ago between us, and which terminated our literary connection, I will not doubt that they are now considered by you as they are by me, as bygones' (BL Add. MS, 46,641 ff 137–8).

117 To Miss Guthmin[1]

Windsor Nova Scotia
26th. June 18[51]

Dear Miss Guthmin –

I have just this moment received your note 19th-June and have I hope time to answer it by return steamer –

I am delighted to hear you think of visiting this far west – I have alwys been unambitious & never sought power, now I wish I had it, for if I was supreme, I would lay an embargo on you when once here, & never take it off –

You shock me beyond measure by yr. account of poor old Stephen[2] – I have many reasons to respect and love him – he was the friend of my father in law Capt. Neville,[3] the guardian of my wife, and the confidential correspondent of myself for many years – His death is to me the breaking of the last link of a chain now no longer in existence – He was a worthy – and agreeable man – His family were 'heavy in hand' and I never took to them, but there is something mysterious about their property – To my *certain* knowledge he had a large sum invested, which was left to accumulate – This will turn up some day – Give my love to Mrs. [Dawes?][4] – I rejoice to hear she is well – She was a very – *very* handsome woman, when I last saw her – I hope time has dealt kindly with her but your climate is more merciful to yr. [?] than ours – Here they bud, bloom and wilt like summer flowers – How glad I shall be to see you once more, my dear friend, and to see you here too!!!

Kindest regards to all –
Th. C. Haliburton

Huntington Library MS [*Ph.*]

1 Unidentified
2 John Stephen (1771–1850), army agent, of Church Street, Chelsea. What Miss Guthmin might well have told Haliburton was that his old friend died very soon after the death of his wife, Harriet Stephen; so quickly, in fact, that John Stephen had no time to take out letters of administration for her. As a result, Stephen's son, Henry, took out letters of administration for both his father and mother in December 1851 (PRO PROB. 6/227).
3 John Stephen worked as an army agent for the company of Cox, Cox, and Greenwood. They were the agents for the Nineteenth Light Dragoons when Captain Neville was an adjutant, and they were agents once again for the same regiment when Captain Neville was its paymaster.
4 A Mrs Dawes is listed in the *Post Office Directory* (1851) as living at 9 Carthusian Street, City. The attribution is doubtful.

118 To Richard Bentley

Windsor Nova Scotia
10th. July [18]51

My dear sir –

I had the pleasure to receive your note of the 25th. June – In that and also in the former one you were kind enough to say that you had sent me a book –

As you have been so obliging as to take this trouble, it is but right that your intentions should be carried out and to inform you that it has not come to hand – It might be as well to inquire after it – the address ought to be 'Via Halifax Steamer,' care of 'Honble. S. Cunard Halifax' – Perhaps it got into New York steamer by mistake – The agent at Liverpool is I think McIvor[1] –

I observe with great regret that the border of your notes indicate mourning, and I fear to ask the cause – God knows I have had affliction of this kind enough and the effect it has upon [?] health – If you think a run across the water would do yo[u] good, I shall be most happy to see you at my *wigwam* at this place, and I assure you it would do me great good to see you –

                Yours very truly
                Th. C. Haliburton

Harvard MS *Pub.*: ed. W.I. Morse, 77

1 Charles MacIver. His brother, David, died in 1845.

119 To Richard Bentley

Windsor Nova Scotia
12th. May 1852

My dear sir –

I have a new work in hand entitled 'Sam Slicks Wise Saws & Modern Instances or What He Saw Did or Invented' or some such title, which will be ready by the 1t. Octr – or thereabouts[1] –

You have all my Clock-makers & all *Sams* own works, and I wish you had had all *mine*, it was a small affair that seperated them – I completed my arrangement with Colburne, who has still a *compilation* in hand not advertised, somewhat analagous to his last work[2] – I am therefore free again to act as I like, and I should like very much that you had all these original works of mine to go together and also that *we* should go together again – Would you like to have this work? – It will be in *two* volumes (not capable of stretching into 3, as Colburne very foolishly did, and which I never undertook to furnish to him) – I think I have dug into a rich vein of humor and as far as I have gone like what I have done –

I see you have become a *free trader* in literature and a *radical* among publishers & booksellers[3] – I expect to hear that Murray[4] has broke your nose with a guide book, & Colburn assaulted you on the street with a United Service Journal[5] while Parker,[6] has knocked you down with a theological folio and then revived you with the perfumes of 'Tracts for the Times' –

You had better take care of yourself, you have got a hornets nest about you, and things that cant *bite* can *sting* –

In haste
Yours alwys
Th. C. Haliburton

Harvard MS *Pub.*: ed. W.I. Morse, 78–9

1. Bentley did not publish Haliburton's new work. It was published by Hurst and Blackett.
2. Colburn and Co. published *Traits of American Humour by Native Authors*, 3 vols (1852) and followed it with a further three volumes in 1854.
3. A book had two prices, the publication price at which the public bought it and the trade price, at which the retailer procured it. The difference between these two prices caused a rift between publishers and retailers. The retailers wanted a free hand in the control of their profit margins. The publishers insisted on a lower level of profit. Bentley found himself opposed to the position of the Booksellers' Association, which had agreed not to sell below a 25 per cent profit margin. See *The Times*, 30 March 1852, 5: cols 4–5.
4. John Murray (1808–92), publisher. Murray continued his father's interest in guidebooks, producing the famous red handbooks for tourists.
5. Henry Colburn (d. 1855), publisher and founder of the *United Service Magazine and Naval and Military Gazette* (1828)
6. John William Parker (1792–1870), publisher and printer: 'A handsome volume of specimens and bibles, testaments, and books of common prayer was circulated by him in 1839' (*DNB*).

120 To Richard Bentley

Windsor, Nova Scotia
9th July [18]52

My dear sir

On my return to this place[1] I had the pleasure to receive your note asking me to state confidentially to you what I expected to receive for my new work 'Sam Slicks Wise Saws & Modern Instances &c' – It will be in two volumes, but will not be capable of bei[ng] stretched into three and I think as [far] as I have proceeded it will comp[are] very [fa]vorably with anything I have ever written – I am aware that there is not from one cause or another either the same price or circulation obtained for books as formerly, and am willing to offer you these two volumes for the same sum you used to give me for one, namely five hundred pounds,[2] and only regret that any cause seperated the publication of my books so that they are not capable [of] ever being united again – In the course [of a] few days I shall again have an [in]terval of leisure and will complete the work at once, – I shall be glad therefore to hear from you on the subject before I again leave home – I name this lesser sum to save the trouble & delay of corresponding about it –

I have been a good deal amused at the controversy going on between the publishers & retailers of books, in which you stood at the helm and held such a conspicuous part[3] – So far as the public are concerned I think it not improbable people generally will be benefitted, but I doubt whether publishers and authors will not eventually lose by it, nor am I sure that the character and quality of books will not also deteriorate – What amused me most was that only half the story, as you know, was told – Men who go to law or consult phisicians seldom tell all, I should like to have talked over the subject with you but free trade in literature in America has signally failed – How is our old friend Miss Shillebear[4] who was so shocked at being mentioned in your Miscellany? We have just completed our telegraph here which puts us in communication with Quebec – New Orleans – and St. Louis 2,000 miles up the Missisippi[5] – in a few years we shall be able to talk across the Atlantic[6] –

Yours always
Th. C. Haliburton

Harvard MS *Pub.*: ed. W.I. Morse, 79–81

1 From the summer circuit of the Supreme Court at Antigonish (fourth Tuesday in June) and Guysborough (first Tuesday in July)
2 Bentley's reply reveals the thinking behind his offer: 'I much regret, however, to say ... The state of business is so altered, especially the demand for works of light literature, that the old ratio of price has ceased to be a criterion ... I feel, however, your kindness so much that I have resolved to go to the utmost verge of prudence upon this occasion; and therefore offer you 300 for the copyright.' (BL Add. MS, 46,641, ff 233–4)
3 Bentley's reply alluded to his part in the controversy: 'If the absurd allowances to the carriers of the trade were diminished, there might be a reduction to that extent with great advantage to author and publisher. Never fear that new Books will be too cheap.' (BL Add. MS 46,641, ff 233–4)
4 See letter 242, below.
5 Amherst and Halifax were linked by telegraph in 1849.
6 A transatlantic cable was laid in 1858 but failed after a few weeks. In 1866, the link between Newfoundland and Ireland was established.

121 To Richard Bentley

Windsor Nova Scotia
15th. Sepr 1852

My dear sir –

I received your note[1] from some unpronounceable pl[ace] in Wales, in which you offer [me] three hundred pounds, as the m[ost] liberal proposition you can [make] for 'Sam Slicks Wise Saws & M[odern] Instances' – I feel satisfied you [do] not understand the nature [of the] work, or that I have very un[favora]bly expressed it, for I keep no co[pies of my] letters – It differs essentially [from The] Clockmakers in not depen[ding for its] success on quaintness in American [idi]oms, as any thing *now* new (altho [writ]ten in a colloquial style & in their a[c]cent) – [Its ch]ance for popularity being based upon [clear?] – delineation of character, knowledge [of men?] & things & a vein of proverbial [philoso]phy to sustain its name of 'Wise [Saws'] –

The work will be ready to leave [the co]untry (for it is all drafted) [by] the 1t. Dcr. next & will make [mon]ey –

I find this new vein both [?] & rich, and well calculated [for?] popularity, so much so that [to work?] out the idea would require a second series some 18 months afterwards – Now reconsider your opinions on this subject, & let me know what you can offer for it –

1t. as it stands in two volumes
2y for 1t. or 2d series seperately or collectively –

You have all *Sams own* works I should like you to have these which will terminate them – Write me by early steamer –

I did not know poor Colburn altho I have seen him, but am sorry to learn from your note that he is dead² – You do not say so in express terms but I infer it from your letter, for you say he has '*departed*' and been *Hurst*³ – Placing a man in a *hearse* is the last act of kindness, & I suppose, knowing your *mutual* affection, you was his chief *mourner* – Where was he buried? Not in *Long acre*⁴ certainly for a small corner of that would do for such a *little* man – That cemetery is for *Long man*⁵ the publisher & *Long fellow* the poet⁶ – *Long* may it be before you and I go there – It seems to me but the other day that poor 'Inglesby'⁷ 'Hook'⁸ and myself had our knees under yr mahogany – I believe I have their *knees*, mine dont seem as if they belonged to me – I wish I had their *heads* – I dont know Welsh, which you appear to have been studying & therefore must say in plain English – Good night –

Yours truly
Th. C. Haliburton

Harvard MS *Pub.*: ed. W.I. Morse, 81–2

1 Dated 24 July 1852. The opening informs Haliburton that Bentley had been 'on a tour in Wales, in pursuit of health' (BL Add. MS 46,641, ff 233–4).
2 Colburn had retired from his business. He did not die until 1855.
3 Colburn's company was then taken over by 'Hurst and Blackett.'
4 A part of London, from Drury Lane to St Martin's Lane, famous for its coachmakers. It was a spacious street.
5 William Longman (1813–77) and his brother, Thomas (1804–79), were partners in publishing.
6 Henry Wadsworth Longfellow (1807–82), celebrated American poet
7 R.H. Barham, author of the *Ingoldsby Legends* (1840)
8 Theodore Hook, comic writer and essayist (d. 1843)

---

122 To William Jerdan¹

London 6 Spring Gardens
11th. June 1853

My dear sir –

The welcome sight of your handwriting after a lapse of so many years, has awakened many an agreeable recollection of past days – I thank you for your kind note and for your still kinder notice of my work,² which awaited me on my return from the country –

I assure you it will afford me very great gratification to have the opportunity to renew my acquaintance with one whom I esteem so highly and have received so much kindness from as yourself, and if you will do me the favor to tell me where I can have the pleasure of calling upon you in London, I shall lose no time in doing myself that pleasure – I leave town on Wednesday for the country again & return on Saturday for a few days – previous to a more extended tour – During that interval I trust we can arrange to meet & shake each other by the hands once more – Very truly

          Yours always
          Th. C. Haliburton

Wm. Jerdan Esqr

Yale MS [*Ph.*]

 1 (1782–1869), journalist and editor of the *Literary Gazette*
 2 Jerdan wrote a flattering review of *Sam Slick's Wise Saws* in *Literary Gazette*, 11 June 1853: 573–4.

---

123 To Richard Bentley

6 Spng Gardens [London]
23 June 1853

Will you be so good as to send me by bearer a copy of 1t. series of Clockmaker, if you have one –

          Yours trly
          Th C Haliburton

University of Illinois MS [*Ph.*]

---

124 The Duke of Newcastle[1]

London,
6 Spring Gardens,
28 June 1853.

My Lord Duke,

By an old regulation emanating from the Colonial Office it was directed that half the salary of any provincial officer should be withheld during his absence from the colony. It was doubtless designed as well to check the too frequent application for leave of absence as to provide funds to pay a deputy. This rule is inapplicable to a judge, for neither he nor the crown can appoint a deputy, and if his brethren on the bench cannot perform the additional labor he cannot obtain his leave; still less is it applicable to a judge in Nova Scotia who receives his salary under a public *law* containing *no such condition* and which can neither be abridged or enlarged by any power short of the legislature.

In my case even if it were applicable it ought not to be enforced for I have been *25 Years* on the bench laboriously employed and ought not to be compelled to pay a fine amounting to half my salary for the enjoyment of a short vacation, especially as no duty is neglected; no pension is provided for me and my salary altogether inadequate.

When last in this country Lord Stanley (Derby) took this view of the case and exempted me from the application of the rule when he found that the other judges, as now, had performed my duty and that the public service had not been injured.[2]

I must now beg for the same indulgence (if it be not considered my right) and I trust that the great length of my services and the extreme hardship, not to say injustice of the case will not be overlooked.

> I have the honor to be
> Your Graces' most obedient
> Servant
> Th. C. Haliburton

To His Grace
The Duke of Newcastle,
Colonial Office.

PRO (Kew Gardens, London) copy; signed by Haliburton

1 Clinton, Henry Pelham Fiennes Pelham, fifth Duke of Newcastle (1811–64), colonial secretary, 28 December 1852 to 12 June 1854
2 After due consideration, the duke's secretary (Mr Merivale) declined Haliburton's request, on the grounds that precedent was against it.

---

125 To Barwick Baker[1]

Rectory/Loughboro[2]
1[s]t. July 1853

My dear sir –

I have to thank you for your very kind invitation to Hardwicke Court, for Monday the 11 & subsequent days to attend the Royal Agricultural Society's meeting at Gloucester – It will give me very great pleasure to be present on that occasion, & I have to express to you my most grateful acknowledgement for so kindly affording me the opportunity –

> I am dear sir very [truly?]
> Yours
> Th. C. Haliburton

Barwick Baker Esqr –

UCLA MS [*Ph.*]

1 Thomas Barwick Lloyd Baker (1807–86), philanthropist and prison reformer, who resided at Hardwicke Court, near Gloucester. See Professor Von Holtzendorff, *An English Country Squire as Sketched at Hardwicke Court Gloucestershire*, trans. Rosa Gebhard (Gloucester 1878) 3.
2 In 1853, Loughborough had two churches. Haliburton was most likely staying at the Old Rectory House. According to W.G. Dimock Fletcher, *Historical Handbook to Loughborough* (London 1881) 41, the rector was Henry Fearon, BD.

---

126 To Lady Sitwell[1]

Loughboro
3d. July 1853

My dear Lady Sitwell

I regret very much that our arrangements for travelling are so complicated with those, of some friends whom we are to meet at York that I cannot avail myself of your kind invitation for today – We have received our route as military men say, and leave this at two aclock –

> I am dear Lady Sitwell
> Yours always
> Th C Haliburton

Brotherton MS [*Ph.*]

1 Identification is uncertain. Of the Lady Sitwells listed in *Burke's Peerage*, Lady Sitwell of Barmoor Castle, Northumberland, or Lady Sitwell of Ferney Hall, Craven Arms, Shropshire, are the most likely candidates. We cannot rule out the possibility that this might be Lady Sitwell of Renishaw Hall, Derbyshire, the grandmother of Edith Sitwell.

127 To the Duke of Newcastle

London,
6 Spring Gardens,
31 August 1853.

My Lord Duke,

On the 28th June last I had the honor to address a letter[1] to your Grace, requesting under circumstances therein stated, to be exempted from the operation of a rule emanating from the colonial office, that deprives officers in the civil service in the plantations of half their salary while on leave of absence. Taking it for granted that as there was nothing in my case, to vary it from a similar application made by myself to your Graces' predecessor in 1843 which was acceded to,[2] I confined myself to merely restating the reasons which were then thought sufficient. It was therefore with no little surprise, that I found they were supposed so far to differ from those now existing as to lead to a different conclusion from what was then arrived at.

I have now, while thanking your Grace for an opportunity of being reheard, to add some additional reasons not then supposed to be necessary, which in my opinion render the present application infinitely stronger and one which cannot without great hardship and injustice be refused.

Before however, I state these additional grounds which distinguish my case from all others, I must first state that the legal objection taken by me in 1843 still remains unremoved.

If the order (the date of which I have no means of ascertaining) preceded the law of 1840 by which my salary was fixed, and upon the faith of which I accepted office, then the royal assent to the act, which contains no such proviso as to half pay virtually supercedes & repealed it. If it was subsequent to that date then it was invalid, as no colonial memento can add to or vary the laws as established by the legislature. In this the crown officers of England will, if it requires confirmation, at once concur.

It is said, however, in Lord Stanley's despatch, who admits this to be sound law, that the governor may refuse leave unless this condition be complied with. It is true that a governor may by an exercise of arbitrary power, add to the expense & inconvenience of a judge who requires the benefit of change of scene and climate by compelling him to relinquish half his salary as the price of the restoration of his bodily strength; and if this power exists it can also be extended to a case like mine, in which I have prevailed upon a brother judge to assume my labors in my absence, and where the public service has not been neglected. That such an ungracious power exists, and that a poor judicial officer may be prevented by the withdrawal of his means from recruiting his health cannot be denied, but that it should be claimed and exercised could never have entered into the contemplation of those who framed the rule. The regulation was doubtless made to meet those cases which formerly too often occurred of the repeated and long continued absence of public officers from a colony who left no sufficient deputy to discharge their duties. Admitting however the existence of this extraordinary power, and that though it would not be tolerated by the English bench, colonial judges cannot avoid its operation, it does not apply to my case. No such condition was imposed and had it been, nothing would ever have tempted me to submit to the degradation of first incurring the obligation of asking an aged and over worked judge to undertake my duties in my absence, & then to memorialize the Colonial Office to grant as a favor what I conceive to be my right. My leave of absence was accompanied by a letter containing two conditions, first that I should through some other judge provide for the spring circuit which I have done, and secondly that I should return in time to undertake the autumn one[3] myself which I am now about to do by relinquishing one entire fortnight of the term granted to me.

No such stipulation as that of losing half my salary in addition to these conditions was ever named to me, had it been, the other two would have been unnecessary, on the contrary, when I mentioned this absolute rule myself & stated not only its inapplicability to judges (who can appoint no deputies) but the exemption that had been made both in my case and that of Judge Bliss,[4] I was told there could be no doubt I should be again relieved & all that would be necessary would be to mention it to your Grace.

Without such an impression on my mind I would have sooner submitted to the operations of climate and labor which are inevitable, than have incurred a great obligation on the one hand and a pecuniary injury on the other which are less tolerable because the necessity for them is unnecessary and unjustly imposed.

I turn, however, with some satisfaction to that portion of your Graces' letter in which you mention that the practice has at times been departed from on some ground peculiar to the case. Here I think I can state with some complacency (and without arrogating much to myself) that if ever there was an exceptional case mine is that one.

1st, I have been about twenty five years on the bench; a period which in England enables a judge to retire on a pension, and in a colony at least entitles him to an occasional leave of absence. Few men can count so many years service, and few can ever be found to exceed that term.

2ndly, upon the abolition of the Court of Common Pleas in 1840 (of which I was a judge) I was by law entitled to a pension of £300. per annum. When Lord Falkland offered me a seat on the Supreme Court bench I hesitated about accepting it, but thinking it was wrong to be a burden even to that little extent on the colony, I consented to serve & have therefore actually paid nearly four thousand pounds towards my own salary. I think I may say that this distinguishes my case from all others, for in reality I only receive little more than half my salary, and the whole of that half is now sought to be withheld. It appears to me that it is merely necessary to mention this circumstance at once to enlist your Graces' sense of justice on my side.

3rdly, I will say nothing about my literary labors constituting any claim. It may be replied that they were voluntary and although they may have benefitted my country and made it and its resources better known, still they are purely colonial and not entitled like those of English or Scotch authors to any consideration, or it may perhaps be said that they are not instrinsically deserving of it. It does not become me at all events to speak of them in general, but there is one of my works for which I do claim to be considered in this matter and that is a laborious, authentic, and copious history of the colony, that cost me much time & great expense, and for which all the remuneration I have received is a legislative vote of thanks.[5]

The private business which brought me to this country was mainly the benefit to be derived to my health from change of climate and relaxation, but another minor cause was to endeavour to arrange for a new edition of this expensive (and from its nature not very popular) work which is most important to the home as well as the colonial government.

Having thus stated the grounds of my legal as well as equitable claim upon the government I must trust to your Grace's sense of right to do me justice.

> I have the honor to be
> Your Graces' obedient servant
> Th. C. Haliburton

To/His Grace
The Duke of Newcastle.

PRO (Kew Gardens, London) copy; signed by Haliburton

1 The letter dated 28 June 1853, above
2 The letter dated 21 August 1843, above

3 It started at the end of October.
4 William Blowers Bliss (1795–1874), judge of the Supreme Court of Nova Scotia, 1834–69
5 Published in many of the early editions of the *Historical ... Account*, the vote of thanks was passed in April 1829.

128 To S. Holme[1]

London 6 Spring Gardens
31t. Aug 1853

My dear sir –

Your kind note inviting me to The Judges[2] at Liverpool on the 12th. instant did not reach me until after that day – Had it been possible to have been there, it would I assure you have given me great pleasure to have met you once more at hospitable & convivial table – I regret to say that I embark at Liverpool on Saturday the 3d September at 12 aclock for Halifax – At 10 I shall have the pleasure of calling at your office to bid you adieu & to thank you personally for all your kindness

I am dear sir
Very truly yours
Th. C. Haliburton

S. Holmes Eqr.
&c &c

Huntington Library MS [*Ph.*]

1 Samuel Holme was a partner in the firm of Samuel and James Holme, architects and builders (*Robson's Liverpool Directory* [1840] 167). He also served as mayor of Liverpool.
2 The invitation was to stay at the 'Judges lodgings' or 'Judges Residence,' 62 St Anne Street, Liverpool, used by circuit judges from 1835 until 1868.

129 To Joseph Howe

Halifax, 29 October 1853.

Sir,

I have the honor to request that you will be pleased to lay before his excellency the Lieutenant Governor[1] the following statement of facts and the application based thereon. On the 30th September last, the quarter salary was due to me as a judge of the Supreme Court amounting to £175. My draft for that amount was refused payment by the Accountant General on the ground as I am informed that the 2nd sec. of the instruction regulating leave of absence applied to my case, having been out of the province during a portion of that quarter. This rule is as follows, 'An officer to whom leave of absence has been granted will be entitled to half salary, the remaining half being applied to remunerate the person selected for the performance of his duties &c, &c.' This rule was made in order to secure the selection of a suitable substitute, and was designed for the control of those officers paid by England, as will appear more plainly by reference to sec. 4, where the leave of the clergy (who were then paid by the home government) is regulated, and who on that ground only were under the necessity of asking leave of absence. It is wholly inapplicable to judges for neither they nor the governor can appoint a deputy. In this view of the case, it was not attempted to be enforced on me in 1842, nor subsequently on Judge Bliss, in both cases, our brethren on the bench having undertaken our duties for us. I do not, however, rest my claim on this reading of the rule, but on the plain and intelligible law of the land. In 1840 an act was passed authorising the appointment of an additional judge of the Supreme Court, with a clear net salary of £700. per annum, payable quarterly; that law contained no such provision or condition as that mentioned in the rule referred but is absolute and unqualified. I was selected for that situation and thus became entitled to the full sum therein established without deduction of any part or the interference of any person whatever. The Receiver General of Canada fell recently into the same error that has been committed here and attempted to apply this old rule to the case of Mr Justice Hagerman,[2] who had been absent in England, but he insisted on his right and called the attention of the local executive to the state of the law as I have done and they immediately ordered payment to be made in full to him.

But my case is infinitely stronger than his, for we have another law on our Statute Book, that did not then exist in Canada. It is the 11th Vic., Cap. 21., and is entitled, 'An Act to render the Judges of the Supreme Court, independent of the Crown' by assenting to which the Crown has forever surrendered all power to interfere with, control, or influence these officers in any way whatever.

As a matter of course therefore, no preexisting rule of a Secretary for the Colonies, nor any subsequent one, not adopted or incorporated into our law, can in any way affect the judges. Although it appears to me that it is so plain that the mere statement of the case is sufficient, it may perhaps be satisfactory to his Excellency to know, that as a preliminary step, I submitted the case to two senior and eminent counsel Hon.

James Johnston and James Stewart Esquire,[3] who fully and entirely concur in this view of the law. As the refusal of the Accountant General has already put me to expence and occasioned me the trouble and inconvenience of a journey to Halifax, I must beg the favor of an early reply, in order that I may proceed to my home.

> I have &c
> T.C. Haliburton

PRO (Kew Gardens, London) copy

1 Sir John Gaspard Le Marchant (1803–74), lieutenant-governor of Nova Scotia, 1852–8
2 Christopher Alexander Hagerman (1792–1847), appointed a judge in Upper Canada in 1840
3 James Stewart (1803–61), barrister

130 To Joseph Howe   Halifax, November 17th, 1853.

Sir,

I have the honor to acknowledge the receipt of your letter of the fifteenth instant, in which you state 'That the law officers of the Crown do not concur in the opinion entertained by yourself and said to have been approved by the counsel whom you have consulted, that the act, that fixes your salary, provides that it shall be drawn by warrant of the Governor, not that the judge should draw his salary himself independently of the Governor and in violation of the instructions from the Secretary of State.'

In reply to this I must observe that my letter, as you will perceive by reperusing it, contains no such claim on my part, and no such denial of the governor's authority, or duty to give the warrant. Its purport appears to have been wholly misunderstood. I merely referred to the act that created the office I accepted, and which established the amount of my salary; enacted that it should be paid quarterly and contain no condition or qualification; and then I requested that its terms should be complied with.

A further misapprehension appears to exist as to the funds from which I am to be paid.

You say that 'while the judges were paid out of the funds controlled by the imperial government, the moiety of salary forfeited by an absent judge could only be issued on the order of the Colonial Secretary. Now that the control of the fund has been transferred to the provincial government, a vote of the legislature must precede the drawing of a warrant by the Lieutenant Governor.'

I must therefore again call your attention to the fact, that I never was paid out of monies under the control of the Secretary of State, but from the treasury of the province, in the usual manner under and by virtue of an act of the General Assembly, and that that law, being a permanent one, does not require a vote of the legislature to authorise a warrant for each or any payment, as the act itself contains the authority itself.

Nor have I been less misunderstood in the portion of your letter which refers to the independence of the judges – I have made no claim, as my letter will shew, inconsistent with the act, which was specially passed to place those officers in a situation, to ensure, as in England, the impartial and unbiased exercise of their functions. Above all I have advanced no claims to be relieved from the full and faithful discharge of my duties or the responsibility they impose upon me. The judges of this country ever have been and always will be found not only ready and willing, but most anxious to fulfil to the best of their ability, every obligation that the nature of their high office imposes upon them; and permit me to observe that I cannot understand why the punctual payment of their salaries should be supposed to lead, in their case, to those consequences to which you have alluded, that would so ill become their character and station.

My claim to my salary is founded on the plain, intelligible words of the law, under which I accepted office, and the sole question is, has any officer of the local government the right to withhold it, in contravention of that law? Upon a reconsideration of this subject, with reference merely to its legality, and not expediency or favor, I feel assured that his Excellency will perceive that I am entitled to be paid as I have requested and will issue orders accordingly.

My letter on this matter contained nothing more than a remonstrance against the refusal of those officers, whose duty it is, in obedience to the act, to pay my salary, and also a succinct statement of the law upon which my right is founded.

It was not, therefore, without surprise as well as pain, that I perused your reply, the tone and tenor of which were not called for by anything contained in my communication; and upon reflection, I am sure you will perceive that it is not such an answer as ought to have been sent to one of the judges of the land. You will observe that I have based my claims on the law and not asked it as a favor to myself. I cannot however but feel that there are circumstances connected with my case, that at least entitled me to a courteous and considerate answer. I have been on the bench twenty five years, a period which covers the whole prime of my life. Thirteen years ago I was awarded a pension for past services of three hundred pounds a year which has been merged in my pay; so that I have contributed nearly four thousand pounds towards my own salary. When I was last in England, Lord Stanley (now Lord Derby) exempted me from the operation of this obsolete rule; which he had too much sagacity not to observe was illegal, and at a subsequent period the local Government entertained a similar opinion as to Mr Justice Bliss's case. What decision has been made regarding those officers of the government who have been recently absent I do not know, nor is it necessary to enquire, for they are in different positions from the judges and are not by laws made independent of the Crown, and the example of their losses affords no precedent for me. In my case the public service has not been neglected. My duty has been performed, in my absence, as a personal favor to myself by a brother judge; and I may add the only one on the bench whose strength could enable him to undergo such great additional bodily and mental labor.

With these peculiar claims for consideration, why I should be singled out as one exception, still less why I should be addressed as I have been I am at a loss to understand. Although I cannot but feel this, I do not complain of it, it is merely one incident in my case. I do not ask my salary as a favor, I demand it as a right,[1] and I feel that these explanations cannot fail of satisfying those officers of the government, whose conscientious scruples may have caused them to doubt in a matter of law with which they are not familiar.

I have therefore to request that you will be pleased to lay this letter before the Lieutenant Governor, who, I am convinced, will, without hesitation, issue the necessary orders to the Receiver General, to fulfill the requirements of the law.

In conclusion, I must add that although neither myself nor the eminent lawyers I have consulted entertain any doubt, whatever, as to the soundness of the views I have taken of the law on this subject, yet as it would ill become me to persist, as I am doing, in asserting my claim, if any reasoning can be advanced at all to vary the conclusion I have arrived at, I have to request that the Lieutenant Governor will favor me, as is usual in such cases, with a copy of the opinion of the crown officers, more especially as it happens to have been expressed in such decided terms as to have been the basis of his decision.

As I have already been delayed two months and a half, I must beg the favor of his Excellency to do me the honor of giving me an early reply.

       I have the honor to be
       &c, &c, &c,
       T.C. Haliburton

To the Honble.
Provl. Secretary.

PRO (Kew Gardens, London) copy

1 Haliburton's letter offended Le Marchant, the lieutenant-governor, and Le Marchant's reply, written by Howe as provincial secretary, took exception to Haliburton's use of the word 'right.'

131 To Joseph Howe   [Windsor, November? 1853]

My dear Howe –

If any thing I could say, could have a tendency to alleviate the pain, inflicted by the loss you have recently sustained,[1] most happy would I be to do so – But I know that time & reason can alone be serviceable – All I shall say therefore is, that I beg you to be assured that I deeply, sincerely (and from sad experience)[2] *feelingly* sympathise with you –

       Yours always
       T C Haliburton

Dalhousie MS *Pub.*: *Catalogue of the William Inglis Morse Collection ... at Dalhousie University Library* (London: Curwen Press 1938) 90

1 Howe's daughter, Mary, died, aged twenty-one, on 1 November 1853 (see the *Morning Chronicle*, 3 November 1853).
2 He alludes to the loss of three infant children and the deaths of his wife, Louisa, in 1841 and his son Tom in 1847.

132 To Joseph Howe   Halifax, December 6, 1853.

My dear sir,

Twelve or thirteen years ago when the Courts of Common Pleas were abolished,[1] I was awarded by law a pension of £300 per annum for past services as a judge. Immediately afterwards, Lord Falkland tendered me a seat on the bench of the Supreme Court. At first I hesitated to accept it as my time was of more value to me than the salary, but I felt that at the age I then was I ought not to be a burden on the treasury of the province even to that small amount while I could work without personal inconvenience.

In accepting this seat, my pension merged in my salary so that I have effected a saving to the province of nearly four thousand pounds.

The time has now arrived when I think myself entitled to resume my pension and resign my office. I shall feel obliged therefore if you will do me the favor to communicate my wishes on the subject to his Excellency the Lieutenant Governor and to state to him that as soon as that pension is again sanctioned by a permanent and unconditional act of the legislature I shall be prepared to send him my resignation, as I cannot afford to retire without my former pension, so of course the enactment will have to precede the resignation.[2]

> I am my dear sir
> Yours very truly
> T.C. Haliburton

The Honourable
Joseph Howe.

PANS copy *Pub.*: *Journals ... of the House of Assembly* (1854) Appendix 24, 206; Chittick, 565–6

[1] By an act of the Legislature, passed on 29 March 1841. See *Journals ... of the House of Assembly* (1841) 193.
[2] The copy of this letter is part of a file at PANS concerning Haliburton's pension dispute with the Nova Scotia government.

133 To Richard Bentley

Windsor Nova Scotia
21t. Decr. [18]53

My dear Bentley –

I am very desirous, if it be practicable that there should be a uniform edition of my works, but as part of them are in your hands & part in Hursts I hardly know how it is to be done by either of you –

As you have in one form or another pretty well exhausted the demand for those in your possession, it has occurred to me you might feel disposed to reconvey to me the copyright – If so what sum would you demand for them collectively, or for each severally? Will you be kind enough to consider the subject & let me know what you think of it –

Yours truly
Tho. C. Haliburton

Richd Bentley Esqr
Harvard MS *Pub.*: ed. W.I. Morse, 83

134 To Joseph Howe

Windsor Nova Scotia
[1855?]

My dear Howe

I have had my attention called to your speech on the union of the colonies lately[1] in consequence of the subject turning up incidentally in the new work which goes to England by next steamer[2] – The speech I consider the best ever delivered in any of these colonies, and the illustrations very happy & well grouped and arranged – I shall refer to it in a note to my new book in these terms[3] – My object now is to ask you if I quote your figures if I can depend upon them? – are they correctly reported? I have only Croskills[4] paper containing the speech – I have no time to verify them, am I safe in taking them as I find them,[5] or is some of the 'totals' as Hume calls them bunkum[6] – ? Drop me a line please & if there is a second pamphlet send me one –

Yours
Th C Haliburton

Dalhousie MS *Pub.*: *Catalogue of the William Inglis Morse Collection ... at Dalhousie University Library* (London: Curwen Press 1938) 90; in part by Chittick, 410

1 Howe's speech on the 'Union of the North American Colonies' was delivered in the Nova Scotia Legislature on 11 March 1854 and later published.
2 *Nature and Human Nature*, 2 vols
3 See *Nature and Human Nature*, vol. 2; 214, n., where Howe's speech is described as 'incomparably superior to any one delivered during the last session of the Imperial Parliament.'
4 John H. Crosskill (d. 1857), Halifax publisher
5 The printed *Speech of the Hon. Joseph Howe on the Union of the North American Provinces, etc.* (London: James Ridgway 1855) contains several mistakes in addition: Imports for the year 1853 (20); 'Revenues' (22), and 'Lists of Inhabitants' (44).
6 An allusion to Joseph Hume (1777–1855), nabob and radical politician, whose eloquence was famous

---

135 To Joseph Howe (Provincial Secretary)   Antigonish 12th. July 1855

Sir

I have the honor to acknowledge the receipt of your letter enclosing a petition of Duguld McNab praying for a remission of the sentence passed upon his son by me at the last sittings of the Sup. Court at Baddeck[1] –

The petitioner is a highly respectable man, and has ever borne a reputation for integrity, – It is natural that he cannot bring himself to believe in the guilt of his son, and should attribute his conviction to a conspiracy among those who testified against him, but he is evidently under a delusion on this subject[2] –

The witnesses thrice in number (one of whom was the sherriff of the county) are people of undoubted veracity, and most unwillingly appeared against the unfortunate man – The petitioner mentioned his suspicions to me after the trial, and I enquired of the magistrates and others friends of the family, but they all concurred in the opinion, that there was no ground for supposing that the charge was preferred from ill feeling –

I sympathise most deeply with the family in their affliction, and would have rejoiced if he could have cleared himself from the accusation, but the impartial administration of justice forbids us making or knowing any distinction of persons –

         I have the honor to be
         Your obt
         Th. C. Haliburton

To the Hon.
The Pro Secty –
&c &c

PANS MS

1 Held on the fourth Tuesday in June at Antigonish
2 'Remarks' on Haliburton's letter, written by Dugald McNab the elder, survive at PANS, RG 5, 'GP' Misc 'A' 1855–9, vol. 3, no. 21.

136 To the House of Assembly of Nova Scotia

Clifton Windsor 12th. Feby [18]56

The memorial[1] of the undersigned humbly sheweth –

That in the year 1828–9 – your memorialist was appointed First Justice of the Courts of Common Pleas and President of the several Courts of Sessions in the middle division of Nova Scotia comprising the counties of Liverpool Lunenburg Hants & Kings – That in the year 1841 these courts were abolished and a pension of three hundred pounds a year was assigned to him, and others holding similar offices – That the act that thus reconstructed the judicial establishments of this country provided at the same time for the appointment of an additional judge of the Supreme Court at a salary of seven hundred pounds per annum –

That his excellency Lord Falkland who was at that time Lt. Governor of Nova Scotia tendered the office to your memorialist as will appear by his letter dated the 29th. March 1841 hereunto annexed – That it was not without much hesitation he accepted it, his desire being to retire into private life and devote himself to literary pursuits, but he felt he was then too young to be a burden on the civil list of the province, and that at all events he would for a few years assume the office and responsibilities, and perform its duties knowing full well that this course would be duly appreciated by the legislature, who would in consideration of the saving this effected to the province, at any time restore to him his pension, and permit him to retire from the service and leave him as it found him –

Your memorialist now begs leave to call your attention to the following facts – 1st. That the office sought him & not he the office, as appears by the original letter of Lord Falkland hereto annexed – 2y – That owing to the present infirm state of his health (which altho for the present sufficient to enable him to perform his duties, taxes all his mental & bodily powers to their utmost and render them daily more irksome & onerous) he is desirous of withdrawing from the bench, provided the legislature shall see fit to revive his pension to which he was entitled on accepting office – 3dly He asks no pension or allowance as judge of the Supreme Court, and altho he has affected a saving to the province of a very large sum of money by merging his pension in his salary he merely asks the legislature to replace him where [they?] found him, and permit him to withdraw on the retiring allowance to which he was entitled – 4y Your memorialist considers that his case is an exceptional one – and can now be drawn into a precedent for pensions in as much as he seeks no retired allowance and merely asks leave to return to the station, from which the govt. of the day, solicited him as a matter of economy in their arrangements to assume his present position – 5y Your memorialist while distinguishing his case from that of any other provincial judge might perhaps advance claims of a peculiar nature as the historian of Nova Scotia, and an author who has advocated its claims & made it better known than it was before, but he prefers to found his application on the just and reasonable grounds above stated, and he feels there is too much honor & liberality in the Assembly of his native country, to compel him to labor till he falls in that harness in which he has so long & faithfully toiled –

> All which is respectfully submitted
> Th. C. Haliburton

PANS MS

1 The memorial was presented in the legislature on Haliburton's behalf by John Joseph Marshall (1807–70), MLA for Guysborough County. He was John George Marshall's nephew.

---

137 To Sir John Gaspard Le Marchant

Windsor, 11th August 1856.

Sir,

Having made up my mind to retire from the public service, I beg leave to tender to you the resignation of the situation I now hold as judge of the Supreme Court.

Hereafter I shall have the honor to address to your Excellency another letter on the subject of the pension to which I was entitled when I accepted the commission I now hold.

> I have
> etc., etc.,
> Signed, T C Haliburton.

PANS copy *Pub.: Journals ... of the House of Assembly* (1863), Appendix 24, 9

5
A New Life, 1856–1859

Following his visit to England in 1853, Haliburton sought to release himself from his judicial duties and to claim whatever pension he could secure from the Nova Scotia government. The government was unwilling to recognize his claim, and no pension materialized. He therefore tendered his resignation to the lieutenant-governor in August 1856, moved to England, and promptly married Sarah Harriet Hosier Williams, a widow, who lived in Shropshire. She was the daughter of William Mostyn Owen, of Woodhouse, and had been the childhood friend of Charles Darwin and his sisters.[1] Her marriage to Haliburton brought her out of a quiet rural life and into the drawing rooms of London. The newly married couple chose Gordon House, Isleworth, Middlesex, for their home. Sarah Harriet was well suited to her new surroundings and the new life she was about to lead. She collected china, liked books and prints, and had good connections in London society. She supported Haliburton when he became an MP and, although she was not vastly rich, she did bring an element of comfort to his declining years. When Haliburton suffered from gout she solicitously nursed him and kept up his correspondence.

Haliburton did not finish wrangling with the Nova Scotia government over his pension until 1862; his pension case was tried twice, and both times he received a judgment in his favour. The story of the pension dispute has been told by Chittick in detail.[2] The evidence of the letters suggests that Haliburton tried hard to secure a favourable result by enlisting the support (surprisingly, considering their former estrangement) of Joseph Howe.

Time is a great healer. Perhaps no better illustration of this can be found than in the fluctuating accord between Haliburton and Joseph Howe. Their friendship developed from the turbulent days of Haliburton's legislative career (1826–9), when Howe watched and listened to the new member from

Gordon House, Isleworth, 1869

Haliburton and his wife, Sarah Harriet, at Gordon House

the Press Gallery. When Howe published Haliburton's *Historical ... Account* (1829) the relationship was established. Haliburton's withdrawal from active politics and Howe's emergence into the political sphere in the eighteen-thirties marked the beginning of a rift between the two men: 'you wont advance your own interest by going there [i.e., the Legislature],' argued Haliburton in 1835. The immediate and wide success of *The Clockmaker* published by Howe in the columns of his newspaper, the *Novascotian*, and then in book form, led to a further strain in their relationship. Letters entered by Howe into his *Letterbook* in 1841 chart the angry end to their relationship.[3] Howe took exception to passages in Haliburton's Third Series of *The Clockmaker*. He unleashed a torrent of frustration at Haliburton, who he felt was unaware of the sacrifices he had made thus far as Haliburton's publisher. Howe felt, moreover, that he was being cast aside for Richard Bentley.

The silence in their relationship was interrupted, in the eighteen-forties, only by business dealings. Howe was provincial secretary and obliged to answer Haliburton's complaints about receiving half-salary while absent in England. One senses from Haliburton's side of the correspondence that Howe's tone was still testy. See letters 129 and 130 above. Curiously, in the same month that Haliburton sent several official letters of complaint to Howe, he also wrote a personal message of sympathy (letter 131) at the death, on 1 November 1853, of Howe's twenty-one-year-old daughter, Mary. From this point onwards and until Haliburton's death, we see a continued improvement in their relationship. After visiting Nova Scotia in 1860, Haliburton went immediately on an errand of mercy to seek Howe's son who had been wounded in the Crimea and was recovering on the HMS Victory in Portsmouth. In return for such favours Haliburton hoped that Howe would assist him in securing 'a paltry pension' from his native province.

One of the reasons he pressed so hard for his pension was the need to offset the incidental expenses of a parliamentary seat. Securing a seat was the inevitable result of a concerted effort to launch himself as a public figure on colonial matters. Haliburton addressed the Manchester Athenaeum in December 1856 and an audience in Glasgow in March 1857, on the subject of the colonies. As a speaker he was much in demand. In response to an invitation that he could not take up he published the lecture he gave at Glasgow and declined any further offers to speak throughout England and Scotland. Though Haliburton's speeches during his later years have never been collected, they are an interesting guide to his thinking during this period.[4]

His high profile as a public speaker on North American subjects led (as he wished) to his entry into Parliament. The offer in April 1859 of a seat as MP for the rotten borough of Launceston in North Cornwall came suddenly, and I have related the full story elsewhere.[5] Suffice it to say here that Haliburton's entry into Parliament was the result of a concerted effort to focus public interest in England on North American subjects and to capitalize on the attention he commanded as the creation of the best-known Yankee character of the day, 'Sam Slick.' Haliburton's physical presence in London society, as a solid middle-class citizen, surprised and genuinely pleased his English audiences.

Now that he was once more in England, Haliburton's old friendship with Richard Bentley prospered. During the years from 1857 to 1859, Haliburton became one of Bentley's literary advisers, dined with him frequently, often invited him to Gordon House for the weekend, and proffered advice and assistance on projects of mutual interest. But after two years of regular social contact and amicable relations, Haliburton's friendship with Bentley became strained once again. The immediate source of the difficulty was an article that Bentley solicited from Haliburton on the 'Overland Route' for a new journal he was launching, *Bentley's Quarterly Review*. Expecting his article to be needed for the first issue of the new quarterly, Haliburton worked on it while away from home in North Wales. But Bentley had neglected to clear the article with his editors, Sir Robert Cecil and William Cook, who, after asking for revisions, decided not to include it in the first or any issue of the magazine (there were only four issues). The dropping of the article irritated Haliburton considerably.

In March 1860, the curious circumstances surrounding the publication of *The Season Ticket* resulted in further coolness between the two. If we can judge by the later letters (191, 192, 195, 198, and 199, in section 6, 'Parliamentary and Business Interests') in the months preceding the publication of *The Season Ticket* Haliburton offered Bentley a manuscript on behalf of an impatient author (for whom he acted as intermediary). When it came to the publication of his own book he sold it to Bentley at a reduced price, wishing it to appear anonymously. Although he did not use the name 'Sam Slick' on the title page, the attempt at anonymity failed (the book had been serialized in the *Dublin University Magazine*, 1859–60, and was widely understood to be Haliburton's). The result was so great a disappointment to Haliburton that he accused Bentley of knocking his pen from his hand for ever. A projected continuation of *The Season Ticket* was never executed.

Despite these irritations, Haliburton enjoyed his life in England. In addition, Haliburton's friendship with shipping magnate William Schaw Lindsay and with the lord mayor of London, Alderman Thomas Quested Finnis, helped to maintain his high profile in fashionable society. He became, for example, one of the committee members for the lord mayor's 'Indian Mutiny Appeal Fund' in 1857.

As a result of his marriage to Sarah Harriet, Haliburton also met William Benjamin Watkins (1788–1864), a Manchester alderman and businessman. The friendship that developed was one that defied politics: Watkins was a Liberal and a Free-trader, Haliburton was a Conservative and a Protectionist. But it made no difference. Watkins lived at Legh House, Ardwicke, Manchester, and Haliburton visited there frequently, finding Watkins a wise and congenial companion. Watkins was a former (1845) chief magistrate of Manchester and a man who had played a prominent role in Manchester politics (declining a seat in Parliament when it was offered to him under the auspices of the Anti-Corn Law League). Like most Victorian gentlemen, Watkins enjoyed combining business, civic, social, and philanthropic interests. Their friendly visits, one with the other, continued in 1858, 1859, and 1860. The letters to Watkins stop after 1860, but there is no reason to suspect that their friendship lapsed in any way before Watkins died on 24 June 1864, aged seventy-five. Haliburton did not, however, attend his friend's funeral.[6]

When Haliburton wasn't visiting Watkins, he was often spending time with one of his other old friends, Edmund Hopkinson (1787–1869), of Edgeworth Manor, near Cirencester, Gloucestershire, to whom he dedicated two of his works (*The Attaché*, First Series, 1843, and *Nature and Human Nature*, 1855). Hopkinson was married to Octavia Burton, Decimus Burton's and James Haliburton's sister. The Hopkinsons had made their money as army agents in the early part of the century and were now private bankers in London. Haliburton enjoyed visiting the thousand-acre estate that Hopkinson had purchased from the Earl of Bathurst in 1836. No letters to Hopkinson have been found, and only one in the collection is written from Edgeworth, yet Haliburton's friendship with Hopkinson spanned twenty years.

1 See H.E. Litchfield, *Emma Darwin, Wife of Charles Darwin: A Century of Family Letters*, 2 vols (Cambridge: Cambridge University Press 1904) 1: 180.
2 Chittick, 565–73
3 A letter sent to Thomas C. Haliburton, Halifax, 2 January 1841 (PAC, MG 24, B 29, vol. 33)
4 See 'Haliburton's Speeches in England,' 269–70.
5 See Richard A. Davies, '"Not at all the man that we have imagined": Mr. Justice Haliburton in England 1853–65,' *Dalhousie Review* 59 (1979): 683–95.
6 See Watkins's obituary in the *Manchester City News*, 2 July 1864: 2, col. f.

138 To Joseph Howe

Gordon House
Isleworth
4th. Nr. 1856

My dear Howe –

I hear from Porter[1] with great satisfaction of your return for Windsor,[2] not only without opposition but in a most gratifying manner in other respects – You ought on private as well as public grounds to be in the assembly, and I am glad you have at last a constituency, that will give you no trouble, and one that is not in the hands of those who expect a member to be a mere mouthpiece of a religious party and to have no independent opinion of his own, a position than which nothing can be more degrading to a man of spirit – Since I saw you I have become a married man,[3] and am settled down quietly at the above address in one of the most beautiful villas on the banks of the thames, ten minutes walk to the Richmond station, & the same distance from those of Twickenham, and Isleworth, and by either train 20 minutes from London[4] – By a singular coincidence it belongs to Lord Hallyburton[5] who is married to a sister of Lady Falkland the place was a present from Wm 4th. to his daughter[6] – When you come to England I hope you will make your head quarters with me, as I shall be delighted to see you at Gordon House – This letter goes by my son Arthur,[7] who you may recollect went into the commissariat about 15 months ago and proceeded direct to Constantinople[8] – He returned about 3 weeks ago, and leaves on Saturday by Halifax steamer to Canada where he is to be stationed at present – He has returned with the highest testimonials & will be made a depy asst. comy[9] as soon as the rules of the service will admit – He has been very fortunate having already obtained the first step & been confirmed as clerk in the establisht, since February last, while almost every other supernumerary but himself has been discharged[10] – I believe he will only be able to be in Halifax during the brief detention of the steamer, should he apply for a fortnights leave he will see you – I shall be very glad to hear from you when you can find time to write – When you do so let me hear how the railway progresses, particularly the Windsor end of it,[11] as I have not heard a word about it since I wrote – When it is all finished I must come out and take a ride up in it – How does the stately born get on as a judge, for by this time he must have performed a circuit & tried his wings[12] – That fool bird 'West'[13] tried to play him a trick at last – How strange it is he cant do any thing like another man – I am going to lecture by invitation at Athanaeum at Manchester[14] – I shall try colonies for a subject, pray send me your Speech & Letter to Gladstone on *that subject* (not on enlistment bill)[15] by return steamer – It will arrive just in time dont forget – I want to use you as an illustration of a colonial statesman[16] – Can I do anything for you here? – If so command me – Kind regards to Mrs Howe –

Yours always
Th C Haliburton

PANS MS

1 Reginald Porter (1813–66), lawyer and partner to Perez Cunningham, Haliburton's former school friend at King's College, Windsor
2 Howe was returned as MLA for Windsor in 1856. But his seat was insecure and he resigned it in the same year following the defeat of the Liberals in an election.
3 Haliburton married Sarah Harriet Hosier Williams, a widow of Eaton Mascott, Shropshire, on 30 September 1856, at St George's Church, Hanover Square, London.
4 Isleworth was a salubrious suburb of London, linked by railway to Waterloo, pleasantly situated on a bend in the Thames and on the edge of the Duke of Northumberland's estate at Syon Park. See Richard A. Davies, 'Thomas Haliburton in Isleworth, 1856–65,' *Dalhousie Review* 57 (1977): 619–27.
5 Had Haliburton written in the past tense here, his views would have accorded with those of local historian Alan C.B. Urwin, whose accounts of the ownership of the riverside villas are given in his book *Railshead Isleworth* (Newport, Mon.: Hounslow and District History Society 1973). Haliburton claimed that the Gordon House property where he was living belonged to Lord Hallyburton, i.e., Lord Frederick Gordon, who changed his name to Hallyburton in 1842. But Urwin's examination of the rate book for Gordon House suggests that ownership had already passed in 1851 to the Earl of Kilmorey, who rented it to the Haliburtons (Kilmorey's estate was in Shropshire, the home county of Sarah Harriet) until 1867, when he moved into it himself.
6 This was true.
7 Arthur Haliburton (1832–1907), Haliburton's youngest son
8 See J.B. Atlay, *Lord Haliburton: A Memoir of His Public Service* (London 1909) 8.
9 Atlay dates Arthur's departure for Canada as 1857, but clearly Arthur left for Canada before the end of 1856.
10 Atlay confirms Haliburton's statement (*Lord Haliburton*, 9).
11 Howe was chief commissioner of railways for Nova Scotia in 1856.
12 Haliburton was succeeded on the Supreme Court bench by Lewis Wilkins, Jr. See the *Acadian Recorder*, 29 March 1856.
13 The 'fool bird' might refer to Samuel C. West (1824–58), an attorney in Halifax.
14 Haliburton lectured at the Manchester Athenaeum, a prestigious business and literary club, on Tuesday evening, 16 December 1856. His subject was 'The Position and Prospects of the North American Colonies,' and the entire speech was printed in *The Times*, 19 December 1856.

15 Haliburton wants Howe's *Speech ... on the Union of the North American Provinces* (1855), not Howe's *Letter to the Right Honorable William E. Gladstone, MP. ... Being a Review of the Debate on the Foreign Enlistment Bill, and Our Relations with the United States* (London 1856).
16 Haliburton did not use Howe as an example in the speech he delivered at the Manchester Athenaeum.

---

139 To Rev. Edward Girdlestone[1]

Gordon House
Isleworth
23d Decr [18]56.

Revd & dear sir

I have only this moment recieved your letter of the 19th. which by accident was sent to my son in law's address at Torquay,[2] where it was redirected by him, & forwarded to me –

This accidental delay in its delivery, will, I hope, be accepted as an apology for my not having more promptly replied to you – I beg you to accept my best thanks for the very kind and flattering expressions contained in your note, and for the hospitable invitation you are so good as to give me to become your guest, during the meeting of the members of the Athenaeum on the 19th. of January next –

It would have afforded me very great pleasure, if I could have availed myself of your kindness, but unfortunately, engagements both at home and abroad, from which I cannot extricate myself, preclude the possibility of my doing so –

I enclose a letter for the president and officers of the Athenaeum (in answer to that you were so obliging as to forward to me,) expressing the regret I feel at not being able to be present at their meeting, which regret is, I assure you, greatly increased by losing the opportunity of having the honor, and advantage, of making your acquaintance –

I am Revd and dear sir
Yours always
Th. C. Haliburton

Revd
E Girdlestone
&c &c

Acadia University Library MS

1 Rev. Edward Girdlestone (1805–84), canon residentiary of Bristol from 1854 onwards. Girdlestone was known affectionately as the 'Agricultural Labourer's Friend' because of his interest in the well-being of agricultural labourers.
2 Alexander Fowden Haliburton (d. 1873), who married Haliburton's daughter Augusta in 1854. Haliburton dedicated *Sam Slick's Wise Saws* (1853) to him.

140 To Joseph Howe

Gordon House
Isleworth
15th. Jany [18]57.

My dear Howe –

Porter[1] sent me the Chronicle[2] containing your admirable Letter to the Catholic[3] – I am delighted you have a seat[4] where they cant touch you – It is a bold – lucid excellent letter & I am glad there is one person in the country manly enough to say what all think but few like even to breathe – It is time they understood other people have rights as well as them –

Last mail I sent to Willy Cunard[5] a petition to the House about my pension to give somebody to present to legislature[6] – The difficulty hitherto has been in jealousy about my successor, that is now over & I hope justice will be done me – By last mail also I sent you paper (Times) containing a [full?] report of my speech at Manchester on colonies.[7] It took wonderfully & has drawn forth a general expression in their favor – I have been requested to address meetings at Bristol Leicester Leeds & other places on same subject and have had to decline, as I do not feel authorised to speak any opinions but my own – I have also had an offer of a seat in Parliament,[8] which I should have liked, but it is attended with expence I cant afford – I dont mean expence of seat for that was offered free, but the incidental expence of attendance – If I could get my pension I should feel I could accept – I think by my writings I have done something to make our colony known & am in a position to do them service – I am about bringing out a work recommending it to emigrants of property[9]

Considering that I possessed the pension & that it is not creating a new one, & my general claims, as well as what my accepting office again saved the province, that my case ought to be considered an exceptional one, and I confidently rely upon your friendship to do what you can for me –

Did you see that d——d foolish speech of Sir Robt. Peel at Birmingham[10] – He has made govt. perfectly ridiculous – I never knew any thing make such a 'hurrussh' as your Irish friends call it – By the time you get this I hope Cunningham[11] will be at Gordon House – I long to have a good talk over Nova Scotia &c.

When shall you be here again? When you do come, come & stay with us – The way here is by Richmond Rail – We are ½ mile or mile from station – distance to Waterloo Bridge 25 minutes –

The climate agrees very well with me & I am in better health & stronger than I have been for years, I want nothing but my pension to ensure long life for pensioners never die –

I hear you have had a tremendous fire at Halifax but know no particulars[12] –

>In haste
>Yours truly
>Th. C. Haliburton

King's College, Halifax, MS *Pub.*: Chittick, 413, first paragraph only

1 Reginald Porter
2 Howe's 'Letter to William Gladstone' on the subject of the foreign enlistment question was published in the *Halifax Morning Chronicle*, 12 August 1856.
3 Haliburton refers to a letter from Howe that appeared in the *Novascotian*, 23 June 1856, giving an account of the violence that had broken out on the Windsor Railroad between Irish Catholic workers and local Protestants. Another letter of Howe's appeared in the *Halifax Morning Chronicle*, 27 December 1856, attacking the Catholics of the Province.
4 Howe was returned as member for Windsor Township on 9 September 1856 and took his seat on 5 February 1857.
5 Samuel Cunard's second son, who married Haliburton's daughter Laura in 1851
6 The petition was presented in February 1856 (*Journals ... of the House of Assembly* [1856] 46). A bill granting Haliburton his pension passed a first reading in the Nova Scotia Legislature in March 1857, but was quickly dropped before its second reading (Chittick, 567). A court case followed in 1860–1.
7 *The Times*, 19 December 1856
8 Chittick mentions that Haliburton was offered a seat for Middlesex in 1857. His actual entry into Parliament was a sudden affair in 1859, when he accepted the seat offered at Launceston, at three days' notice. See Richard A. Davies, '"Not at all the man that we have imagined": Mr. Justice Haliburton in England 1853–65,' *Dalhousie Review* 59 (1979): 683–95.
9 Not traced
10 Sir Robert Peel spoke on 6 January 1857 to an after-dinner audience in the new library at Adderly Park and indulged himself in a series of anti-Russian remarks while relating his tour of St Petersburg and the Royal Palaces.
11 Perez Cunningham
12 The fire destroyed much of Hollis Street. In 1859, another fire destroyed most of Granville Street. See Raddall, 191.

141 To Richard Bentley

Gordon House
Isleworth
3d Feby [18]57.

My dear sir –

When I went to town yesterday I found Lady Falkland disposed to accept another offer[1] – I could have wished you had taken the work, but am glad it is terminated, as I live too far from London to manage any affairs but my own –

       Yours very truly
       Th. C. Haliburton

Harvard MS *Pub.*: ed. W.I. Morse, 83

1 Haliburton acted as intermediary between Bentley and Lady Falkland in the unsuccessful negotiations to publish her travel journal, *Chow-Chow* ('odds and ends').

142 To W.B. Watkins

Gordon House
Isleworth
7th. March [18]57.

My dear friend –

Since I saw you last, or rather wrote to you last, notwithstanding I have hitherto declined every invitation to lecture, I have been over-persuaded to do so at Glasgow[1] – The day will be the 25 or 26 instant, the precise one I shall know by return of post –

My object in troubling you with this uninteresting piece of information, is to ask you if you feel inclined to spend a day at Glasgow, with me – If so I will take Manchester in my way thither, for the sake of our meeting & going together. I feel 'auspice tenero'[2] I should have good luck, at least I shall be certain of a pleasant trip – I hope you will be able to do so –

Cobden[3] has 'gone and done it' and like a housemaid that has smashed a *glass cabinet* seems astonished at what he has done – He and the govt. are both wrong – He is wrong in condemning the govt. for enforcing the observance of treaties on the Chinese – The govt was wrong in attempting it until they had collected a force sufficient to have looked down all resistance[4] – More prudence & more energy and all this bloodshed might have been avoided – I am delighted to hear such good accounts of dear Helen,[5] and we hope she will be able to come & complete her restoration to health at Gordon House, with the return of good weather – Present my kindest regards to dear Mrs Watkins[6] & your daughters and believe me –

> Yours always
> Tho. C. Haliburton

W.B. Watkins Eqr

Massey College MS [*Ph.*]

1 See the *North British Daily Mail*, Friday, 27 March 1857, for a report on Haliburton's arrival and lecture in Glasgow.
2 With slight hope
3 Richard Cobden, radical MP, by an unholy alliance with Disraeli and Gladstone, managed to bring down the government over the incident at Canton concerning the Chinese boarding of the vessel *Arrow*. A general election followed, returning Lord Palmerston to power with a majority of seventy. Cobden lost his seat.
4 When Palmerston was returned to power he sent Lord Elgin to China with a list of demands and accompanied by a strong force of British and French troops.
5 Helen Watkins, W.B. Watkins's daughter, who stayed at Gordon House in 1857
6 Ellen Wynne Watkins, good friend of Sarah Harriet Haliburton

143 To 'Gentlemen'[1]

> Gordon House
> Isleworth
> 15th. March [18]57.

Gentlemen –

In reply to your letter of the 13th. Inst, I have to inform you, that I do not propose to deliver an address in any other place than Glasgow –

> I am yr. obt. sevt
> Th. C. Haliburton

Columbia University MS [*Ph.*]

1 Unidentified

144 To Dr Browne[1]

Gordon House
Isleworth
17th. March [18]57

My dear sir

I have the pleasure to acknowledge the receipt of your very kind letter of the 14th. inst. and regret extremely that it will be out of my power to visit Dumfries, as my time is so very limited, that I shall be compelled to leave Scotland almost immediately after the delivery of my address at Glasgow – I beg to thank you very cordially and gratefully, for the very kind expressions in your letter and to assure you of my great regret, at not being enabled to make your acquaintance & have the opportunity of thanking you in person – As it is my intention to publish my address for general circulation,[2] the object I had in view in availing myself of the invitation to Glasgow to deliver it, will I hope be obtained and therefore I do not propose to address any other audience on the subject – Indeed in the present excited state of public feeling,[3] I cannot hope that it will excite the attention the importance of our colonies merits –

With many thanks for your kindness believe me to be

My dear sir
Yours very truly
Tho. C. Haliburton

Dr Browne –

Acadia University Library MS

1 Dr William Alexander Francis Browne (1805–85), medical commissioner of the Crichton Royal Institution, Dumfries, and author of *What Asylums Were, Are, and Ought to Be* (1837). In the autumn of 1857 he was appointed medical commissioner of lunacy for Scotland.
2 Published as *An Address on the Present Condition, Resources and Prospects of British North America* (Glasgow 1857).
3 Haliburton is probably alluding to the recent fall of the two-year-old Palmerston government (3 March) over the bombarding of Canton by the British.

145 To Richard Bentley

Gordon House
Isleworth
28th. May [18]57

My dear sir –

When I had the pleasure of seeing you at the Lity Dinner,[1] you said you would do me the favor to spend Sunday next with me –

I write to remind you – we expect you to stay over night with us – I hope you will come early in the day, so as to enjoy the scenery and fresh air –

The Richmond railway, is the proper one from Waterloo –

Yours truly
Th. C. Haliburton

R. Bentley

Harvard MS

[1] The occasion was the sixty-eighth anniversary festival of the Royal Literary Fund at the Freemason's Tavern, London, on 29 May 1857. Haliburton was one of the stewards of the Royal Literary Fund dinner for 1857, at which he responded to a toast on 'The Literature of the Colonies.'

146 Thomas Quested Finnis[1]

Gordon House
Isleworth
28th. July [18]57.

My dear Lord Mayor –

Not knowing the locality of Wansted,[2] or the mode of getting there from the Waterloo station, would you do me the favor, to ask the chaplain,[3] to drop me a line to inform me of the proper route to take from that place – With a thousand apologies for troubling you I am my dear Lord Mayor –

Yours alwys
Th. C. Haliburton

NY Univ. – Fales Library MS

[1] Alderman T.Q. Finnis, lord mayor of London

2 Haliburton was to join Finnis on Friday, 31 July 1857, to participate in the 'London Shoeblacks' annual treat at the lord mayor's residence at Wanstead. The occasion is reported in the *Standard*, 1 August 1857.
3 Unidentified

---

147 To W.B. Watkins

Gordon House
Isleworth
8th. Aug [18]57.

My dear sir –

Many thanks for your kind letter – I have been so dissipated lately, dining out or *aquaticising* every day, I have hardly had time to put pen to paper – Right glad was I to see your handwriting again – I cant tell you how much I missed you, in my evening session in the temple with a cigar, and the chats that added to their flavor nor do we less miss dear Helen at our every turn, sometimes when I hear a footstep I think it is hers, but alas 'we miss her at her accustomed haunts'[1] – I am afraid she found it very dull here, but I assure you, it has made this place very dull without her – The weather has been fearfully hot here, altho I think it is now passing off – I believe it has been very hot every where, for I had a letter from my son[2] at Montreal who says 'I am writing without coat waistcoat or cravat, half dead with the heat' – Mrs Owen[3] arrived here night before last, and yesterday accompanied us up the River in the Lord Mayors state barge, in which we dined, a little above Richmond Bridge[4] – It was a very jolly time, so jolly that when we left, Anderton the Under Sherriff aged 74 was dancing a quadrille – It was a state dinner & the toast master Harker[5] was there to give out the toasts – Helen recollects him at the Mansion House,[6] giving out in a voice of thunder the toasts – Tell her I heard a good story of him – He is a crier of the Old Bailey Court, and one Sunday fell asleep in church and suddenly waking up, on hearing the noise of the congregation rising, called out as he awoke – 'Silence in court' – Alderman Sydney[7] asked me across the table if there were not two 'ls' in my name which he *aspirated* – I said no – and that I was very glad of it – Why he asked? Because it would make a 'hell' of a difference – Give our united love to Mrs Watkins & the young ladies & believe me my dear friend

Ever yours
Th. C. Haliburton

PANS MS

1 Unidentified
2 Arthur, stationed in Montreal
3 Possibly Sarah Harriet's mother, Mrs Frances Owen (d. 1908)
4 *The Times*, 7 August 1857: 5, col. e, reported the 'Royal Thames National Regatta.' Although Haliburton is not listed by name in the report, it is likely that he was present on the occasion, as his own description of the festivities matched that of the account in *The Times*.
5 Mr Harker was still functioning with 'undiminished impressiveness & vigor' on 2 April 1861, according to an account of him in the *Standard* of that day.
6 At the 'Grand Banquet to the Archbishops and Bishops,' held in the Egyptian Hall. The account in the *Standard*, 17 June 1857, reported the presence of 'Mr Justice and Mrs Haliburton and Miss Watkin.'
7 Thomas Sydney (1805–89), MP, former alderman, and mayor of London

148 To Richard Bentley

Gordon House
[Isleworth]
Wednesday [2 September 1857]

My dear sir –

On my way to town yesterday I received yr. letter and was indeed much grieved to hear of your indisposition – Pray drop me a line and assure me if you can that you are better –

I attended the dinner[1] and had a pleasant afternoon there – Many regrets were expressed at your absence and especially at the cause of it –

Either Friday eveng or very early on Saturday morning I go to Southampton to go to sea with one of the Peninsular and Oriental Companys boats on a trial trip[2] – I dont know how far they intend to go –

I hope to have a line from you before I go –

Mrs H desires to unite in kind regards & good wishes – She has read the msst. and thinks there is no evidence of [Mevis?][3] identity – While the nervous excitement he appears to have laboured under all his life induces her to think he is under an hallucination on the subject of his birth[4] –

She happens to know almost every lady he refers to in Shropshire –

Yours alwys
Th. C. Haliburton –

Harvard MS *Pub.*: ed. W.I. Morse, 102–3

1 Possibly a 'public meeting,' held at the Mansion House, to devise means for the relief of

the sufferers from the mutinous outbreaks in India (the *Standard,* 26 August 1857: 5, cols e, f; 6, col. a)
2 Haliburton left Southampton on Monday, 7 September 1857 (see the *Standard,* 8 September 1857: 4, col. e), and returned on 23 September (the *Standard,* 24 September 1857: 5, col. c).
3 Haliburton's hand is hard to read here, and I have been unable to verify this unlikely sounding name.
4 Haliburton might be referring here to the celebrated 'Shrewsbury Peerage case,' which was much before the public at this time.

---

149 To Richard Bentley

Gordon House
Isleworth

My dear sir –

25th. Sepr. [18]57.

I have but just returned from Lisbon,[1] rather suffering from its malaria – When I am able to go to London I will call and see you –
  I am ashamed to say I have been very idle since I saw you –

Yours truly.
Th C Haliburton

Harvard MS

1 Haliburton returned on Wednesday, 23 September, at 12:30 PM.

---

150 To W.B. Watkins

Gordon House
Isleworth

My dear old friend –

6th. Nvr [18]57

I have just heard a passage read from Helens[1] letter and am grieved to find that you are not well – She says you talk of going to London – Dont do so just now, for we go to Gloucester[2] on Wednesday next for a few day and want you to wait till we return, so that you can come & stay with us – I will under take your cure – It will do us both good – In the mean time here is a prescription equal to your silk belt for lumbago, that *I will warrant* for your throat –
  Dissolve in brandy as much salt as it will take up – Take a desert spoonful occasionally (3 or 4 times a day) raw – *I knew* this cure an awful astma (is that spet right?) of 25 years standing –

It operated like a miracle –
I want you to clear your throat before you come, for I have stories that will choke you otherwise –
I will write you the day I return –
Love to all yr family in whch Sarah unites & believe me

        Yours always
        Th. C. Haliburton

Massey College MS [*Ph.*]

1 W.B. Watkins's daughter. She stayed with the Haliburtons at Gordon House during July.
2 To stay with his old friend Edmund Hopkinson at Edgeworth Manor, Cirencester, Gloucestershire

---

151 To Richard Bentley

Gordon House
Isleworth
25th. Novr [18]57.

My dear sir –

Will you do me the favor to dine with me quietly on Saturday at 6½, and spend Sunday here – if not better engaged –
 The Richmond train is the nearest –

        Yours always
        Th. C. Haliburton

R Bentley Esqr

Harvard MS

---

152 To W.B. Watkins

Gordon House
Isleworth
23d Decr [18]57.

My dear friend –

If you will look at your watch, at 8 precisely on Christmas day a.m. it will remind you at that moment I shall propose a toast at my table – 'All our friends at Leigh House'[1] a merry Christmas & many of them to you –
 And if you will search the records of your memory, you will find there an overdue 'I.O.U.' for a visit to Gordon House, on the subject of which I

beg to suggest, if you cannot conveniently liquidate it, that you will do me the favor to renew it at a short date –

You will still be in time for the launch of the Leviathan[2] – Railway trains *can run* on a level, but it has been reserved for Brunel[3] to discover that a vessel can be *launched* on a level – Had he given a decent incline, he would have needed neither capstans nor hydraulic rams, a greater piece of presumptious ignorance was never heard of – The whole affair is a disgrace to England – If you dont come here soon, I shall think it is not from want of an *incline* but want of *inclination,* so come & redeem your promise – I have had an awkward attack of gout[4] in my right hand, which has been very uncomfortable, but thank God I am all right now –

With our united & kindest regards to Mrs. Watkins & your daughters, I am very truly

> Yours always
> Th. C. Haliburton

Massey College MS [*Ph.*]

1 Haliburton consistently spelt 'Legh' as 'Leigh.'
2 The *Great Eastern* steamship, designed by Isambard Kingdom Brunel, from 1852 to 1858, and the largest ship in the world at its launching. Haliburton was writing to Watkins after repeated attempts had been made to launch it. See L.T.C. Rolt, *Isambard Kingdom Brunel: A Biography* (London 1957) 266.
3 Isambard Kingdom Brunel (1806–59), one of the great civil engineers of the Victorian era
4 The start of a series of gout attacks that troubled Haliburton over the next few years. They did not, however, curtail his dining habits and prandial delights.

---

153 To ———[1] [Isleworth? 1858?]

Mr Christie[2] is a chamber counsel of the highest eminence confidentially consulted by the Lords Chancellors. It was he who selected for the govt of the day the Commrs of Encumbered Estates in Ireland, who were anxious to get first rate men.

He was an old friend of Lord Jeffreys[3] and Lockhart,[4] and Sir Walter Scott,[5] and an early cooperator with J. Wilson Croker in Quarterly Review.

PANS copy; fragment only

1 The copy, an 'Extract of a letter from Judge Haliburton,' is written on the verso of a judgment of J.H. Christie, QC, 24 March 1858.
2 I have been unable to corroborate Haliburton's biographical references to Christie.
3 Francis, Lord Jeffrey (1773–1850), Scottish judge and critic, founder of the *Edinburgh Review*
4 John Gibson Lockhart (1794–1854), biographer of Sir Walter Scott, editor of the *Quarterly Review*, 1825–53
5 Sir Walter Scott (1771–1832), celebrated novelist and poet

154 To Richard Bentley

Gordon House
Isleworth
18th. Feby [18]58

My dear sir –

Will you dine on Saturday with us & spend Sunday – Our hour is 6½ –

Yours truly
Th. C. Haliburton

Harvard MS

155 To Richard Bentley

Gordon House
[Isleworth]
23 Feby 58

My dear sir –

I concluded from not having heard from you or seeing you on Saturday last, that you were from home –

We shall be at home next Saturday & shall be happy to see you then if not better engaged –

Yours truly
Th. C. Haliburton.

R. Bentley Eqr.

Harvard MS

156 To Richard Bentley

Gordon House
Isleworth
17th. March 1858

My dear sir –

I shall be delighted to see you on Saturday next, to spend Sunday here – I shall dine out at orphan charity in London that day,[1] but return by 10 train in time to discuss a glass of whiskey & a cigar with you in the evening before bed – Mrs Haliburton will be delighted to have you to dine with her at 6.½. – She has a piece of Nova Scotia moose meat for your dinner – When you come I will talk over the Inglis book with you[2] – I can point out a track for you, that I think may answer

> Yours alwys
> Th.C Haliburton

Many thanks for Sherman,[3] I have been laid up the whole week past with gout, but am now convalescent, & hope soon to be able to give 'leg bail' to the disease – Le Marchant[4] could help you with Thesiger, Inglis father in law[5] – When you come I will instruct you what to say to Mrs Inglis the Genls. mother,[6] who is an old friend of mine & lives at Tunbridge Wells –

Harvard MS *Pub.*: ed. W.I. Morse, 84–5

1 At the anniversary festival of the British Orphan Asylum (*The Times*, 22 March 1858: 10, col. b).
2 Lady Inglis's *Siege of Lucknow: A Diary*. Haliburton allowed his name to be used in Bentley's approaches to Lady Inglis because he knew the General's (Sir John Inglis's) mother, who lived at Tunbridge Wells, the widow of Bishop John Inglis, bishop of Nova Scotia, 1824–50. Negotiations for the book were not successful, and the diary of the siege of Lucknow remained unpublished until 1892.
3 Unidentified
4 Sir Denis Le Marchant, chief clerk to the House of Commons from 1855
5 Frederick Thesiger, first Baron Chelmsford (1794–1878), barrister
6 Widow of the former bishop of Nova Scotia, John Inglis (d. 1850)

---

157 To Richard Bentley Brighton 9th. Ap. [18]58

My dear sir –

I find it impossible to get away from here tomorrow as my friends[1] wont hear of it – So if you will be good enough to substitute tomorrow week, for tomorrow I shall be at home to receive you –

> Yours always
> Th C Haliburton

R. Bentley, Esq

Harvard MS

1 Unidentified

158 To Richard Bentley

Gordon House
Isleworth
14th. Ap [18]58

My dear sir –

Your letter crossed mine from Brighton on the road – Many thanks for the books –

I am very sorry indeed to hear of the continued indisposition of your son, I think after all London advice much the best for him –

I shall be most glad to see you on Saturday –

Yours
T C Haliburton

University of Illinois MS [*Ph.*]

159 To Richard Bentley

Gordon House
Isleworth
Tuesday – [*c.* May–June 1858]

My dear sir –

I return the proof sheets[1] with a few alterations, especially in leaving out one name & merly giving the initial of Gen W—— (yndham)[2] which are too personal, the others are verbal – From page 144 to page 169, proofs were not sent, you can look these over yourself –

I enclose a suggestion for preface[3] which you can send to Mrs Case[4] –

Yours truly
Th. C. Haliburton

I would call it
   'Day by Day in Lucknow'
   or a Narrative of the
   Siege &c &c
I do not mean the enclosed to be *the* preface, but to serve as a suggestion for one –

Where Polehamptons death is mentioned in Mrs Case work, I would insert *as note* the enclosed paragraph,[5]

It will help to fill up your *empty pages* –

T.C.H.

I have opened this letter to enclose one from the Revd Mr. James[6] who saw Mrs Polehamptons father Mr. Allnutt[7] – The latter appears to be a fool – The journal *is* at Shrewsberry,[8] in Mrs Allnuts hands, fairly written out – The Queen has seen it – & Mrs Kenyon[9] read several pages, or the whole of it & spoke enthusiastically about it to me. Mr James will be written to again –

Harvard MS *Pub.*: ed. W.I. Morse, 87–8

1 The proof sheets of Mrs Adelaide Case's *Day by Day at Lucknow: A Journal of the Siege of Lucknow* (1858). An offer went out to Mrs Case on 22 May 1858. Her preface is dated 5 June. Bentley suggested that the proofs be sent directly to Haliburton.
2 Major General Windham, MP for East Norfolk, commander in India. General Windham's name appears on pages 305–6 of *Day by Day at Lucknow*.
3 The preface acknowledges the help of friends in presenting the journal to the public.
4 Mrs Adelaide Case, the wife of Colonel Case, Thirty-second Foot, lived at Bute Place, Old Trafford, near Manchester.
5 The death of the Rev. Henry Stedman Polehampton is recorded in *Day by Day at Lucknow*, 67.
6 The Rev. William J. James was curate of Can Hop (a small village near Eaton Mascott, the former home of Haliburton's wife, Sarah Harriet). See S. Bagshaw's *Shropshire Gazetteer* (1851) 500–1. In 1856, he is listed in the Shrewsbury *Post Office Directory* as living in Coton Hill.
7 Possibly Charles Blake Allnatt, listed in the *Shropshire Gazeteer* (1851) as a barrister-at-law, the Crescent, Shrewsbury
8 The journal referred to here is that of the Rev. Henry S. Polehampton, chaplain at Lucknow. Bentley published the journal later the same year.
9 Unidentified

---

160 To Richard Bentley

Dear Mr Bentley

St Anns' Hotel
Buxton
Saturday [4 September 1858][1]

Your kind letter, & *too* liberal donation of books reached us safely this morning, pray accept our best thanks for both – We arrived here on Thursday, the Judge is at present rather worse from the effect of the baths – We are told this is generally the case, but we have every hope that a few days more, will make a wonderful improvement in him – The pain has shifted into the knee, which makes him more of a cripple than he was before – This is a very quiet place, but the accommodation is good – The

Judge delivers his kindest regards, he will write to you as soon as he is able – He does not like the last new title of the Review, he thinks 'Imperial' even, is better – What do you say to Cosmopolitan?[2] –

I hope you are quite recovered, for I did not think you as well as usual, when you were last at Gordon House – Believe me –

Very truly your's
S.H. Haliburton

Harvard MS

1 The date is provided by the postmark, 'TUNBRIDGE-WELLS SP 4 58.' The letter is written on Haliburton's behalf by his wife, Sarah Harriet.
2 According to Gettmann, 146: 'Bentley ... recommended a neutral title such as *Great Britain, a Quarterly Review*, the one finally chosen was *Bentley's Quarterly Review.*'

161 To Richard Bentley

Gordon House
Isleworth
26th. Oct [18]58

My dear sir –

I have been laid up ever since I saw you – I was attacked on the 9th. of August, and have not yet shaken it off, as on Sunday it returned suddenly, and seized me in the left arm – This second advent I impute to going to Manchester[1] before I was able to stand the fatigue – You may judge how severe & continuous the attack has been when I tell you, that today I walked as far the edge of Richmond Green[2] – Still I hope I shall soon be all right altho my suffering at Buxton was something quite dredful –

I am sorry to find from your letter that you too have been an invalid, and trust you have derived benefit from the change of air – I hope you will come to us on yr. return, when I will have your prospectus[3] ready for you – In the mean time drop me a line & tell me how you are –

Mrs Haliburton sends her kind regards to you & yours

Yours always
Th. C. Haliburton

Harvard MS *Pub.*: ed. W.I. Morse, 85

1 Haliburton visited W.B. Watkins in late September / early October.
2 Richmond Green is approximately a mile from Gordon House.
3 Unidentified

162 To W.B. Watkins

Gordon House
Isleworth
27th. Oct [18]58.

My dear friend –

I have not been in spirits to write to you since my return – On Sunday morning when I awoke I found a tumor on the point of my left elbow about the size of a plumb – Whether it was a boil, or a contusion arising from some little injury to a nerve on the journey, I could not tell, so I went to London and showed it to a Dr. who pronounced it gout, and I am now under medecine for it, and a good deal of pain in the arm – How lucky it is that I was so abstemious at Manchester, or I should have been under the impression it was owing to my having deviated from a course of diet, of which I retain the same indifferent opinion I always have – A three months gout is no joke is it?

I observe by todays paper you have been successful in obtaining a general vote in favor of Mr Basely,[1] – I hope there will be no contest, for such things leave stings behind –

Mrs H. who is getting ready to drive out with me, this day is so fine, being unable to write – desires me to say, she has seen Mr Brown, and given him Mrs. Watkins china – He pronounced the priest old Bow[2] (he dont mean the priest is an old *Beau*) and valuable – and that this other strange to say has both the Chelsea & Dresden mark on it,[3] a thing he never saw before and very strange & unaccountable as a thing cant be made in two places –

To mend them nicely will cost a pound, so she awaits Mrs Watkins answer as to expence before she orders it –

I will write on a separate sheet and send you *the clauses* I spoke of, as I am up I can sit to write with ease

Pray give our united love to Mrs W & your daughters & believe me with a thousand thanks to you & them, for all your kindness –

Yours always
Th. C. Haliburton

W B Watkin[4] Eqr.

Massey College MS [*Ph.*]

1 Sir Thomas Bazley (1797–1885), manufacturer, politician, Manchester cotton spinner, and merchant. He was MP for Manchester from 1858 to 1880, a Liberal and Free-trader. Haliburton might well have been reading *The Times* for Wednesday, 27 October 1858, 12, col. f: 'Election Intelligence, Manchester.'
2 'Bow' china, manufactured in Stratford High Street, Essex, c. 1747–76
3 See Alfred Beaver, *Memorials of Old Chelsea* (London 1892) 101, for examples of china marks variously attributed to Bow and Chelsea.
4 Haliburton normally refers to his Manchester friend as 'Watkins,' but occasionally, as here, he drops the final 's.' The 'Watkin' family was a rich and influential one in Manchester at the time but I have been unable to establish Watkins's relationship to them.

---

163 To Richard Bentley

My dear sir –

[Gordon House
Isleworth]
Friday 29th. Oct. [1858?][1]

I dine out tomorrow[2] so if you can manage to come early on Sunday I shall be delighted to see you –

                Yours always
                Th. C. Haliburton

Harvard MS

1 This note and the one following are undated but might have been written on the same day.
2 At the Walpoles. See the next letter.

---

164 To Richard Bentley

My dear sir –

Gordon House
Isleworth
Friday 29th. Oct [1858]

I have just received your note in time to say we dine out on Saturday (tomorrow) at Mr Walpoles[1] but will *be very glad* indeed to see you on Sunday morning –

                Yours in haste
                Th. C. Haliburton

Harvard MS

1 Spencer Horatio Walpole (1806–98), MP for Cambridge University, 1856–82; home secretary, 1852, 1858–9, and 1866

165 To Richard Bentley

Gordon House
Isleworth
5th. Nvr [18]58

My dear sir

Recollect we expect you to dine with us tomorrow Saturday at 6½ aclock –

> Yours always
> Th C Haliburton

R Bentley Eqr

Harvard MS

---

166 To Anthony Trolloppe[1]

Gordon House
Isleworth
12th. Novr. [18]58

My dear Trolloppe –

I have just received your letter of the 10th, and I assure you it has given me very great satisfaction to hear *directly* from you, *indirectly* I often hear of you from our mutual friend Bentley upon whom, poor fellow, sorrow & years have made unmistakeable traces – I have also had the gratification of reading your singularly clever works, and congratulate you with all my heart, upon attaining the enviable distinction of being by far the best delineator of female character of the present day – If I were capable of entertaining a feeling of envy, it would be of that masterly & delicate hand that so truly & so skilfully pourtrays the feelings, impulses and instincts of the fair sex – Go on and prosper –

I look back with great pleasure and great gratitude, to the days & they were not a few, spent in your mothers hospitable house, in bygone times, – When you write to her next, pray remember me most affectionately to her – How glad I should be to renew our acquaintance –

It is probable you will visit London before you depart for the west[2] – If you do, pray ... [3] me – I am only a short mile [from?] [Ri]chmond to which there are trains from Waterloo station every half hour, a distance that hundreds on both sides of me think not incompatible with even daily business in town – If you cant do this pray give me what time you can – The address on this letter is known to every cab man in Richmond, as this house, before I obtained it, was occupied by people of some distinction –

I send you a letter to my daughter at Halifax Mrs. Cunard,[4] who will not only shew you any attention in her power, if you visit that place but introduce *your identity*, for your name will be a letter of introduction throughout the provinces –

Do you think of [visi ?] ... if you do I will give you letters to people there that may be serviceable to you – There is a delegation of their *head men* in London now, – If you reach London before they leave, I will do that personally – If they have gone by letter – But let me know –

Yours always
Th. C. Haliburton

Anthony Trollope Esqr.

University of Illinois MS *Pub.: The Letters of Anthony Trollope*, ed. N. John Hall (Stanford, Calif.: Stanford University Press) I, 78

1 Anthony Trollope (1815–82), the celebrated novelist. See *DNB*.
2 Trollope was about to leave for the West Indies on post office business.
3 Hiatus in MS
4 Haliburton's daughter Laura, who married William Cunard, second son of Samuel Cunard, in 1851

---

167 To Richard Bentley

Gordon House
Isleworth
22d Novr [18]58

My dear sir –

Enclosed is the prospectus – It was so carelessly done, I have had a great trouble in correcting it –

It would have been much easier to have re–written it –

It will do now to submit and may be added to or improved by others –

Yours always
Th. C. Haliburton

I will send the other on Tuesday –

Harvard MS *Pub.*: ed. W.I. Morse, 86

---

168 To Richard Bentley

Gordon House
Isleworth
24th. Nor [18]58

My dear sir –

Enclosed is a letter my son enclosed to me from Montreal,[1] your son did not leave his address with him, & he inferred from his talk he had left for England –

My people in setting my room *to rights* have put my papers *away* & mislaid your proof of your new work[2] – Pray send me another copy –

Can you spend next Sunday with us – I dine in London on Saturday,[3] but if you will spend the evening & dine with Mrs Haliburton & my daughter that day, she will be happy to see you & I will join you in the evening –

> Yours alwys
> Th. C. Haliburton –

Harvard MS *Pub.*: ed. W.I. Morse, 86

1 Arthur Haliburton (1832–1907), stationed with the army commissariat in Montreal
2 Perhaps the *Memoir, Letters, and Diary of the late Revd Henry S. Polehampton, Chaplain of Lucknow,* second edition (BL Add. MS 46,637, f. 117 verso), published by Bentley on 19 November
3 The occasion was the farewell dinner to 'Dr P. Colquhoun,' held at the Freemason's Tavern, upon his appointment as 'judge of the Supreme Court of the Ionian Islands' (the *Standard*, 29 November 1858: 3, col. b).

169 To Richard Bentley

[Gordon House
Isleworth]

Dear Mr Bentley   Decr 2d [1858]

The Judge's fingers being still disabled, I must thank you on his behalf,[1] & my own, for your kind present of books, we are indeed very much obliged to you for them, & I anticipate much pleasure in their perusal these long winter evenings – The Judge will carefully return the prescription after the druggist has copied it –

We hope very soon to have the pleasure of seeing you here again, you are always a welcome guest, & whenever you are disposed to pass a Sunday with us, a line from you the day before, will always ensure our being at home – With the Judges's kind regards, believe me

> Very truly your's
> S.H. Haliburton

Harvard MS

1 Written on Haliburton's behalf by his wife, Sarah Harriet. Haliburton was still suffering from the gout: but did manage to pen the acceptance note that follows.

---

170 To ——?[1]

Gordon House
Isleworth
2d Decr. [18]58

Dear sir

I shall have great pleasure in accepting the invitation, the Committee for the National Celebration of the Centenery Birth day of Burns have done me the honor to forward to me, to dine with them at Glasgow on the 25th. January next –

                Your obt servt.
                Th. C. Haliburton

City of Glasgow, Mitchell Library MS [*Ph.*]

1 Unidentified

---

171 To Richard Bentley

[Gordon House, Isleworth?]
7th. Decr. [1858]

My dear sir

Enclosed is a letter to send Miss Pardoe[1] – I am very sorry I was not more successful –
   I hope to have the pleasure to see you next Saturday –
   I received Lord R Cecils[2] note –

                Yours alwys
                Th. C. Haliburton

Harvard MS

1 Julia Pardoe (1806–62), travel writer, novelist, and historian. It was probably either her *Episodes of French History* (1859) or *A Life's Struggle* (1859) that Bentley was seeking.
2 Lord Robert Cecil, one of the editors of the ill-fated *Quarterly Review*

172 To Richard Bentley

Gordon House
Isleworth
16th. decr [18]58

My dear sir –

We hope to have the pleasure of seeing you on Sunday next, on Saturday I am sorry to say we shall be full –

           Yours always
           Th. C. Haliburton

Harvard MS

173 To Richard Bentley

Gordon House
Isleworth
29th. Dcr. [18]58

My dear sir –

I am rejoiced to hear that you are now quite well again – We shall be delighted to see you on Saturday and will expect you at dinner – Pray present our kind regards to your family and accept the best wishes for the new year to come from

           Yours always
           Th. C. Haliburton

I am reading up for the article[1] and ready to put pen to paper –

Harvard MS *Pub.*: ed. W.I. Morse, 87

1 The first number of the ill-fated *Bentley's Quarterly Review* appeared in March 1859. The quarterly published only one leading article per number, the remaining space being taken up with book reviews.

174 To Sir Edward Bulwer Lytton[1]

Private
Gordon House
Isleworth
27th Jany [18]59.

My dear Sir Edward B. Lytton

With reference to the conversation I had with you, a short time ago, as to the employment of my son, Robert Haliburton, (of the Nova Scotia bar)² & your very kind assurance, that you would bear him in mind, whenever a suitable opportunity should occur, I beg to say I have just heard that Mr Kennedy,[3] the Colonial Secretary of Bermuda, has either sent in his resignation or is about to do so immediately –

For such a situation, my son, Mr R. Haliburton, is eminently qualified, as well by his high legal attainments, & general knowledge of colonial affairs, as by his proficiency in both ancient & modern languages –

He certainly would be 'the right man, in the right place,' there, & I am convinced the appointment of a *colonist*, to such an important post in another colony, would be as acceptable to the bar, & the people of both provinces, as it would be gratifying to myself –

Thanking you for the very kind reception you were so good as to give me, when personally introducing the subject to you, I am, dear Sir Edward,

Yours always
T.C. Haliburton

To
Sir Edward Bulwer Lytton Bart.
&c &c.

Lytton MS [*Ph.*]

1 Edward George Earle Bulwer Lytton (1803–73), novelist and statesman. He was secretary of state for the colonies, 1858–9.
2 Robert Grant Haliburton (1831–98)
3 Sir Arthur Edward Kennedy (1810–83), colonial governor of Gambia (1851–2), Sierra Leone (1852–4), Western Australia (1854–62), and Vancouver Island (1863–7)

---

175 To Richard Bentley

Woodhouse[1]
Shrewsberry
28th. Janury. [18]59

My dear sir –

On my return from Glasgow I got your letter here – I will write you from Coed Coch, Abergele, Wales,[2] a memorandum such as you require – From there I will send you the first part of article for review –

I saw two notices in the times of Mrs Elliotts book[3] – They seem puzzled to know where it came from and appear to doubt its authenticity, but yet admit it throughout – It will help the circulation –

We had a jolly time at Glasgow[4] – My speech they tried to flatter me was the best of the evening[5] – I had an unexpectedly warm & enthusiastic reception – It was badly reported in the Glasgow papers & wholly omitted in The Times – I will talk over these and other matters with you when we meet –

If you write to me next week write to Coed Coch Abergele, N Wales –

      Yours always
      Th. C. Haliburton

Shirley Brooks[6] was at Glasgow and promised to propose a toast, but at the last minute gave them the slip and young Jerrold[7] did it very badly for him –

Harvard MS *Pub.*: ed. W.I. Morse, 88–9

1 Woodhouse was the family seat of the Mostyn-Owen family, thirteen miles north-north-west of Shrewsbury.
2 The home of John Lloyd Wynne (1807–87) of Trofarth and Coed Coch, Abergele, a JP, and high sheriff of Denbigh in 1865
3 Entitled *Narrative of the First French Revolution. The Times* doubted its authenticity as a personal account of the French Revolution and criticized Bentley's slovenliness as publisher (26 January 1859: 12, cols a–c; 27 January 1859: 8, cols a–c). Bentley replied on 28 January.
4 Haliburton attended the Robert Burns Centenary Festival, Tuesday, 25 January 1859, held at the city hall, Glasgow. See the *North British Daily Mail*, 26 January 1859.
5 Haliburton proposed a toast to 'The Clergy of Scotland,' but spoke mainly about the activities of the Scottish clergy in North America.
6 Charles William Shirley Brooks (1816–74), editor of *Punch* magazine
7 William Blanchard Jerrold (1826–84), journalist and author, son of Douglas Jerrold (1803–57)

6
Parliamentary and Business Interests, 1859–1865

Haliburton enjoyed his parliamentary career as much as he enjoyed his club life. He declared his intention to serve the four million North Americans who had no representation in the English Parliament, hoping thereby to achieve reparation for the sin of entering Parliament by means of one of the few surviving rotten boroughs, Launceston in North Cornwall.

Haliburton's literary and other energies did not wane during his years in Parliament. In 1859, he published *The Season Ticket* in the *Dublin University Magazine*. Two visits to North America followed, in successive years, 1860 and 1861. In North America during September 1860, Haliburton spent time in Halifax trying to untangle the legal impediments of his pension dispute and then travelled to Toronto, meeting with Sir John Beverley Robinson's son to lay the basis of a venture that became the 'Canada Land and Emigration Company.'[1]

The Canada Land and Emigration Company was incorporated in April 1861 for the purpose of settling a tract of land near the centre of Canada West, approximately 450,000 acres, divided into townships, a large proportion being surveyed and ready for immediate settlement. Haliburton polished the company prospectus in March 1861 for the public announcement. He became the company's first chairman, responsible for a capital of £250,000. In 1863, delays were reported in concluding final arrangements with the government of Upper Canada and in the actual settlement of the lands, although the problem was regarded as only a temporary setback to the profits that the directors were confident they would eventually reap. Despite Haliburton's hard work, there was no immediate financial reward for the shareholders.[2]

Throughout his later years in England, Haliburton's contacts with visiting North American businessmen were frequent, and some of the

Photograph of Haliburton by Mayall, published in D.J. Pound, *The Drawing-Room Portrait Gallery of Eminent Personages*, 1860

Photograph of Haliburton by Parish and Co., Halifax

surviving notes hint at a broad range of business activity. Haliburton's involvement from 1864 to 1865 with the activities of two highly successful joint-stock ventures, the Credit Foncier Company Limited and its successor, the Credit Mobilier Company Limited, suggest that had he lived longer he might have begun to derive some real financial benefits from his business contacts in England.[3]

Wood-engraved portrait of Haliburton, published in the *Illustrated London News*, 9 September 1865

Haliburton did not live to reap many rewards. His health deteriorated slowly but surely after 1863, and he did not long survive the closure of Parliament in July 1865. He died at Gordon House on 27 August 1865. His life in the community of Isleworth had been as full as his business life in London, in addition to his activity as an MP. He died leaving effects of less than six thousand pounds, hardly a great sum, for he never recovered the full cost of building Clifton. Mrs Haliburton lived on at Gordon House for only two more years. She then moved to Bridge House, Richmond, and died almost two decades later in 1886.

Haliburton's parliamentary and business career at the close of his life reveals his tireless interest in almost every aspect of development in the nineteenth century. He was always championing railways, bridges, steamships, and North America. Politically, Haliburton remained a Tory, unable to co-ordinate his interest in mechanical advance with the political changes that accompanied them. He was well aware of the social changes they brought, for his response was typically Victorian: he was a devotee of philanthropy and down-to-earth good works.[4] What has been forgotten is how successful he was in England during his last years. Although he fell in and out of friendship with men like Joseph Howe and Richard Bentley, and although he fought long and hard against his native province over a 'paltry pension,' he was always a proud ambassador for Nova Scotia. His life was characterized by bouts of high energy followed by moments of extreme frustration and despondency. But he was never despondent for long. His personality was both complex and resilient and is of compelling interest to the student of Canadian literary and political history.

1 See Julia Jarvis, *Three Centuries of Robinsons. The Story of a Family* (Toronto [?] 1953) 154.
2 *Money Market Review*, 2 August 1862: 83 and 104
3 *Money Market Review*, 5 March 1864: 245; and the *Banker's Magazine*, October 1864: 967–72
4 See Richard A. Davies, 'Thomas Haliburton in Isleworth, 1856–65,' *Dalhousie Review* 57 (1977): 619–27.

---

176 To Richard Bentley

[Coed Coch, Abergele, Wales?]

Dear sir

30th Jany – [1859]

I send you the first sheets of the article,[1] I will continue to supply them as fast as Mrs Haliburton can copy them – Could you send me those two or three Times newspapers, containing the correspondence on Vancouver's Island – about ten days or a fortnight ago[2] –

My address till the 8th Feby I will give you on the other note, & will you forward the proof sheets there –

Always yours
T.C. Haliburton

Honble
Mr Justice Haliburton
Coed Coch
Abergele
N.W.

Harvard MS *Pub.*: ed. W.I. Morse, 89–90

1 The article on the 'Overland Route' solicited for *Bentley's Quarterly Review*. The letter is in Sarah Harriet's hand, not Haliburton's.
2 *The Times*, 19 January 1859: 6, cols c–f: a lead article 'From our own correspondent,' on the subject of 'British Columbia'

---

177 To Richard Bentley

Coed Coch
Abergele
North Wales

My dear sir –   1st. Feby [18]59

I enclose another sheet of msst.[1] *pray send proofs daily* as time is short –
What do you think of Miss Howes msst.[2]
This is 3d letter with enclosure –

Yours alwys
Th C Haliburton

Harvard MS *Pub.*: ed. W.I. Morse, 89

1 The article for *Bentley's Quarterly Review*.
2 Julia Ward Howe (1819–1910), American poetess and philanthropist, author of the 'Battle Hymn of the Republic.' The manuscript is possibly her travelogue, *A Trip to Cuba*, published in book form in 1859.

178 To Richard Bentley

Coed Coch
Abergele
4th. Feby [18]59

My dear sir –

I received your note by yesterdays mail – You misunderstood me, when you supposed I intended the article to be unfinished and continued – I meant merely to exclude Vancouver & Columbia from it & to conclude it with the overland route – I intended to reserve those two colonies for an entirely seperate and distinct article, for the subject is too large for one article –

As far [as] this article goes it will be complete, the title[1] of it only will be changed – I have had no proofs & if they do not come tomorrow pray give orders that they may be sent to me to the underneath address –

      Yours trly
      Th. C. Haliburton

Address
Otely Park
Ellesmere[2]

Harvard MS *Pub.*: ed. W.I. Morse, 90–1

1 The MS reads 'tittle' or 'titlle.'
2 The home of Charles Kynaston Mainwaring (1803–61). Ellesmere is a market town sixteen miles north-north-west of Shrewsbury.

179 To Richard Bentley

[Otely Park, Ellesmere?]
Sunday – 14th Feby. [1859][1]

My dear sir –

I now send the last manuscript of the article[2] – I also return proof as far as it has gone –

 My address will be till you hear from me
      Justice Haliburton
      Miss Darwin[3]
      Shrewsberry –

Let me see the last proofs –
I shall be home next Saturday ni[ght[4] – Will] you come & dine?
      T.C. Haliburton

Harvard MS *Pub.*: ed. W.I. Morse, 84

1. The next letter helps to confirm the date here.
2. On the 'Overland Route' for *Bentley's Quarterly Review*
3. The Darwins were a well known Shrewsbury family. Besides the eminent naturalist Charles Darwin, there were four daughters and one other son. At this time, two of the daughters remained unmarried, Susan Elizabeth (1803–66) and Emily Catherine (1810–66). The 'Misses Darwin' lived at Mount Frankwell, Shrewsbury.
4. Haliburton arrived home on Thursday, 18 February.

---

180 To Richard Bentley

Gordon House
Isleworth

My dear sir –

18th. Feby [18]59

I have just time to say I have arrived at home, and the first thing that met me, was a letter of Lord Robert Cecil,[1] saying that the article on the overland route, was to be postponed, as it would be too extended, if completed on the present scale – This is a mistake, as the article is completed – No one article can embrace those colonies, on the Pacific and the overland route, to do justice to the subject – Nor is it necessary that it should be continued, as far as it goes it is complete –

I had no idea, when I undertook this at your request, that I should be first hurried, and then told it was not required, for it has occupied me, while away from home, in a manner very inconvenient –

I should prefer not to continue to write for the quarterly, and as it can be dispensed with in this number, it will be no inconvenience to dispense with future contributions – The proof of the last sheet has not come – Will you send it to me, and if you can, The Times of yesterday, & the day before 16 & 17th.[2] –

I hope to see you at dinner tomorrow –

Yours alwys
Th C Haliburton

– I have not time to write to Lod. R. Cecil tonight, but will when I see you –

Harvard MS *Pub.*: ed. W.I. Morse, 91–2

1. Editor of *Bentley's Quarterly Review*
2. Haliburton wanted a report of 'Exploration of the Rocky Mountains,' delivered to the Royal Geographical Society (*The Times*, 16 February 1859: 12, col. d). In *The Times* of 17 February 1859 is another long report on the goldfields of British Columbia (9, cols b, c, and d).

181 To Richard Bentley

Gordon House
[Isleworth]
19th. Feby [18]59

My dear sir –

Last night on my return home, I found a letter from Lord Robert Cecil, saying that there would not be room for the article on the overland route in your forthcoming quarterly – I suppose this means that it is too long – If so I am of the same opinion – I wrote it on this extended scale because you said the longer the better – If it is too long it can be easily cut down, and perhaps much expunged with advantage – Let me know what number of pages you require and I can very easily reduce it to the size you require –

It is to be regretted that you or your editor had not communicated this to me while it was in progress, for it would have saved me a great deal of trouble – One reason for making it so long, besides your express wish, was that the evidence given as to the nature of the country thro which this route is to pass, is of a very contradictory character – The Hudson Bay Co having denied every statement in its favor – I thought it best therefore to examine the testimony so as to prove the accuracy of the view I had taken – Much however can be struck out some with great advantage and more without any injury – Let me know the size you wish it reduced to at once and you can have it on Tuesday morning – As it is I have been put to much needless trouble – Yours T.C.H.

Harvard MS *Pub.*: ed. W.I. Morse, 92–3

182 To Richard Bentley

[Gordon House,
Isleworth]
Wednesday evening [24 February 1859][1]

I have revised the sheets, – You will see I have struck *out 8 pages* – I cant strike out more without spoiling it – But I have marked a few passages that may go into small print as they are extracts –

You need not send it again to me – It is all right –
I shall be in town tomorrow and will try to see you –

I think the article as it stands, a very good one, in all respects –

Harvard MS *Pub.*: ed. W.I. Morse, 95–6

1 I have dated this letter 24 February 1859, as Haliburton is still checking proofs for the ill-fated 'Overland Route' article. On 25 February, Bentley wrote to say that the article would not, after all, appear in the first issue of the new quarterly.

183 To Richard Bentley

Gordon House
Isleworth
25th. Feby [18]59

My dear sir –

I have just received your note, saying that the article on the overland route, will not appear in the first number of your quarterly –

I acquit you of all blame, and it is a matter of indifference to me, whether it is used or not –

You must excuse me however, from ever looking at it again, or in any way revising it – You can either use it, or burn it – I can only say, if you do use it, the shape it was in, before the last pencil revise at your office, was the best, and that what was then struck out, rather injured, than improved it –

If it was originally too minute, and diffuse, (which I think myself it was,) you must recollect, it was extended in compliance with your opinion, that the longer it was, the more acceptable it would be to you –

I have had a great deal of trouble with it, as you know, *and really cannot consent to touch it again* – It is not for me to express an opinion upon the article, but I sincerely trust, on your account, that its place has been filled by a better one,[1] and on a subject of more importance, as well as more general interest –

Wishing you every success in your undertaking, I am, my dear sir

Yours always
Th. C. Haliburton

To
R. Bentley Eqr.

Harvard MS *Pub.*: ed. W.I. Morse, 93–4

1 The first number contained an uninspiring article on 'English Politics and Parties.'

184 To Richard Bentley

Gordon House
Isleworth
9th. March [18]59

My dear sir –

If you will send me from library Grattons work,[1] I will review it for you & begin in time – I heard it denounced greatly the other day in a company where I was, a person saying it was enough to close every door in America against an English traveller –

With reference to the article on the overland route to express candidly my opinion to you, as it was written to order, and cost me great labor, I think you ought to send me a cheque for twenty guineas[2] – But I leave this to yr. own idea of what is right –

I can return Grattons book when I have done with it

Yours always
Th. C. Haliburton

R Bentley Eqr.

Harvard MS *Pub.*: ed. W.I. Morse, 94

1 Thomas Colley Grattan (1792–1864), British consul at Boston, and author of *Civilised America*, 2 vols (London 1859). The book was characterized by rash and sometimes abusive generalizations about the Americans.
2 Rates of payment were ten guineas per sheet of sixteen printed pages (Gettmann, 145).

185 To the Electors of the Borough of Launceston[1]

Launceston, April 29, 1859.

Gentlemen,

I have now the agreeable duty to perform, of thanking you for the honor you have done me, in electing me to represent you in Parliament.

The manner in which this has been done has greatly enhanced the value of the election, and has left an impression on my mind, that neither time nor distance can obliterate. I have endeavoured as far as possible, to see every elector, and to visit every part of the borough, and I have every where met with a kind and courteous reception, not merely from the conservative party, but from those who entertain political opinions at variance with my own. This is not always the case in elections, where party feeling not infrequently assumes a hostile character, and I beg to assure you, that it is particularly gratifying to a man like me, who while conceding to others, what he claims for himself, an independent exercise of judgment, is most desirous to be considered the representative of all classes and interests in the borough. To each and all of you therefore gentlemen, I return my most heartfelt acknowledgements.

The present crisis both in our domestic and foreign policy,[2] requires the exercise of anxious deliberation, and great caution in the representatives of the people and I assure you that it is a great source of satisfaction to me, to know that Her Majesty's ministers are fully equal to the emergency, and that I shall best serve the interests of the country, by giving them such support, as it is in the power of an humble individual like myself to afford.

The present is not a suitable occasion to discuss the particular topics of national interest that are likely to be considered in Parliament. I solicited the honor of your support, upon conservative principles, which, (however they may have been misrepresented by those who appropriate all liberality exclusively to themselves,) will be found in practice, to combine security with progress, in the only manner in which a constitutional monarchy can be maintained. By those principles my public conduct will be regulated, and by those alone.

As regards your local interests, I invite your cooperation and assistance, and assure you it will be my pleasure as well as my duty, to promote them in any way within my power.

In conclusion, gentlemen, I cannot but express a hope, that my public duties may be so discharged, that you will not have reason to regret your choice.

> I have the honour to
> remain gentlemen,
> Your faithful and obedient servant,
> Thomas C. Haliburton

Pub.: *Launceston Weekly News*, 7 May 1859

1 Launceston was in North Cornwall. The Duke of Northumberland, Haliburton's near neighbour at Syon Park, Isleworth, Middlesex, had owned this borough since 1832, and usually selected the member himself.
2 The Franco–Austrian War in Italy broke out in April 1859 and ended in July of the same year.

186 To Richard Bentley

[Gordon House,
Isleworth?]
5th. May [18]59

Did I understand you right, that your review[1] did not come out till 1st. July –

> Write immediately
> Yours alwys
> Th C Haliburton

Harvard MS

1 Haliburton means the second issue of *Bentley's Quarterly Review*, which appeared in July 1859.

187 To Sir Edward Bulwer Lytton

Gordon House
Isleworth
3d June [18]59

My dear Sir Edward Bulwer Lytton

Some time ago you were so kind as to say, you would think of my son Robert Haliburton, a barrister of the Nova Scotia bar, for a legal appointment, in some of the recently formed colonies –

I have written out to Nova Scotia, and been furnished with testimonials, from all the judges, of the most laudatory & satisfactory character, ready to be laid before you, when occasion may require – My object in writing now, is to keep him before you, if a suitable opportunity offers[1] –

Hoping to hear of your renewed health, and the resumption of your official & Parliamentary duties,

> I am
> My dear Sir Edward Bulwer Lytton
> Yours
> Th. C. Haliburton

Lytton MS [*Ph.*]

1 According to the docketing to the letter, Bulwer Lytton replied: 'I am down &/shall have a place/when vacant.'

188 To Richard Bentley

Gordon House
Isleworth
17th. June [18]59

My dear sir –

Will you come to us on Sunday to dine & take a bed?
It is a long time since we have foregathered –

> Yours always
> Th. C. Haliburton

Harvard MS

189 To ——?

Gordon House
Isleworth
17th. Oct [18]59

My dear sir –

I shall have great pleasure in complying with your request to attend on Wednesday the 16 Nov, at the lecture of Mr. Owen[1] –

> I am dear Sir
> Yours alwys
> Th. C. Haliburton

Penn. State Univ. MS [*Ph.*]

1 Sir Richard Owen (1804–92), naturalist and lecturer

190 To Sir Richard Owen

Gordon House
Isleworth
28th Oct [18]59

My dear sir –

I beg your acceptance of a brace of Nova Scotia partridges and a steak of the moose meat of that country, just received by last steamer –

> Yours always
> Th C. Haliburton

BL Add. MS 39,954

191 To Richard Bentley

Gordon House
Isleworth

My dear sir –

7th. Decr. [18]59 –

I am grieved to say Mrs Haliburton is still confined to her bed, from internal inflammation – Yesterday & today she shews symptoms of amendment for the intervals of ease between the paroxisms of pain are of longer duration, & I hope she is now out of danger –

I have been commissioned to offer you a manuscript, please read it over & say what you will give for it, or on what terms you will publish it – I am not at liberty to say anything about the author, beyond having consented to have it dedicated to me[1] – Let me know soon your mind, for authors think the world must stand still for them – I have not read it –

If you will come on Sunday & dine with me I will give you some [fresh?] game the Duke of Northd[2] has sent me –

Yours alwys
Th. C. Haliburton

Harvard MS *Pub.*: ed. W.I. Morse, 95

1 Unidentified. See letters 195 and 196 below.
2 Sir Algernon Percy, fourth Duke of Northumberland and first Baron Prudhoe (1792–1865), admiral and patron of the arts

192 To Richard Bentley

Gordon House
Isleworth

My dear sir

4th. Jany [18]60

Pray give me your answer about manuscript in yr. hands or I shall be in a scrape –

If you do not bid for it, tell me to whom to offer it (other than Hurst and Blackett)[1] –

Write answer unmixed with other matters, for transmission to the author –

We are both improving in health –

Yours always
Th C Haliburton

Harvard MS *Pub.*: ed. W.I. Morse, 96

1 Publishers of *Sam Slick's Wise Saws* (1853), *Nature and Human Nature* (1855), and the *Address ... on North America* (1857)

193 To Richard Bentley

Gordon House
Isleworth
6th. Jany [18]60

My dear sir –

Many thanks for apprisoning me of the price of the prize book[1] – It is beyond my mark – I will send one from my library instead –

Yours alwys
Th. C. Haliburton

Harvard MS

1 Unidentified

194 To Sir William Jolliffe Bart[1]

private
Gordon House
Isleworth
7th. Jny [18]60

My dear Sir William

This will be presented to you by my old friend Mr Bentley the publisher, who has a communication to make to you on a subject which I think will commend itself to you, as most desireable for & serviceable to, the good cause[2] – He will explain his object fully himself & I shall feel greatly pleased to hear that you coincide, in the view that several of my conservative friends entertain in the matter –

Yours always
Th. C. Haliburton

Harvard MS

1 William George Hylton Jolliffe, first Baron Hilton (1800–76), politician and Conservative party whip, 1858–9. See *DNB*.
2 Probably a charity that Bentley, Haliburton, and Jolliffe shared in common.

195 To Richard Bentley

4 George Street
Hanover Sqr[1] [London]
Tuesday [early 1860?][2]

My dear sir –

Pray give me an answer about manuscript –

Yours alwys
Th. C. Haliburton

Harvard MS

1 Number 4 George Street, Hanover Square, in the census of 1862, is a boarding house run by the Peachey family (PRO, RG 9/42, 18).
2 Neither this note nor the next one can be dated precisely.

196 To Richard Bentley

[4 George Street,
Hanover Square, London?]
Thursday [early 1860?]

My dear sir –

Will you be so good as [to] give a reply about msst.[1] or return it, as the author wishes to leave town –

Yours always
Th. C. Haliburton

Harvard MS

1 The reference might be to the MS Haliburton sent Bentley on 4 January 1860. Bentley published Haliburton's *The Season Ticket* on 6 March 1860 (BL Add. MS 46,637).

197 To the Duchess of Northumberland[1]

[London, early 1860?][2]

... election[3] that has occurred ... [in my]
   We have moved into town, to the address of this letter,[4] to remain till Easter, that I may be near the House, & escape the short days, & cold nights of this time of year – Mrs Haliburton begs to unite with me, in kind

regards to your Grace, & the Duke, and I am, dear madam, your obt & very grateful sevt.

Th. C. Haliburton

Penn. State Univ. MS [*Ph.*] fragment only

1 Lady Eleanor Grosvenor (d. 5 May 1911), eldest daughter of the second Marquis of Westminster
2 The date is conjectural.
3 Unidentified
4 The address is missing. It is possibly 4 George Street, Hanover Square, although Haliburton did stay at other addresses in successive winters.

---

198 To Richard Bentley

Dear sir –

[Gordon House, Isleworth?]
Monday night [early 1860?]

I am very much annoyed to find that you have ordered the press to continue before you had the revise – It is full of errors & I feel very ill used in the matter – The tittle page is not complete nor the preface, nor the notice of its being copied from the D–U Magazine[1] –

Above all things it cannot be issued till after the magazine reaches London[2]

I wouldnt for fifty guineas this should happen – Indeed [i]t must not occur – It will compromise my character – I did not think you could treat me this way –

Pray stop it at once & let me see you or your clerk –

Yours
Th C Haliburton

Harvard MS *Pub.*: ed. W.I. Morse, 100

1 A note indicating its prior publication in the *Dublin University Magazine* was inserted.
2 Bentley called on Haliburton personally (21 February) and the next day wrote a terse note to the editor of the *Dublin University Magazine* to say that he would be publishing *The Season Ticket* simultaneously with the appearance of the magazine's last instalment of the work. Bentley did not think it would interfere with sales of the magazine (BL Add. MS, 46,642, f. 348).

199 To Richard Bentley

Gordon House
Isleworth –
2d Apl. 60

My dear sir –

It is impossible for me to express my astonishment on perusing this sheet in the Dublin University Magazine[1] – you bought an *anonymous work*,[2] & have nailed the authorship on me and made it an *avowed one* – I ask you if this is fair? There is no mistake in this matter – I told you over and over again I could not and would not avow this work, for many reasons, *for any price* – I sold it low on that account, – You immediately fasten my name to it, and get the advantage of that name – I dont mind other peoples ascriptions, but see what you have done – You advertise it with a notice from the critic 'that it is well known to be from the pen of Sam Slick' – Who is supposed to know better than the publisher, who is the author of a work put forth by him – If I was not the author, then you were not authorised to attribute it to me – If I am, you are precluded by agreement from saying so –

How can I go on writing after this,[3] you have knocked my pen out of my hand – I hardly know what to do – I am quite dumbfoundered – As you yourself said it would be worth more if my name was attached to it, now that you have used that name, having purchased it at the anonymous price, I feel myself entitled to compensation in this matter – For knocking up my pen nothing can compensate me –

Let me hear from you at Leigh House, Ardwicke, Manchester[4] where I go on Wednesday morning

Yours always
Th. C. Haliburton

There was another advertisement to which I objected, and Mr Marsh[5] said it was a mistake and should not occur again –

Harvard MS *Pub.*: ed. W.I. Morse, 96–7

1 The 'sheet' might well have been a loose-leaf insertion, sent as an advertisement to subscribers.
2 Bentley's reply alludes to the rumours of Haliburton's authorship originating in the Manchester Review (BL Add. MS 46,642, f. 209 verso, a letter sent 4 April 1860).
3 The final words of *The Season Ticket* are: 'Whether I shall renew it ... I have not yet

decided, but this sheet completes the memorabilia of my present "Season Ticket."' The *Dublin University Magazine* for April 1860 advertised 'No 1 of A New Series of Sketches By the author of the "Season Ticket,"' but none appeared.
4 Haliburton was staying with W.B. Watkins.
5 Bentley's manager

200 To W.B. Watkins

Gordon House
Isleworth

My dear friend –

12th. June [18]60

Mrs H tells me she has received a letter from Helen saying you will be here on Saturday – We shall be delighted to see you, and I assure you the sight of you will do me much good, for I have been a great invalid lately –

I am like a railway engine, I have a '*tender behind*' – which reminds me to advise you to provide an air cushion for yr. journey, I find great relief from one – I had hoped that dear Mrs Watkins would have accompanied you, but I hope she will follow with Helen – Counting the time till you come I am my dear friend with kindest love to all yr. circle in which Mrs H cordially joins –

I am yours always
Th. C. Haliburton

PS. As our old ferryman[1] says, 'I say *en core* to this' –

S.H.H.[2] –

Massey College MS [*Ph.*]

1 The Railshead Ferry crossed the Thames from just outside the grounds of Gordon House. See also Alan C.B. Urwin, *Railshead, Isleworth* (1973), plate 8. An ordnance-survey map of 1865 clearly indicates the ferry's route.
2 The last remark is in Sarah Harriet Haliburton's hand.

201 To Sir John Beverley Robinson

Toronto 16th. Sepr [18]60

My dear Chief Justice –

I had hoped to have had the pleasure of calling upon you this morning but the heat of yesterday has fevered me and rendered me otherwise so poorly that I am obliged to keep house today – I suffered so severely from the heat yesterday that I have abandoned the idea of going southward & shall leave tomorrow for N York & Boston en route for Halifax – Please to present my respects to Lady Robinson[1] & believe me my dear Sir William[2] –

Yours always
Th. C. Haliburton

PAC MS

1 Emma Walker, who married John Beverley Robinson in 1817
2 The manuscript reads 'Sir William,' even though the letter is addressed to 'My dear Chief Justice,' i.e., Sir John Beverley Robinson. One explanation might be that Haliburton was still feverish and not thinking clearly. Sir William Robinson died in 1836.

---

202 To Joseph Howe

Gordon House
Isleworth
20th. Oct [18]60

Dear Howe –

Immediately after my arrival in town,[1] I proceeded according to promise on Thursday morning to Portsmouth to see your son – On my arrival there I found that Haslaar hospital[2] was not at Portsmouth but at Gosport,[3] and I took a cab and went to the chain point to cross in the steamer – When I got there I found there was a furious gale blowing, the steamer had smashed her chain, & could not run, and that the only way of crossing was by a wherry,[4] while I saw that those who landed were drenched through –

Full of gout as I am, I was afraid of a ducking, and in great perplexity got another cab and returned to station to ascertain, if I could get round by rail – I found I could but that I should have to stay all night at Gosport – Having a return ticket and not money enough by me, to meet such charges & a fresh ticket I enquired if they had an officer of intelligence, that I could send across in a boat, and having found one to my mind, I gave him your letter to me & my card and told him to go to the hospital see the surgeon & get his report & above all to see your son, to tell him I was at Portsmouth, where I had come for the purpose of seeing him, to ask him how he was, and to enquire if he wanted any thing or if there was any way I could serve him, but above all to write me a line that I might know my commission was executed –

Having despatched him, I waited four hours for him at the station when he returned half drowned – He reported he had gone to the hospital, & the surgeon told him your son had been discharged from hospital the day before (Wednesday the 17th.) and was then on board The Victory[5] – Having enjoyed on the man to see your son personally, he got a boatman with some difficulty (for it was blowing like the devil) to take him off to the ship – He saw your son, who said he had quite recovered, tho he looked as if he had been ill & his hair looked short as if it had been cut off in hospital, and that he wanted for nothing, & expected leave of absence in a few days, – He had just received yr. letters by mail – I enclose his letter to me – I have written to him to invite him to come & see me as soon as I return from Paris – I didnt get home till near midnight – Give my love to Mrs Howe and tell her, she has now no cause for uneasiness –

       Yours alwys
       T C Haliburton

King's College, Halifax, MS

1 Haliburton had been in North America during September and had seen Howe.
2 A hospital ship
3 Not far from Portsmouth
4 A light, shallow rowing boat used for carrying passengers
5 Nelson's famous flagship at Trafalgar, a hospital ship for most of the century

---

203 To Richard Bentley

Gordon House
Isleworth
30th. Ocr. [18]60

My dear sir

Your letter has only just this minute 6 aclock p m been handed to me –

I have enclosed it to Mr. Porter[1] one of the committee of the Athenaeum[2] an old friend of mine and formerly (last year I believe) in direction of Union Club[3] begging him to do what he can for your son –

I wish I had known of it before – I have also written to a Mr. Parker[4] a member of that club – I do not know the committee –

I am sorry to hear that you have a lame foot but hope you will soon be enabled to come & see us – I have much to tell you of a most charming visit to America – in haste

Yours alwys
Th. C. Haliburton

Harvard MS *Pub.*: ed. W.I. Morse, 98

1 'Edward Porter' is listed as a committeeman '(C)' in Francis Gledstanes Waugh's *Members of the Athenaeum Club, 1842 to 1887* (London 1888).
2 Founded 17 February 1824, devoted to the association of authors, literary men, MPs, and promoters of the fine arts
3 The Union Club was a non-partisan club for politicians and professional and mercantile men.
4 Three Parkers are listed in Waugh: '1858, Parker, Charles Stewart'; '1844, Parker, James'; '1826, Parker, Right Hon. John (C).'

---

204 To Richard Bentley

Gordon House
Isleworth
2d Nor. [18]60 –

My dear sir –

I am shocked at both the ingratitude & falsehood of the govt. in saying that they have no power to grant a public funeral to Lord Dundonald[1] – No man ever merited so well all the honors a nation could pay him as his Lordship did, which is not a matter of opinion, but of history – The Duke of Wellington if my memory serves me died in September,[2] at a period when Parliament was not sitting, and the same power which conferred upon him a public funeral, exists now to pay a similar honor to the gallant admiral –

If he were my father, England under such circumstances should not hold his remains, for I should convey his body to that channel in which he defended his ungrateful country, and commit it to the sea, with the funeral rights of a sailor – His honors are immortal, and he should repose in a temple not built by hands – Every man, possessing a generous mind must blush for his country, when he hears of this decision of the govt.

Yours always
Th. C. Haliburton

Harvard MS *Pub.*: ed. W.I. Morse, 98–9

1 Thomas Cochrane, tenth Earl of Dundonald (1775–1860), admiral. The announcement of the death of the Earl of Dundonald at his residence in Kensington appeared in *The Times*, 1 November 1860: 9. Cochrane had at one time been commander-in-chief of the North American station.
2 Arthur Wellesley, first Duke of Wellington (1769–1852). He died on 14 September and was given a monumental funeral.

---

205 To Richard Bentley

Gordon House
Isleworth
5th. Nor. [18]60

My dear sir –

I shall be going to town in a day or two, and will stop at Wandsworth[1] on my way & see you – I am very sorry indeed to hear you are still laid up with your foot – I know what that is –

If you come here arrange to stay over night – Mrs H. sends kind regards – Yours always

Th C Haliburton

Harvard MS

1 Bentley lived at East Hill, Wandsworth, Surrey, south of the Thames, which happened to be on Haliburton's route from Isleworth to the City.

---

206 To Richard Bentley

[Gordon House,
Isleworth]
Saturday 10th. Nr. [1860]

My dear sir –

I begin to doubt the evidence of my own senses, and to question whether the real and substantial Mr. Bentley whom I thought I had had the pleasure of seeing, is not after all, an unreal and unsubstantial phantom, for I cannot get a sight of him again –

Here have I been for two weeks endeavouring to come in actual contact with you, and cant find you, there being nothing but a 'habitation and a name'[1] –

Now I really do want to see you, as at last I am actually off for Gloucester,[2] and if you will put this matter out of all doubt by saying either that you will meet me, or that 'you will see me damned first' you will very much oblige –

Yours always
T C Haliburton

Harvard MS *Pub.*: ed. W.I. Morse, 99

1 *A Midsummer Night's Dream*, v, i, 7:
   'And, as imagination bodies forth
   The forms of things unknown, the poet's pen
   Turns them to shapes, and gives to airy nothing
   A local habitation and a name.'
2 Probably to stay with Edmund Hopkinson

---

207 To Richard Bentley

My dear sir –

Gordon House
Isleworth
15th. Dcr. [18]60

Many thanks for the valuable parcel of books you were so kind as to send to me –

I hope to see you on Monday night at Mr Moodys[1] party, & thank you personally – If I miss you, what night can you come and dine & take a bed? I have a good deal to say to you –

       Yours always
       Th C Haliburton

Harvard MS *Pub.*: ed. W.I. Morse, 100

1 A 'Literary Reunion' given by Charles Edward Mudie (1818–90), London stationer and bookseller. (See the *Standard* 18 December 1860: 3, col. c.) 'Judge Haliburton' is listed as one of those in attendance, but not Richard Bentley.

---

208 To Richard Bentley

My dear sir –

Gordon House
Isleworth
21st. Feby [18]61

You have a difficult person to deal with,[1] and one that requires careful handling – If you will come to us on Saturday or Sunday we shall be glad to see you & we can talk it over, there will then be time enough for answer –

If you mean by the 250, the residue of 500 I should not think of depositing it – All she is entitled to is the first moiety – I shall be absent all day tomorrow –

       Yours alwys
       Th C Haliburton

Harvard MS *Pub.*: ed. W.I. Morse, 101

1 No obvious clues can be found in Bentley's *Letterbook* as to the subject of this discussion. Haliburton usually assisted Bentley with authors that he (Haliburton) knew personally.

209 To H. Montgomerie[1]

Gordon House
Isleworth[2]
4th. March [18]61

My dear sir –

I have made some alterations in the prospectus[2] which I now return to you – Some of them are mere verbal corrections, which I think may improve it, others are more substantial –

I think something should be said of the climate, as the severe frosts & heavy snows of the lower province many people think are applicable to the whole country – I have therefore added a paragraph on that subject – The reference to the Canada Company,[3] is renewed in another place, I have condensed the two & placed them together – You can adopt or reject any or all of these as you think proper –

Dont wait for me tomorrow as I fear I cannot be punctual –

The Hold Company,[4] meets tomorow not at 74 Old Broadstreet, but at Mr. Abrahams office[5] in Westminster at 1, so as to enable the promotors to attend on the Committee on Bills to see whether they have complied with the standing orders[6] – This is very inconvenient to me, and will prevent my keeping time at the Land Companys meeting –

I shall however be there shortly after ½ past 2 –

It would be adviseable therefore not to wait but to proceed to business, at once – I think it would be adviseable to appoint the chairman tomorrow, so as to perfect the prospectus –

When you have gone through that document, it may be considered as finally settled, but before it goes to the press I should like to see Lord Bury[7] (having missed him on Friday) about Sir Allens[8] name, which is of more use now than it will be here after –

I shall endeavour to see him Monday night, & obtain his consent – I will write you from the House,[9] immediately –

Yours always
Th. C. Haliburton

H. Montgomerie Esqr –

University of Iowa MS [*Ph.*]

1 The initial of the correspondent looks like 'R,' but Haliburton's dealings at this time were with Hugh Edmonstone Montgomery, a merchant of Gracechurch Street, London, one of the directors of the Canada Land and Emigration Company.
2 The prospectus was announced in *The Times*, 25 April 1861.
3 The Canada Land and Emigration Company, which purchased land through the Canada Agency Association
4 Most likely a reference to the Canada Agency Association, incorporated in April 1861.
5 Probably 'Abraham J. Roberts, Esq. 15 Lombard Street,' who was a director of the Canada Land and Emigration Company
6 Exchequer bills were government bills of more than twelve months' duration.
7 William Coutts Keppel, seventh Earl of Albemarle and Viscount Bury (1832–94), MP, former superintendent of Indian affairs in Canada, 1854–7, and one of the directors of the Canada Agency Association
8 Sir Allan Napier MacNab, first Baronet (1798–1862), politician, businessman, land speculator, lawyer, and soldier. See *DCB*.
9 The House of Commons

---

210 To Richard Bentley

Gordon House Isleworth
26th March [18]61

My dear sir

How could you be so absurd as to write me such a foolish letter? – How could it ever enter your head that I could say or write anything to hurt your feelings? I cant tell you how much you have astonished me, upon my word I should have as soon expected to be had up for stealing, or what is still more impossible, for committing a rape –

There was an old maid died last week under very similar circumstances to what you describe – Her father left her 5,000 a year on condition that she would never marry –

Well she never thought of marriage, such an idea never entered into her head, but the moment she found she could not marry, if she did wish to, she fretted so, she died in two months – I think you are about as reasonable –

But as offence has been taken I wish distinctly to say I never intended to give it, and am very sorry for it, & beg your pardon, sincerely regretting having written anything so carelessly as to admit of an unpleasant construction

On Thursday I am off to Launceston[1] – I wish the journey was over –

Yours always
Th. C. Haliburton

Harvard MS *Pub.*: ed. W.I. Morse, 101–2

1 The *Launceston Weekly News*, 6 April 1861, reported Haliburton's visit to the borough. He arrived on 1 April, delivered a lecture on North American law at the Mechanic's Institute, and the next day (a Tuesday) laid the foundation stone of the Launceston Grammar School and participated in the civic celebrations.

211 To Richard Bentley

My dear sir –

Gordon House
Isleworth
Saturday [8 June 1861][1]

I am very sorry indeed that you did not receive my letter of Tuesday morning last – On that day I received a summons to attend the division on the Maynooth Grant,[2] and immediately sat down and wrote to you expressing my regret that it would deprive me of the pleasure of dining with you at the Stationers Hall[3] that day – The letter was posted at 11 on Tuesday and fearing it might miss you if addressed to New Burlington St[4] I directed to Stationers Hall & marked it immediate and in due course it ought to have reached you before 5 – I enclosed also the card that it might not put you to the expense of a guest who could not be there –

I am very sorry indeed that this incident should have annoyed you, and assure you it was a great disappointment to me –

Yours always
Th. C. Haliburton

Harvard MS *Pub.*: ed. W.I. Morse, 103

1 The letter can be dated precisely by his presence at the vote on the Maynooth College Bill. See note 2 below.
2 Since 1845, the Board of Works had been responsible for the upkeep of the buildings of the College of Maynooth in Ireland. In 1853 the usual vote to grant the necessary money was narrowly lost, which forced Parliament to introduce an annual 'Maynooth College Bill' to enable repairs to take place. Haliburton refers to the attempt to defeat the bill on Tuesday, 4 June 1861, an attempt that failed by seventy-seven votes. Haliburton is listed among those who voted for a committee to explore the withdrawal of support for Maynooth College (the *Standard*, 6 June 1861: 2, col. d). Haliburton was not present for debates on the Maynooth grant in other years.
3 The Stationers' Company had received its charter from Philip and Mary in May 1557. It was originally established to inspect printing offices and to seize and destroy offending material in the presses. Later, Stationers' Hall, situated between Ludgate Hill and Amen Corner, became a registry for copyright publications. The hall was used for dining purposes by publishers and their guests.
4 Bentley's office

212 To Arthur Haliburton[1]

Gordon House
Isleworth.

Dear Arthur –

22d Aug [18]61

I enclose Weldons[2] and Susans[3] letters for you to read –
   I am off to Liverpool tomorrow and embark on Saturday at 9 a.m.[4] –
   I see by papers Robert[5] is appt. Secretary to Industrial Exhibition whatever that is[6] at salary at rate of 300 per annum –
   Wilkins[7] is sanguine about pension, non ego –

                      Yours always
                      God bless you
                      Th C Haliburton

Penn. State Univ. MS

1 After his posting to Montreal, Arthur returned to London, where he worked until his retirement in 1897.
2 The Hon. John Wesley Weldon, St John, NB, judge of the Supreme Court of New Brunswick, who married Haliburton's eldest daughter Susannah in 1848. She was his second wife.
3 Susannah Lucy Anne Haliburton (1817–99). She had one child, Haliburton Weldon, who died in 1873, aged twenty-four.
4 For a trip to Nova Scotia, possibly to argue his pension case
5 Haliburton's second son. He was appointed secretary to Nova Scotia's exhibit at the International Exhibition in London, 1862. See *Catalogue of the Nova Scotian Department* (Halifax 1862).
6 The International Exhibition of 1862 was modelled on the Great Exhibition of 1851 and designed to reflect the great advances of the previous decade.
7 Lewis Morris Wilkins (1801–85), politician and judge, successor to Haliburton on the Supreme Court bench and son of the Supreme Court judge of the same name who died in 1848. Haliburton's pension dispute was in its fifth year.

213 To W.H. Merritt[1]

Gordon House
Isleworth

My dear sir –

[21 November 1861?][2]

I have just had the pleasure to receive your note – and am delighted at the prospect of seeing you again – I'll call on you at the British Hotel

Cockspur St.³ at 1 aclock on Thursday next – If that hour will not suit you
– name another & I will 'like a *wooden clock*' keep time exactly –

        Yours always
        Th. C. Haliburton

PAC MS

1 William Hamilton Merritt (1773–1862), soldier, merchant, promoter, and politician
2 The letter lacks a date. At the top of the manuscript is 'Nov 4 56,' in a hand other than Haliburton's. At the foot of the manuscript is '21 Nr 61,' also in another hand. The manuscript also contains other illegible docketing.
3 The British Coffee House, No. 27, Cockspur Street, London, designed by Robert Adam, was a 'great resort of Scotsmen,' and, along with the adjacent No. 26, was known as the British Hotel.

---

214 To Joseph Howe

        Gordon House
        Isleworth
My dear Howe   25th. Nor [18]61

I was very much disappointed at not seeing you, when Mrs Haliburton & myself called the other day – I shall try to get to town tomorrow, if possible, but in the event of my not being able to do so, will you & Mrs Howe come & dine with us on Saturday & stay over Sunday? – The way here is by the Richmond line from Waterloo to Richmond, where all the cab-drivers know where I live – If you can come Arthur shall shew you the way – Drop me a line –

        Yours always
        Th. C. Haliburton

Harvard MS

1 Howe was visiting London.

---

215 To Richard Bentley

        Gordon House
        Isleworth.
My dear sir   Thursday [30 January 1862]¹

I return you the chapter on wines, which is a most valuable addition to the Cooks Guide² – This chapter alone is worth the price of the book – It is also well written – The other chapters are for *the cook*, this is for *the host* –

It might suggest almost a new tittle, if there were added some instructions for keeping wine &c –

'The Cook and Butlers Guide' – or perhaps it might suggest another volume called 'The Butlers Guide'[3] – My instructions for that person in the various branches of his duty –

A point worth thinking of, for it would have an *immense* sale[4] –

We expect you on Sunday – a meal and bed awaits you –

Did you see my lecture in Standard of Tuesday,[5] or Morning Herald of that day?

If so I hope it met your approbation –

Yours alwys
Th. C. Haliburton

Harvard MS *Pub.*: ed. W.I. Morse, 104–5

1 The letter can be dated by the allusion to Haliburton's 'Speech on the American Crisis.'
2 Charles Francatelli's *The Cook's Guide* was published on 30 August 1861. Bentley reprinted it several times in 1861 and was considering additions to it in early 1862.
3 Haliburton's advice does not appear to have been taken as the book continued to sell under its original title.
4 Haliburton was right. Fifteen hundred sold at once, enabling Bentley to print another 500. During October and November 1861, Bentley reprinted 8,000 copies of *The Cook's Guide*. Sales continued to be enormous: they rose to 30,000 by 1872 and 84,000 by 1898 (Gettmann, 81–2).
5 Reported in the *Standard*, 28 January 1862: 2, cols d–f: 'The Hon. Mr. Justice Haliburton, M.P. On the American Crisis'

---

216 To Joseph Howe

Gordon House
Isleworth
20th. Feby [18]62

My dear Howe –

I was very much disappointed at not hearing from you by the last mail, relative to the pension, and the course the government intended to take thereon – I must now appeal to your sense of justice in this matter – The govt. has had the advantage of two trials, and have had two judgements against them[1] – Surely this will warrant them in paying me what is my due, unless they want to make popularity out of resistance – As a friend, when right is on my side, and law, surely I might expect consideration from you – It is not the way I acted to you, when you were out of power, in former days – to run a muck against you – Recollect money is the smallest part to me, if there is an appeal – How will it look here, that my native country, one too which I have advanced and illustrated, has fought me for five years, on a paltry pension of £40 (for that is what it is in our money) had two trials, & still appeals?

Why it will be said, if I was what I ought to be, they would have submitted to the decision of their own courts, & have been glad, of the opportunity of rewarding an old servant, especially one who cant long receive it, by paying him at once –

It will look like personal hatred, and surely, in regard to me & the memory of past days, you will not subject me to this indignity – I dont ask you, to assent to an unjust demand, because of old friendship, but to give me the benefit that the poorest man is entitled to, to be paid when the court has decided twice in his favor – But I do ask you not to put me in a position here, by appeal, to be considered as a man, that his own country men, would die rather do justice to him –

Recollect there has been no appeal that I can recollect, since 1818 from the court in N.S., and could you make that appeal, against a man the country owes more to than his pension –

I rely on your justice – & I hope from your friendship, what it appears, the courts are compelled by law to grant me –

> In great haste
> Yours alwys
> Th. C. Haliburton

Pray drop me a line –

PANS MS

1 See Chittick, 565–73.

---

217 To Hodgson[1]

Dear sir –

Gordon House
Isleworth
15th. May [18]62

Mr. A Owen[2] is very anxious that I should see you upon the subject of a controversy he has had with the magistrates of Chester, in reference to the [Perkens Act?][3] – I am desirous of serving him if I can, but am not in possession of the facts of the case, which he tells me you are – I shall be in the House tomorrow (Friday) from ¼ past 4 till late in the evening and if you should be in town would feel much gratified if you would favor me with an interview at that time, and if not convenient to you, I will meet you at any time and place that will suit you on Monday or Tuesday –

Yours alwys
Th. C. Haliburton

Hodgson Eqr.

Dalhousie University MS

1 Identity uncertain. Circumstantial evidence suggests Haliburton might have been writing to Richard Hodgson (1812–?), MP for Tynemouth, 1861–5, whom he would have known through William Schaw Lindsay, MP for Sunderland. Hodgson was chairman of the North British Railway. However, my assumption that the letter concerns railway business is conjectural. The recipient might have been Sir Robert Hodgson, lawyer, land agent, politician, judge, and administrator (1798–1880). He was chief justice of Prince Edward Island for twenty-two years. See *DCB*.
2 Arthur Owen of Woodhouse, Sarah Harriet's uncle
3 Not traced. The reference might have something to do with a controversy then currently raging between the town council of Chester and the Birkenhead, Flintshire, and Holyhead Railway Company, over the bridging of the River Dee near Chester. See the *Chester Chronicle*, 10 May 1862.

---

218 To Rev Dr Cranewich[1]

Gordon House
[Isleworth]
June 14th 1862

Sir,

In answer to your enquiries respecting my History of Nova Scotia, I believe it is now out of print, but I think you will be able to procure a copy at Sampson Lewis' the American bookseller in the Strand.

I am, sir,
Yours obediently
T.C. Haliburton

Revd. Dr Cranewich
&c &c –

PANS MS

1 Unidentified

219 To Richard Bentley

My dear sir –

Gordon House
Isleworth
Tuesday [August/September 1862]

As your messenger waits for an answer, I opened your letter to Mrs Haliburton who is at the Exhibition[1] with some friends –
  We shall be delighted to see you & your daughter tomorrow –
  Mrs H at three goes out to drive with Lady Francis Russel[2] but will be back to dinner –
  So that if you will come at one aclock, she will be home at lunch and if you can stay to dinner I shall be here all day – the other parts of your letter she had better answer personally – Glorious weather for the harvest, tho the glass has fallen a little during the night –

Yours always
Th. C. Haliburton

Univ. of Illinois MS [*Ph.*]

1 The Industrial Exhibition opened 1 May 1862 and closed on Saturday, 1 November 1862. Haliburton's son Robert Grant was secretary to the Nova Scotia exhibit.
2 Possibly Lady Frances Anna Maria Russell, wife of the Rt Hon. Lord John Russell. Lord Russell lived at Pembroke Lodge, Richmond Park, not far from Gordon House.

220 To Mrs Fletcher?[1]

Gordon House
Isleworth
Novr 15th 1862

Mr Justice Haliburton has been from home, or would have forwarded the enclosed sooner to [Mrs Fletcher?]. He will be happy to furnish Mr Fr with any information he may require, if Mr Fr. will inform him what is the nature of that information.

PANS MS

1 Haliburton's hand is difficult to decipher. The name seems to be 'Fletcher,' but as he then abbreviates the name for the remainder of the letter it is hard to be certain.

221 To W.B. Watkins

Gordon House
Isleworth
28th. Jany [18]63

My dear sir –

I understand this note will arrive in time to congratulate you on the anniversary of your 50th. marriage day – God bless you & your excellent and most amiable wife, and may you both not only live to see but to enjoy many succeeding returns of the day – I recollect when a similar event happened to my grandfather & grandmother,[1] and a happy day it was to us all – It seemed then a very long time, but as I grow older, the time seems shorter, for you will be surprised to hear that my *first* wedding day wants but three years to complete the half century – It is not often both live to see the 50th. anniversary –

In Germany the parties are remarried again, so I shall look in the papers for an announcement of that ceremony with you –

If you were to publish the re-marriage between yourself & Mrs Watkins under her maiden name, you would puzzle your friends & acquaintances more than the last new conundrum, which is why is a bridegroom worth more than a bride? – Because a bride is always *given* away, but a bridegroom is often *sold* –

How I wish we were with your family circle on that day, to give you both our warmest & most heart felt congratulations, but as we cant have that pleasure, I must have the privilege of an old friend & write them – Mr. Mason the confederate envoy[2] dines here tomorrow, – I have asked several people to help each other to [stare?] –

Love to your daughters from
self & wife
Yours alwys
Th. C. Haliburton

W. Watkins Eqr

PANS MS

1 William Haliburton married Susannah Otis, his first cousin, on 9 April 1761, and they celebrated their fiftieth wedding anniversary in 1811, when T.C. Haliburton was fifteen.
2 James Murray Mason (1798–1871), US senator, appointed commissioner of the Confederacy to Great Britain and France. See *DAB*.

222 To J.E. Bradfield[1]

18 Park Street
Westminster[2] [London]
13th. Feby [18]63

Dear sir –

I shall be happy to see you at 10 aclock any morning that may suit you at the above address on the subject of Mr. Hodges mileage bill[3] – My removal from Isleworth for the present, to London has prevented me from fixing any appointment until the present –

Your obt
Th. C. Haliburton

J.E. Bradfield Eqr

Acadia University Library MS

1 Unidentified
2 According to the 1864 *Robson's Court Guide*, John Ball, Esq., FLS, lived here.
3 Possibly James Hodges (1814–79), civil engineer

223 To Lambert Smith[1]

8 Albert Terrace
Knightsbridge[2] [London]
6th. Jany [18]64

My dear sir –

Will you be so good as to send over to Sir Samuel Cunard[3] the enclosed note –

Also to add the address of Mr Lambert of Anglo Egyptian Paper Company[4] (having mislaid it) and forward that also –

Yours always
Th. C. Haliburton

L. Smith Esqr

Haverford College MS

1 Unidentified
2 The occupant of 8 Albert Terrace, Knightsbridge, is 'J Halleburton' in *Whibley's Shilling Court Directory and Fashionable London Guide for 1864* (1865), 360.

18 Park Street
Westminster
13" Feby 63

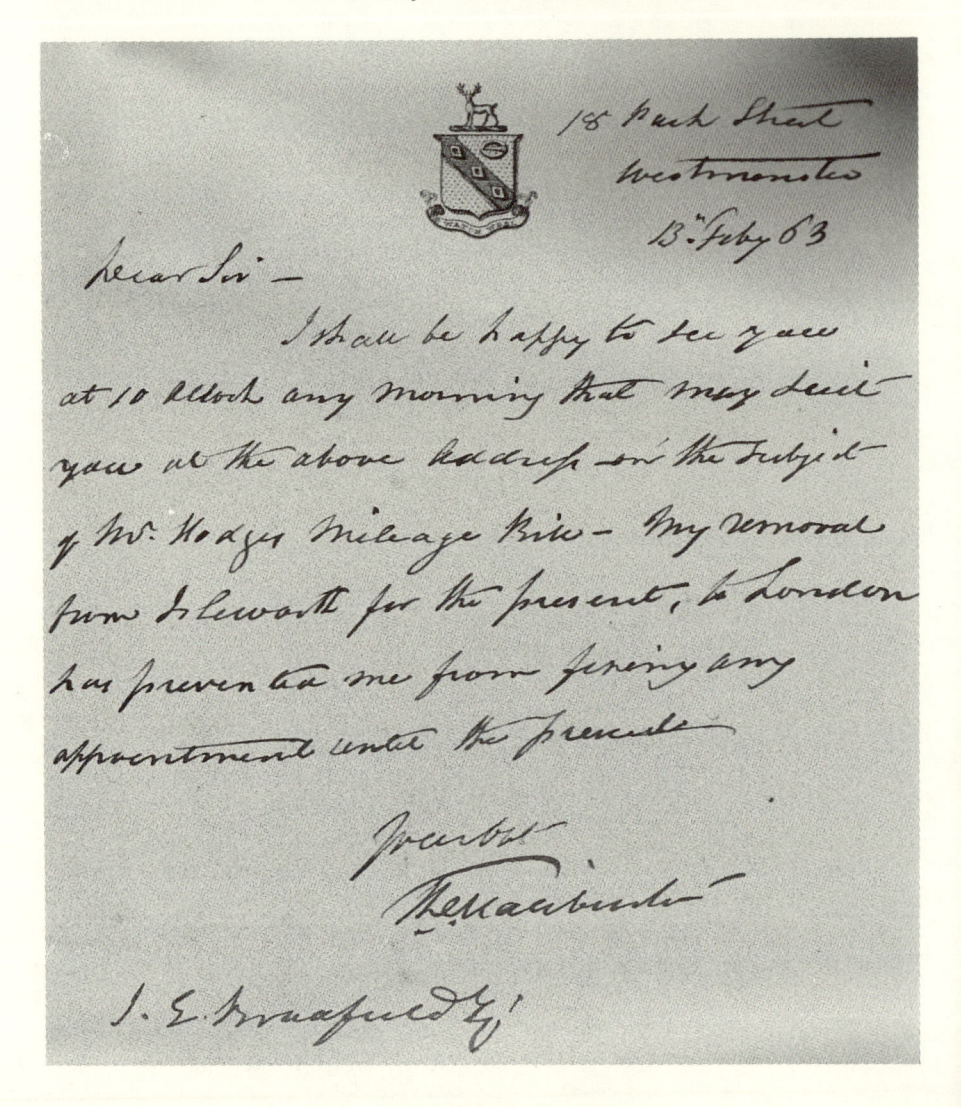

Dear Sir —

I shall be happy to see you at 10 o'clock any morning that may suit you at the above address on the subject of Mr. Hodges Mileage Bill — My removal from Isleworth for the present, to London has prevented me from fixing any appointment until the present

Yours &c
T.C.Haliburton

J. E. Bransfield Esq'

A letter in Haliburton's hand

3 Lambert Smith worked in the vicinity of Sir Samuel Cunard's office, the British and North American Royal Mail Steam Packet Co., 52 Old Broad Street, in the City (*Whibley's ... Directory* [1866]).
4 Unidentified

---

224 To Sir George Broke-Middleton[1]

Gordon House, Isleworth,
June 1st, 1864.

My dear Sir George,

I have received your note requesting me to state my reminiscences of the arrival at Halifax (Nova Scotia) of H.M.S. the *Shannon* with her prize the *Chesapeake*.[2] I have much pleasure in complying with your wishes; but, more than fifty years having elapsed since that event, I can now only recall to my mind some few of the leading incidents that at that time impressed themselves strongly on my youthful imagination.

The action was fought on the 1st June, 1813, and on the *Sunday* following the ships reached the harbour of Halifax. I was attending divine service in St. Paul's Church at that time, when a person was seen to enter hurriedly, whisper something to a friend in the garrison pew, and as hastily withdraw. The effect was electrical, for, whatever the news was, it flew from pew to pew, and one by one the congregation left the church. My own impression was that there was a fire in the immediate vicinity of *St. Paul's*; and the movement soon became so general that I, too, left the building to inquire into the cause of the commotion. I was informed by a person in the crowd that 'an English man-of-war was coming up the harbour with an American frigate as her prize.' By that time the ships were in full view, near George's Island,[3] and slowly moving through the water. Every housetop and every wharf was crowded with groups of excited people, and, as the ships successively passed, they were greeted with vociferous cheers. Halifax was never in such a state of excitement before or since. It had witnessed, in former days, the departure of General Wolfe for an attack on Louisburg, with a fleet of 140 sail, and also his triumphant return.[4] In later years the people had assisted in fitting out the expedition, under Sir George Prevost, for the capture of Martinique and Guadaloupe,[5] but nothing had ever excited the Haligonians like the arrival of these frigates. It was no new thing to see a British man-of-war enter the port with a prize of equal or greater size than herself; they regarded success as a matter of course. When, therefore, the news came, some time previously, of the capture of the *Guerriere* by the *Constitution*,[6] men were unwilling to believe it, considering such an event simply impossible. I can well remember the gloom that hung over the community when the official account was received. In common with all others, old and young, although I participated in the general sorrow that event occasioned, I was not surprised; for, though unable myself to judge of the cause of the defeat, I had heard an experienced old friend of mine (the Hon. S.B. Robie) foretell the occurrence of disasters when our frigates should encounter those of the United States. He said the latter had the scantling[7] of seventy-fours, and were equal to sixty-gun ships; that they were built with remarkable strength, mounted heavier and more guns than our ships of the same nominal rate, and were commanded by very experienced officers. He added that the American Government, by suddenly placing an embargo on all the shipping in their ports, had the seamen of the whole mercantile marine of their country at their disposal, and were thus enabled to man their little navy with crews of picked men; while the system they had adopted of seducing, by means of extravagant bounties, the most skilled gunners to desert from our ships, supplied their men-of-war with a class of able-bodied and disciplined seamen who would fight like demons, as the gallows awaited them if taken prisoners.

In addition to all these disadvantages our naval officers, he said, held their enemies too cheap, and would some day be awakened to a knowledge of their fatal mistake. The people of Halifax were under the same delusion as the navy, and equally ill-informed and rashly confident. The encounter of the *Guerriere* with the *Constitution* fully justified these forebodings of my friends.[8] The relative strength of those ships was first made known after the action, the former mounting (if my memory serves me) only forty-nine guns, with a compliment of 263 men, while the latter carried sixty guns, and had a crew of 450 men. The action was fought with great gallantry on our part, but with a want of discretion that, notwithstanding this great disparity, was said to have occasioned the loss of the ship. Other actions soon followed, with the same inequality, and with a similar fatal result. It was, therefore, no wonder that the people of Halifax were so elated by what they considered a turn in the tide of luck, for it is now known that the action of the *Shannon* and the *Chesapeake* was the commencement of a series of signal victories. It proved the absolute necessity of filling up the crews of our fleet to their full complement, of introducing a stricter discipline, and maintaining a greater state of efficiency.

It soon became known in Halifax that the ships now approaching were the *Shannon* and the *Chesapeake*, and that the former was in charge of Lieutenant Provo Wallis,[9] a native of Halifax, who was in temporary command in consequence of the severe and dangerous wounds of her gallant captain. This circumstance naturally added to the enthusiasm of the citizens, for they felt that through him they had some share in the honour of the achievement. No one could have supposed that these ships had been so recently engaged in mortal combat, for, as they slowly passed up to the dockyard, they appeared as if they had just returned from a cruise, their rigging being all standing and wholly uninjured. They were tolerably well matched in size – the *Chesapeake* being only seventy tons larger than her antagonist, and her broadside only fifty pounds heavier. The greatest disparity was in their respective crews, the American force outnumbering the British by 110 men – a superiority which would probably have proved fatal in a contest finally decided by boarding had not her losses in killed and wounded reduced them to a nearer equality. Nor was the American commander (Lawrence)[10] inferior to his opponent in courage and weight of character. He had, a short time previously, while in command of the United States sloop-of-war *Hornet*, captured, after a short and gallant contest, the sloop-of-war *Peacock*, one of the first ships of her class in the British navy. The prestige of his name was such that the inhabitants of Boston regarded the capture of the Britisher who had so presumptuously challenged the *Chesapeake* as a matter of positive certainty. Lawrence was especially popular with the American seamen, who, when they heard he had received the command of the *Chesapeake*, flocked to his standard in great numbers from all the adjacent ports, and enabled him not only to fill up the full complement of the ship's crew with picked men, but to add to their number many additional volunteers selected from the best seamen in the eastern states. No ship ever left an American port so fully and so ably manned as this frigate. So entirely did the people of Boston anticipate an easy and a speedy victory, that they prepared a banquet for the captors on their return from the conflict, to which they magnanimously resolved to invite Captain Broke and his officers. The wharf from which the last boat was despatched to the ship was crowded with an excited and exulting throng, who cheered their departing countrymen. The feeling of confident triumph was, with one exception, unanimous. A negro in the crowd, who had spent the greater part of his life about the dockyard of Halifax, observing in the boat a coloured friend, gave vent to his humour or patriotism by saying, 'Good-bye, Sam, you is going to Halifax before you comes back to Bosting; give my lub to requiring friends, and tell 'em I is berry well.' For this harmless but inappropriate sally he was instantly thrown into the dock, amid the execrations and derision of the enraged citizens, and narrowly escaped with his life.

Of the action it would be presumption in me to speak. You are in possession of official documents and authentic details, while all I know about it is what I heard after the arrival of the belligerents in the harbour. In fifteen minutes after the first broadside was fired both ships were under weigh for Halifax, the *Shannon* leading the way and her prize following. The Bay of Boston at the time was filled with schooners, sloops, and sail-boats, to witness the combat; and the adjoining headlands, between the scene of the action and Cape Cod, were crowded with people striving to catch a glimpse of the capture of the British frigate. When it was observed that she was in advance, and the *Chesapeake* following, it was unanimously agreed that she was endeavouring to escape, and that the latter was in full chase. The event was hailed with every noisy demonstration of joy, and was communicated to the city, where the only fear entertained was that she would not overtake her flying foe in time for the victorious officers to partake of the splendid banquet which had been provided for them. It was the last view the Bostonians were ever destined to have of their frigate, which had fulfilled the prophecy of the negro, and gone to visit Halifax.

As soon as possible after the vessels had anchored near the dockyard there, a young friend and myself procured a boat and pushed off, to endeavour to obtain permission to visit them. We were refused admission to the *Shannon*, in consequence of Captain Broke requiring quiet and repose on account of his severe wounds; but we were more fortunate in obtaining access to the *Chesapeake*. Externally she looked, as I have already said, as if just returned from a short cruise; but internally the scene was one never to be forgotten by a landsman. The deck had not been cleaned (for reasons of necessity that were obvious enough), and the coils and folds of ropes were steeped in gore as if in a slaughter-house. She was a fir-built ship, and her splinters had wounded nearly as many men as the *Shannon*'s shot. Pieces of skin, with pendant hair, were adhering to the sides of the ship; and in one place I noticed portions of fingers protruding, as if thrust through the outer wall of the frigate; while several of the sailors, to whom liquor had evidently been handed through the portholes by visitors in boats, were lying asleep on the bloody floor as if they had fallen in action and had expired where they lay. Altogether it was a scene of devastation as difficult to forget as to describe. It is one of the most painful reminiscences of my youth, for I was but seventeen years of age, and it made upon me a mournful impression that, even now, after a lapse of half a century, remains as vivid as ever.

The guns of the *Chesapeake* had all names given to them, which were painted in large white letters, such as 'Free Trade,' 'Sailors' Rights,' 'Bloody Murder,' 'Sudden Death,' 'Nancy Dawson,' &c., &c. In looking back on these arrangements, one cannot help regarding with a feeling of contempt this incessant and vulgar appeal to popular prejudice, now so common among the Americans. The two first mottoes, 'Free Trade' and 'Sailors' Rights,' are those which the Yankees have the least pretence of any civilised community on earth to claim to respect or protect. In trade they are close protectionists, and ever have been; and as for 'Sailors' Rights,' it is well known that there is more tyranny, oppression, and cruelty practised towards seamen in their navy and mercantile marine than in that of all other nations of the world combined. I observed on the quarterdeck the figure of a large man wrapped up in the American flag. I was told it was the corpse of the gallant Captain Lawrence, who fell in the discharge of his duty, and whose last words are reported to have been, 'Don't give up the ship.' He was buried at Halifax, with all the respect due to his bravery and his misfortune.

With the subsequent history of the *Chesapeake* you are better acquainted than myself. She remained a long time in the harbour of Halifax, and finally proceeded to England, where she was broken up.

The annals of the British navy furnish numerous instances of gallant frigate actions, but that of the *Shannon* and the *Chesapeake* is equalled by few, and surpassed by none, while its consequences and effects on the subsequent events of the war render it, in my opinion, the most important one on record.

The name of Broke will ever be regarded with pride and pleasure by that service of which he was so distinguished a member; and it must be a great gratification to his family and friends to know that that feeling is fully participated in by a grateful country.

> I am, my dear Sir George,
> Your's always,
> Th. C. Haliburton –

Pub.: *Admiral Sir P.B.V. Broke, Bart., K.C.B., &c: A Memoir*, compiled by Rev. J.G. Brighton (London 1866) 225–33, reprinted by Hutchinson and Co., 1896, 104–15. In part, Beamish Murdoch, *A History of Nova Scotia, or Acadie*, 3 vols (Halifax 1867) 3: 352–5 (reprinted from a review of Brighton's book in the *Pall Mall Gazette*). Reprinted also in the *Acadian Recorder*, 16 January 1913, and Chittick, 35–7

1 Fourth son of Sir Philip Bowes Vere Broke (1776–1841)
2 See Raddall, 149.
3 At the mouth of Halifax harbour
4 Wolfe left to attack Louisbourg on 28 May 1758, with 150 sail and 14,000 men.
5 Sir George Prevost was second in command when Martinique was captured in 1806.
6 See note 8, below.
7 The phrase 'the scantling of' is an uncommon one and means 'the equal of.'
8 See Raddall, 146–7, for an account of the altercation.
9 Sir Provo William Parry Wallis (1791–1892), admiral of the fleet, son of Provo Featherstone Wallis, chief clerk to the naval commissioner at Halifax, NS. He was second lieutenant in the *Shannon* upon the capture of the *Chesapeake*. It was he who took over the ship when Captain P.B.V. Broke was wounded.
10 James Lawrence (1781–1813), commander of the *Chesapeake*

225 To J. Sandfield Macdonald[1]

Gordon House,
Isleworth.
11 Sepr. [18]64

My dear sir –

I have inserted your name for 100 shares in the Guarantee Book & you will get them[2] –

I enclose another letter from Mr Gilbert,[3] from which I infer you forgot to write to him – May I beg the favor of you to answer this to his new address –

       Yours
       Th. C Haliburton

PAC MS

1 (1812–72), premier of the Province of Canada, 1862–4, and premier of Ontario, 1867–71
2 These were shares in the newly created Credit Mobilier Company, which held its first general meeting on 5 September 1864 at the London Tavern. See the *Bankers' Magazine*, October 1864: 967.
3 Possibly James William Gilbart, FRS (1794–?), general manager of the London and Westminster Bank until his retirement in 1860

226 To Richard Bentley(?)

Gordon House
Isleworth
2d May [18]65

My dear sir –

I was very sorry to find by your letter, that you had met with an accident in your recent tour, but I hope that rest and care will soon restore you –

Mrs Haliburton desires me to thank you for the books you so kindly sent her, and I beg you to accept my acknowledgements for Lord Burys,[1] which I hope to get at soon to read carefully –

Mrs Haliburton desires me also to say that 'Crawcour' Baker Street is the name of the shop, where you will, she hopes, get accomodated with an exchange of furniture –

What do you say to Saturday, or Sunday next for coming to Gordon House, if you are able to do so, we shall be most happy to see you, if not whenever you are, you will find a hearty welcome –

> Kindest regards
> To all your family
> Yours always
> Th. C. Haliburton

NY Univ. – Fales Library MS

1 Viscount Bury, *Exodus of the Western Nations*, 2 vols (London 1865), a book concerning his North American experience as civil secretary and superintendent-general of Indian affairs

---

227 To Robert Kempt

Gordon House,
Isleworth.
June 19th 1865

Dear sir

I have to offer you my best thanks for your very kind letter, & for the flattering expressions it contains, & I am also much obliged to you for the book[1] which accompanied your letter – I think it is an admirable compilation, & one that was required[2] – it does you much credit, shewing as it does, your keen appreciation of humour – Many of the facetiae, are, I perceive being copied into the papers, a sure sign of popularity –

It will give me much pleasure to accept your dedication[3] of the forthcoming edition, & wishing you all success, I am, dear sir –

> Your's very truly
> T.C. Haliburton

Buffalo and Erie County Public Library MS

1 Robert Kempt, *The American Joe Miller: A Collection of Yankee Wit and Humour* (1861). See the *Bookseller*, 31 July 1865: 429.

2 The preface claims that 'no good collection of American wit and humour exists on this side of the Atlantic.'
3 The first edition is dated 2 January 1865. The second edition included the following dedication: 'TO/SAM SLICK, / OF SLICKVILLE, THE FIRST OF AMERICAN HUMOURISTS, /THIS VOLUME / IS/(BY PERMISSION)/ADMIRINGLY AND GRATEFULLY / DEDICATED.'

228 To the Electors of the Borough of Launceston

Gordon House, Isleworth, July 4th, 1865

Gentlemen,

Nearly two years ago, I caused it to be intimated to you, that in the event of a general election, it would not be in my power, on account of the state of my health, to solicit a renewal of your suffrages. My intention was thus early made known, in order that ample time might be given you to choose a suitable representative.

The approaching dissolution of Parliament[1] renders it necessary that I should now take leave of you in a more formal and public manner, and I avail myself of the opportunity thus afforded me of thanking you, most heartily and gratefully, for the honour you conferred upon me, in electing me your representative, for the confidence you have been pleased to repose in me, and for the kind and cordial manner in which I have been received, whenever I have visited Launceston.

The severance of our political relations is a source of deep pain and regret to me, but my health imperatively demands it. Still, the social and personal ties arising from the connexion, will ever remain, and will be cherished by me as pleasing reminiscences, that the amenities and friendships of life are quite compatible with the utmost freedom of discussion, and differences of opinion in matters of political interest.

When I solicited the honour of representing you in Parliament, I avowed myself a conservative, and as such you were pleased to receive me. Everything I have since said or done, and every vote I have given, has been in strict accordance with that declaration.

Lord Derby was then at the head of the government, and one of the first acts of his administration was the introduction of a well considered Reform Bill, extending the suffrage to various classes of our fellow citizens, who were capable of exercising it with advantage to themselves, and safety to the country, and who had other claims to consideration beyond that of mere numbers. This bill was summarily rejected by the Whig-Radical opposition, as too guarded, and too limited and deficient in that democratic simplicity, which knows no distinction in classes, and regards the suffrage as an inherent and inalienable right of all. They promised, if the government was entrusted to their hands, to satisfy the cravings of all, and to introduce a measure of Reform so ample, and so sweeping, as to embrace all the democratic blessings of the American constitution. They were taken at their word: the reins of government were entrusted to their hands, and they have ever since retained them. When called upon by their followers to fulfil the promises so profusely and so solemnly made, the contemptuous answer of the father of reform[2] was, 'rest, and be thankful.'

The time has now arrived for a fresh appeal to the people, and there are symptoms that those democratic promises will be repeated, and ratified anew, for the Chancellor of the Exchequeur[3] has seriously promulgated the doctrine that manhood suffrage is the true principle of our elective system!!

But I will not farther pursue the subject; such conduct has produced its natural result – want of confidence at home, and of respect abroad. The remedy is fortunately at hand, and it is to be hoped that electors, made wise by experience, will use it firmly and effectively.

And now, gentlemen, in bidding you farewell, permit me to congratulate you on completion of the railway to Launceston, whereby the resources of the neighbourhood will be developed, and the facilities of locomotion greatly augmented. The extension of the line is much required, and I sincerely hope you may be equally successful in overcoming all difficulties in the way of its accomplishment. In everything connected with the welfare and advancement of Launceston, I shall always feel a deep concern, and shall be glad to co-operate with my successor in any way in my power, in promoting and supporting measures for furthering its interests.

Thanking you again for all your kind offices, confidence, and support,

> I am gentlemen,
> Very truly and gratefully
> Your obedient Servant
> T.C. Haliburton

Pub.: *Launceston Weekly News*, 8 July 1865

1 Parliament was dissolved in July 1865.
2 Lord John Russell (1792–1878), architect of the 1832 Reform Act
3 William Ewart Gladstone (1809–98), chancellor of the Exchequer, June 1859–July 1866

229 To Robert Kempt

[Gordon House Isleworth?]
July 29th [1865]

My dear sir

I must offer you my best thanks for the volume[1] which I received last night, which I shall have the greatest pleasure in placing in my library – I have enjoyed a hearty laugh over many of the stories, & I consider you have made an admirable selection – I am at present suffering from indisposition, & going to the sea in a few days – When I return, I shall hope for an opportunity of making your personal acquaintance.

Meanwhile I pray you to accept my 'effigy,' the last that has been taken of me – I am told it is *justice without mercy*.

Your's always
T.C. Haliburton

Acadia University MS

1 *The American Joe Miller*. See letter 227, of 19 June 1865, above.

Letters of Uncertain Date

230 To G.K. Nichols [n.d.]

Dear Nichols

Will you get Bonnell & Morton[1] to sign the order to this petition & send it back as soon as possible – If by post get Muir[2] to cover it as the man is poor & postage high – Look into the Mondays paper & you will see a dnd advertisement of John Lawsons,[3] which of all the damn fooleries of that damn foolish fellow is the most foolish –

T C Haliburton

PANS MS *Pub.*: Chittick, 48, one sentence

1 W.F. Bonnell and Elkanah Morton were assistant judges.
2 The postmaster at Digby
3 John Lawson (1749–1828) was a wealthy Halifax merchant. As Chittick points out (48), a 'John Lawson had been a fellow matriculant of Haliburton's at King's College, Windsor.' I have been unable to find the advertisement alluded to here.

231 To [C.F. Berkely?][1]   Friday evening

My dear sir

I shall leave London on the first of March, but have fortunately Wednesday

27th at my disposal and shall be most happy to accept your kind invitation for that day –

> Yours trly
> Th. C. Haliburton

C F Berkely Esqr.

Pierpont Morgan Library MS

1 Identification is uncertain, as Haliburton's hand is difficult to decipher. The name of the correspondent might be 'Binkly' or 'Barkeley.' The Hon. Craven Fitz–Harding Berkeley was MP for the Borough of Cheltenham, 1832–47.

232 To Richard Bentley [n.d.]

My dear friend –

By the merest accident in the world I looked over the other part of your proof, and what is it? – A murder of a Halliburton – the very name used and in the preceding chapter, – for Heavens sake strike it out and substitute another name (chap 14 pg 9/8/1 of Miscellany)[1] – People will swear *I wrote both* –

I beseech you to alter that name – Heavens what a coincidence! Pray lose no time –

> T.C.H.

Harvard MS *Pub.*: ed. W.I. Morse, 104

1 Possibly *Bentley's Miscellany*, although I have not been able to find any trace of the ambiguity Haliburton disliked. The numbers '9/8/1' are arranged vertically, with 9 at the top, in the original.

233 To Robert Parker [Windsor?]

It is not scarlet fever we had – young ladies are more subject to that complaint in garrison towns than in the country[1] – but a scarlet rash that looks like it and is called, I believe, scarletina.[2] It did not last long or leave any bad effects, and, thank God, we are all in good health, jogging on in the old way, a pretty dull unvarying round, but perhaps better for the body and the mind than a gayer and more dissipated one.

Pub.: *Canadian Magazine*, 1916: 76

1 Haliburton had lived in a garrison town at Annapolis for eight years.
2 Scarlet fever is an acute infectious disease characterized by a high fever, a sore throat, and a diffuse red rash upon the skin. It was caused by infected milk. 'Scarlatina' is a milder condition of fever accompanied by a red rash and enlargement of glands.

234 To Robert Parker [Windsor?]

Your kind letter and its accompaniment met me on my return from the shore circuit,[1] to put me to shame. If you were not the kindest as well as the best of friends my fortunate habit of procrastination would have forfeited for me your good opinion, as it has one by one most of my friends. I have neither wanted time nor opportunity nor inclination to write, nor a faithful monitor to remind me daily that I should write to you, and I have always most sincerely promised myself to do so tomorrow, but, alas, to-morrow has its to-morrow, till to-day and to-morrow cease to be. If you were disposed to censure you could not do so so severely as I do myself, because I feel that I give good ground to distrust my sincerity when I defer that which can be done so easily and which always gives me pleasure to do. Blame me, my dear fellow, as much as you please, for I deserve it for the habit, but pray think kindly of me, notwithstanding, for of all my early and later friends there is none to whom my heart turns so warmly and affectionately as to you.

Pub.: *Canadian Magazine*, 1916: 78–9

1 Lunenburg and Liverpool, on Nova Scotia's south shore

235 To Robert Parker [Windsor?]

...[1] may desire, – that I have little to say that will interest you, & reserve myself for a good long talk for when you return to our little world, little things will begin to be magnified to your optics to things as large as '*a piece of chalk*' as the yankees so eloquently express it.

All my girls unite in the kindest and most affectionate regards to Mrs Parker & your self & believe me dear Parker yours alwys Th. C. Haliburton

Pub.: Fragment reproduced in the *Canadian Magazine*, 1916: 77

1 A. Wylie Mahon's ellipses

---

236 To Mr Gardiner[1]

[London?]
Thursday

My dear Gardiner

A thousand thanks for all your kindness – I am sorry I cant go to the House of Lords – I have to leave London tomorrow & will have to set out *early in the day* to reach Decimus[2] to dine with him –
Kind remembrances to Mr Mason[3] –

Yours alwys
Th C Haliburton

NY Univ. – Fales Library MS

1 Unidentified. Two Gardiners are listed in *Who's Who*, ed. C.H. Oakes (London 1864): John B. Gardiner, Baronet, and Robert W. Gardiner.
2 Decimus Burton, who had associations with Tunbridge Wells and St Leonard's-by-the-Sea. Both places necessitated travel to reach before the end of the day.
3 The reference to Mr Mason possibly dates this letter after January 1863.

---

237 To ―――?

Gordon House.
Isleworth.
May 6th [1865?][1]

Mr Justice Haliburton would be glad to have the two engravings mentioned by Mr Webber,[2] but as he has already purchased several of them at 5/- each, he would not like to give beyond that price for those in Mr Webber's possession –

Free Library of Philadelphia MS

1 The date is conjectural. The orthography resembles Haliburton's letter to Robert Kempt, 19 June 1865.
2 Unidentified

Miscellaneous Additional Letters

238 Sir Rupert D. George
[Annapolis Royal?]
9th March 1829

Sir,

We beg leave to request the favour of you to state to his Excellency the Leut. Governor that in consequence of the dike land in Granville in the county of Annapolis being distributed throughout the front of the township and in the event of accident from high tides or otherwise requiring the attendance of the commissioners of sewers at different places at one time, there exists a necessity for the appointment of another commissioner –

We beg leave (should his Excellency be of the same opinion to the majority of an appointment) to recommend Elias Bent[1] of Granville as a suitable person to discharge the duties of that office. –

We have the honour to be
Your obt
[Timothy?] Ruggles[2]
Tho C Haliburton
James R. Lovett[3]

PANS MS

1 Elias Bent (b. 1785)
2 Timothy Ruggles (1776–1831), MLA for Granville, 1818–20, 1820–7, 1830–1
3 James R. Lovett (1781–1864), MLA for the Township of Annapolis, 1827–36

239 Sir Rupert D. George

[Annapolis Royal]
Thursday
2d. April 1829

Sir,

The act to extend the provisions of the act relating to commissioners of streets to the town of Digby having received his Excellency's assent, and thereby become a law, and the time appointed for the commissioners to enter upon the duties of their office fast approaching, we beg leave to recommend the following persons to his Excellency's notice as proper persons to be appointed commissioners:

                George K. Nichols
                Thomas Small[1]
                James B. Holdsworth[2]

As these persons are men of correct habits, as well as men of property, and who, from their exertions to benefit the road service heretofore, are well acquainted with the duties of the office, we trust our recommendation will meet his Excellency's approval.

                We are sir,
                Your most obedient and
                Humble servants –
                Tho. C. Haliburton
                John E. Morton

To /
Sir Rupert D. George, Bart.
etc., etc., etc.

PANS copy

1 Unidentified
2 James B. Holdsworth (c. 1796–1859), MLA for Digby Township, 1836–40; Digby County, 1840–3; merchant and farmer

240 To William Hill

15th. June 1829 –
Annapolis [Royal]

Sir –

I have been requested to forward to you the enclosed bond so as to enable the commissioners to draw for one third of the monies voted for the

Wilmot pier, with the season rendering it necessary to commence without delay –

I have also been requested to state that James Robertson one of the commissioners for streets for the town of Annapolis has removed from the province, to the city of St. John where he now resides, and that it becomes necessary that another should be appointed –

For this purpose I beg leave to recommend to his Excellency the Lt. Governor Edward Cutler Esqr. the Sherriff of the County, as a fit and proper person and request the favour of you to make the communication to his Excellency –

> I have the honor to be
> Your obt.
> Tho. C. Haliburton

Willm Hill Esqur.
Actg Secrety

PANS MS

---

241 To Joseph Howe? [Windsor, *c.* 9 November 1836]

The Bridge[1] is safely landed on the 4th and last pier. It is a pity it has to be boarded, in its present state it has a most elegant and light appearance – which enclosing will, to a certain extent, destroy. The staging from 4th pier to Windsor abutment was completed last night at sundown, and two women passed it first, after which a vast number of persons crossed till dark. It is only now the magnitude of the work appears. Contractor says he will finish top work to abutment on Saturday – I don't think he will before Tuesday, it will then take a week to fit flooring for horses and carriages.

Pub.: the *Novascotian*, 9 November 1836: 355, col. a, fragment only, possibly by Haliburton

1 The Avon Bridge was opened to the public on 30 November.

242 To H.W. Shillibeer[1] [London, 13 December 1839?]

Sir

Since I had the pleasure of communicating to you the name of my solicitor, I have received a note from the author of the article in the Miscellany, which it appears has so unexpectedly given offence – He assures me, as I make no doubt was the case, that the coincidence of the surname was purely accidental, and that he not only never heard of the young lady, your client, but that he did not know there was a female of that name, in existence –

I need scarcely say that it is utterly impossible that any person at all acquainted with your client, whom you represent as an accomplished young woman, of respectable character and retired habits, would for a moment suppose that she was the prototype of the very dissimalar ideal character there alluded to, from the mere identity of surname. I might also add that the very nature of the periodical is of itself quite sufficient to preclude any such idea being entertained for a moment, even by the most ill disposed person, for being merely a receptacle for works of imagination suited for the taste of the higher orders of readers, its pages are closed to any thing involving controversy on [political] or religious subjects and above all to articles having a personal application –

Had this been the case, in this instance, I should have had quite as much reason to complain as Miss Shillibear, that my Miscellany had without my consent been made the vehicle of a lampoon which tho it could not lessen the esteem in which your client is held among her friends, would aflict much discredit on my judgement as an publisher, and my feelings as a man – In this case I can only express my sincere regret, at the misconception that exists on her part, on the subject, and altho I am satisfied that the most sensitive person would say that she is not warranted in applying to herself, not only what was never intended for her, but what nobody ever thought of imputing to her, yet I feel it equally due to my own character, as to her feelings, thus to disavow in the most unqualified manner, any intentional offence or any personal reference or allusion whatever also to assure her of how much I deplore that she should for a moment have thought otherwise and in order that she may be fully satisfied of my sincerity, to give her my permission to make what use of this letter she thinks proper –

The claim for pecuniary satisfaction stand altogether upon another footing, and I beg most distinctly to say that I will not pay a penalty for an offence which has never been committed –

I can only regret that your clients feelings are so extremely sensitive as to imagine the world will affect to see a resemblance, which she repudiates herself, and which you describe as dissimilar to her in every particular, but I cannot consent on this account to be made liable for the errors of her imagination –

It is unnecessary to observe to you as a profesional man, that as this complaint, has arisen, in the most unexpected manner possible, no compromise with your client, who it appears has only one part of the name, thus fictitiously used, would preclude a claim from any other person that might come forward, having the advantage of both the same christian & surname, a circumstance which tho unlooked for and improbable, is I assure you not more unlooked for and improbable than was the demand of Miss Shillibear your client –

I have the honr to be

P.S. While writing the above I have received another note from Mr Daniel,[2] who informs me that he has been and satisfied you on this unpleasant subject –

Harvard MS A copy of the letter is entered into Bentley's *Letterbook*, dated 13 December 1838 (BL Add. MS 46,640 f. 27).

1 The letter is in Haliburton's hand, but is written on behalf of Richard Bentley.
  Mr Shillibeer, an omnibus company owner, took exception to some innocuous lines of verse, entitled 'I Met Her in an Omnibus,' that appeared in *Bentley's Miscellany* for 1 November 1838. The poem records the encounter of 'Dick Distych' with 'Charlotte Shillibeer' on the omnibus from 'Brixton Mill' to 'Bank.' She is a 'maiden free and frank' and he invites her for a drink at the Bricklayer's Arms. The poet exchanges a 'buss' with her on parting. In response to the poem, Mr Shillibeer felt his daughter ('an amiable accomplished girl of about eighteen, & who is of very domestic habits') had been brought into 'contempt.' Mr Shillibeer claimed he was the 'original and only Omnibus Proprietor of that name' and on 3 December 1838 commenced legal action against the editor (Charles Dickens) and the publisher (Richard Bentley) of *Bentley's Miscellany*. The case dragged on for years, and a full account of it can be found in Bentley's papers at the British Library, Add. MS 46,635, vol. LXXVI.
2 Unidentified

243 To the Lords Commissioners of Customs

Windsor Nova Scotia
28th. Augt 1839

From the year 1821 to 1829 I resided in the county of Annapolis, which at that time embraced the county now forming the counties of Annapolis and Digby, and was the representative of the county in General Assembly. During that period I was well acquainted with the public services of Mr Morton as Judge of the Common Pleas, an office which he served without salary and as a Custom House Officer. He was a most active and zealous officer, highly esteemed by all who knew him and of the greatest service to the county in all local matters as well as to the province in enforcing the revenue laws. His case is one which is well deserving the favorable consideration of government,[1] as well on account of the great length and variety of his services, as his integrity, ability, and zeal, and especially as during the whole period the emoluments derived from every source afforded him nothing beyond a competent support for the time and were wholly inadequate, with great economy, for making any provision for old age and infirmities.

Thos C Haliburton
Chief Justice Common Pleas.

PANS copy

1 Elkanah Morton was making an application for a retirement allowance as an officer of customs. Haliburton's letter of reference is one of several Morton submitted to the commissioners of customs in Halifax.

244 To ——?

19 October 1858

An affidavit signed by Haliburton concerning his pension claim

PANS copy

245 To ——?

Manchester
10th. Ap. 1860 –

... on monday, as usual –

Yours always
Th. C. Haliburton

Penn. State Univ. MS; fragment only

Haliburton's Speeches in England, 1856–1865

Non-Parliamentary Speeches

1856 16 December At the Manchester Athenaeum, 'On British Colonial Policy,' reported in *The Times*, 19 December 1856: 5, cols d–e
1857 26 March At Glasgow, published as *Address on the Present Condition, Resources and Prospects of British North America* (London 1857)
      19 May At the sixty-eighth anniversary of the Royal Literary Fund, Freemason's Hall, on 'The Literature of the Colonies,' reported in the *Standard*, 20 May 1857
      24 August At a public meeting held at the Mansion House to devise means of relief for sufferers in the Indian Mutiny, reported in the *Standard*, 26 August 1857
1859 27 January At the Robert Burns Centenary Dinner, city hall, Glasgow, reported in the *North Mail British Daily Mail*, 28 January 1859
      18 April An election address at Launceston, North Cornwall, reported in the *Launceston Weekly News*, 23 April 1859
      29 April At the Corn Market, Launceston, Cornwall (an election acceptance speech), reported in the *Launceston Weekly News*, 30 April 1859
      23 August At the 'Non-Elector's Presentation to Mr Lindsay at North Shields,' reported in the *Daily Chronicle*

		and Northern Counties Advertiser, 24 August 1859: 3, cols a and b
1860	April	At the fifteenth anniversary of the Royal General Theatrical Fund, Freemason's Tavern, response to toast, 'The Prince of Wales and the British Colonies,' reported in *The Age We Live In*, 7 April 1860: col. a
1861	1 April	At the Central Subscription Room, Launceston, Cornwall, advertised as 'Circuit Reminiscences,' but not given on that topic. Instead, Haliburton lectured on 'Law in North America.' Reported in the *Launceston Weekly News*, 6 April 1861
1862	27 January	At the Isleworth Infants School-Room on 'Our Relations with America,' reported in the *Standard*, 28 January 1862: 2, cols d, e, and f

Parliamentary Speeches

1859: 25 July, maiden speech; 1 August
1860: 28 February; 14 March; 16 March; 21 April, published as *Speech of the Hon. Mr. Justice Haliburton, M.P. in the House of Commons, on Tuesday, the 21st April, 1860, on the Repeal of the Differential Duties on Foreign and Colonial Wood* (London); 13 July; 2 August
1861: 22 February; 12 March; 21 March; 25 April
1862: 21 February; 4 March; 10 March; 21 March; 21 May; 18 June; 3 July
1863: 23 March; 22 April
1864: 19 February; 4 March; 18 March

Sources of Letters

The following details sources for letters owned by the Houghton Library, Harvard University; Public Archives of Canada, Ottawa; Public Archives of Nova Scotia, Halifax; and Public Record Office, Kew Gardens, London:

Harvard	*Letter*
Harvard 45M-537	57, 64, 75, 76, 78, 80, 82, 87, 89, 91, 97, 99, 100, 102, 106, 116, 118, 119, 120, 121, 133, 141, 145, 149, 151, 154, 155, 156, 157, 163, 165, 167, 168, 172, 173, 175, 177, 180, 181, 183, 184, 186, 188, 191, 192, 193, 203, 204, 207, 208, 210
Harvard 45M-538	68, 85, 148, 159, 164, 171, 176, 179, 182, 195, 196, 198, 199, 206, 211, 215, 233
Harvard 45M-539	194
Harvard 45M-540	242
Harvard 45M-542	160, 169
Harvard bmsCan3	67, 71, 86
Harvard bmsCan58	214, 222
Harvard fmsEng936 vol. 1 (p.75)	93

PAC	*Letter*
PAC MG 23, C 10	23

PAC MG 30/O 11	49
PAC MG 17, B1, vol.5, ff 177–9	115
PAC MG , B9, vol. 3, p.84 (Microreel M-203)	201
PAC W.H. Merritt Papers, vol. 24 (MG 24, E1, vol. 26, p.4666)	213
PAC Macdonald-Langlois Papers, 1854–1922 (MG 24, B30, vol. 2, p.1057)	225

PANS

	Letter
MG 1, vol. 194, doc. 261	48
MG 1, vol. 606, folder 3	38
MG 1, vol. 979, folder II, no. 2	2
,, ,, ,, 4	5
,, ,, ,, 6	9
,, ,, ,, 9–10	10
,, ,, ,, 13	11
,, ,, ,, 15	12
,, ,, ,, 11	13
,, ,, ,, 17	14
,, ,, ,, 22	15
,, ,, ,, 25	16
,, ,, ,, 19	17
,, ,, ,, 23	18
,, ,, ,, 28	20
,, ,, ,, 30	28
,, ,, ,, 31	29
,, ,, ,, 34	230
MG 1, vol. 1548, no. 4B	21
MG 1, vol. 1693, no. 10	22
,, ,, 10A	24
,, ,, 6A	132
,, ,, 6A	137
,, ,, 5	147
,, ,, 6C	153
,, ,, 5A	216

Sources of Letters

″	″	5B	218
″	″	9B	220
″	″	6A	244
″	″	7, 7A 7B	45
MG 100, vol.36, no. 60			112
RG 1, vol. 235, doc. 83			30
″	″	98	238
″	″	109	239
RG 1, vol. 236, doc. 70			31
″	″	91	33
″	″	96	35
RG 1, vol. 237, doc. 62			39
″	″	50	41
″	″	161	47
RG 1, vol. 238, doc. 95			37
RG 1, vol. 239, doc. 13			36
″	″	13	40
″	″	25	42
″	″	32	44
RG 1, vol. 241, doc. 56			51
″	″	60	52
″	″	165	53
″	″	181	54
″	″	179	55
RG 1, vol. 242, doc. 91			56
RG 1, vol. 243, doc. 28			59
″	″	35	62
RG 1, vol. 244, doc. 20			243
RG 1, vol. 248, doc. 197			27
RG 1. vol. 253, docs 60–1			96
RG 1, vol. 257, doc. 132			110
RG 5, Series 'GP,' vol. 1, no. 48			32
RG 5, 'GP' A, vol. 3, no. 20			135
RG 5, Series 'U,' vol. 24, no. 87			136
RG 7, vol. 1, no. 123			1
RG 7, vol. 5, no. 96			240
RG 39, 'C,' folder 1849			113
Micro: Biography: Lynch, Thomas; Papers: Reel 3, Box 4, no. 28			6, 8

PRO	Letter
CO 217, 168, f. 221	65
" 172, f. 659 (316)	70
" 212, ff 311–12	124
" " ff 315–19	127
" " ff 52–4	129

Picture Credits

ii Bust of Haliburton at the Isleworth Branch Library, Middlesex (courtesy of Professor Allen Penney)

50 Photograph, by Edward Graham, of Wolfville, NS, of an oil portrait of Haliburton, c. 1831, by William Valentine of Halifax (courtesy of the Nova Scotia Museum; photograph collection, PANS)

51 'Clifton,' the residence of Judge Haliburton, by W.H. Bartlett, 1842 (courtesy of the Public Archives of Canada – C2416)

101 Print by M. Gauci from a painting of Haliburton by E.H. Eddis, 1838 (courtesy of the Public Archives of Canada – C6087)

180 Gordon House, Isleworth, 1869 (courtesy of Alan C.B. Urwin)

180 Haliburton and his wife, Sarah Harriet, at Gordon House (courtesy of the Nova Scotia Museum)

213 Photograph of Haliburton by Mayall, published in D.J. Pound, *The Drawing-Room Portrait Gallery of Eminent Personages* (London 1860; courtesy of the Nova Scotia Museum)

214 Photograph of Haliburton by Parish and Co., Halifax (photograph collection PANS)

215 Wood-engraved portrait of Haliburton, originally published in the *Illustrated London News*, 9 September 1865 (courtesy of the Nova Scotia Museum)

248 A letter in Haliburton's hand (courtesy of Acadia University Library)

Index

(Figures within parentheses refer to letter numbers.)

Aberdeen, Earl of (George Hamilton Gordon) 139n
Acadian Recorder 32n, 38n, 185n
Adam, Robert 241n
Alexander, Sir James E., *L'Acadie: or, Seven Years' Explorations in British America* 117n
Alexander, Sir William 42, 43
Allnatt, Charles Blake 201, 201n
Allnatt, Mrs 201
American Traveller 17n
Amero 38, 38n
Anderton (under sheriff) 193
Annapolis Iron Works 31, 32n
Anson, H.J.W. 22, 24n
Appleton, Colonel 42
Archibald, Charles D. 86, 90, 91n, 105
Archibald, S.G.W. 18, 18n, 19, 20n, 25, 27nn11, 13
Athenaeum Club 87, 89, 102n, 186, 233
Atlay, J.B., *Lord Haliburton: A Memoir* 117n, 185
Avon River Bridge 49, 80, 265, 265n
Avon River Bridge Company 49, 79, 80, 80n

Bacon, Francis 14
Bagshaw, S., *Shropshire Gazetteer* 201nn6, 7
Bailey, Rev. Jacob 42, 44n
Baillie, Alexander F., *The Oriental Club and Hanover Square* 102n
Bainbridge-Smith, John 116
Baker, Thomas Barwick Lloyd 164n
Bakewell, Mr, Jr 28, 29n
Bakewell, Mr, Sr 29n
Ball, John 247n
Banker's Magazine 216n, 254
Barclay, Colonel Delancey 31, 32n
Barclay, Thomas 32n
Barham, Richard H. 86, 87, 108, 114, 120, 123, 161, 161n; *The Garrick Club Notices* 130n; *Ingoldsby Legends* 86, 87, 161n
Barry, John A. 45n
Barry, Robert 82, 83n
Bartlett, James Russell, *Dictionary of Americanisms* 120n
Bartlett, W.H. 115
Bates, Joshua 101, 102n
Bates, Miss 102
Bates, Mrs 102n
Bath, John 28, 29n
Bathurst, Earl of 183

278 Index

Bazely, Sir Thomas 203, 204n
Beaver, Alfred, *Memorials of Old Chelsea* 204n
Belcher's Almanack 27n, 78n
Belknap, Jeremy 42; *American Biography* 13, 14n
Bent, Elias 263, 263n
Bentley, Richard 86, 87, 88, 89, 90, 91n, 94, 103n, 110n, 113, 114, 116, 120nn1, 4, 120, 127n, 130, 138n, 143n, 155n, 158nn1, 3, 160nn2, 3, 161n, 181, 182, 189n, 199n, 201nn1, 8, 205, 207n, 208n, 211n, 216, 221n, 227, 227n, 228n, 235n, 235, 236n, 237n, 242nn2, 4, 267, 267n
Bentley's Miscellany 87, 114, 118, 119, 120n, 126, 126n, 128, 129n, 159
Bentley's Quarterly Review 182, 202, 202n, 209n, 217n (176), 217n (177), 219n, 219, 221n (182), 221, 221 (183), 224, 224n, 260, 260n, 266, 267n
Berkeley, Craven Fitz-Harding 260n
Birkland, Rev. John 42
Bishop, Daniel 85n
Black, Mr 106n
Blackwood's Magazine 94, 94n
Blair, Richard 19, 20n
Blanchard, William A. 99n
Blanchard and Lea. *See* Lea and Blanchard
Bliss, Henry 106n
Bliss, J. Murray 79n
Bliss, Lewis 106n
Bliss, William Blowers 135n, 166, 168n, 169, 172
Blowers, Sampson Salter 7n, 11, 12n
Boas, Guy, *Garrick Club* 90n, 130n
Bogart family 21n
Bonnell, Anna 29n

Bonnell, W.F. 28, 29nn4, 5, 48, 48n, 259, 259n
Bookseller 255n
Boyle, Colonel Gerald Edmond, *Rifle Brigade Century* 127n
Brenton, Edward 25, 27n
Bristol Mirror 89
British and American Steam Navigation Company 118n
British and North American Mail Steam Packet Company 249n
British Orphan Asylum Anniversary Festival 199n
Broke, Sir Philip Bowes Vere 251, 252, 253, 254nn1, 9
Broke-Middleton, Sir George 254n
Bromley, Walter 12, 14n
Brooks, Shirley 211, 211n
Brown, Mr (unidentified) 203
Browne, Dr William Alexander, *What Asylums Were, Are, and Ought to Be* 191n
Brunel, Isambard Kingdom 197, 197n
Buckingham, James S., *Canada, Nova Scotia, New Brunswick etc* 117n
Budd, Elisha 8n
Burton, Decimus 87, 89, 103n, 105, 106n, 128n, 140n, 183, 262, 262n
Burton, James. *See* Haliburton
Burton, Octavia 183
Burton, Septimus 140, 140n
Burton, William 87, 128n
Burton family 87, 106n, 114, 117
Bury, Viscount (William Coutts Keppel) 237, 238n; *Exodus of the Western Nations* 255, 255n

Campbell, Sir Colin 76, 76n, 79, 80, 83, 84, 93, 95, 99, 100, 109
Campbell, Donald 23, 24n

Index

Canada Agency Association 237, 238nn4, 7
Canada Club 98n, 105, 105n
Canada Land and Emigration Company 212, 238nn1, 3, 5; *Prospectus* 237, 238n
Canada, Viscount 124n
Canadian Review and Literary and Historical Journal 29, 29n
Carey, Lucius Bentick. *See* Falkland, Lord
Carey, Lucius William 152, 153n
Carey and Lea. *See* Lea and Blanchard
Carlton Club 89
Carter, D. (unidentified) 29
Case, Mrs Adelaide 200, 201n; *Day by Day at Lucknow* 200, 201nn1, 2, 5
Case, Colonel 201n
Cassilis, Rev. John 22, 24n
Catalogue of the Nova Scotia Department 240n
Cecil, Lord Robert 182, 208, 208n, 219, 220
Chambers, William 74
Champlain, Samuel de 42, 44n; *Works* 45n
Charnisay, Charles de Menou, sieur d'Aulnay de 43
Chester Chronicle 244n
Chipman, Jared 20n
Chipman, Ward, Jr 22, 23n, 107; *Remarks upon the Disputed Points of Boundary* 107n
Chipman, Ward, Sr 23n
Chipman, William Henry 77n
Chittick, V.L.O. 78n, 90nn6, 8, 98n, 99n, 110n, 112n, 179, 183n, 188nn6, 8, 243n, 259n
Christie, J.H. 197, 198n
Cist, Lewis 141n

Clarence Club 103, 103n
Clark, Roger D. 78, 78n
Clifton 51, 113, 115, 116, 216
Clinch, Rev. Joseph Hart 144n
'Club, The' 5–6
Cobden, Richard 189, 190n
Cochran, Rev. James 67, 69n
Cochran, Terrance 53–4, 54n
Cochran, Dr William 19, 20n, 69n
Cochrane, Sir Thomas 25, 27n
Colburn, Henry 110n, 113, 116, 117, 119, 120n, 149n, 157, 158, 158n, 160–1, 161nn2, 3
Collections of the Massachusetts Historical Society 44n
Collections of the New Brunswick Historical Society 23n
Colmer, J.G., *Canada Club (London)* 105n
Colquhoun, Dr P. 207n
Cook, William 182
Corcum, Mrs 62–4, 64–5, 66n, 67–8, 69nn3, 4
Corkum, Henry 66n
Cornwallis River Bridge 69, 70n
Coutts and Company 109, 120, 137
Cox 102, 103n
Crawley, W.H. 24n
Credit Foncier Company 214
Credit Mobilier Company 214, 254n
Croker, John Wilson 87, 89, 106nn1, 4, 197
Croker, Mrs 89, 105, 107
Cromwell, Oliver 43
Cross, Lieutenant Richard 25, 26nn4, 5
Crosskill, John H. 175, 176n
Cunard, Mrs Laura. *See* Haliburton, Laura

Cunard, Samuel 18n, 116, 136, 137, 137n, 145n, 157, 188n, 206n, 247, 249n
Cunard, William 116, 145n, 187, 188n, 206n
Cunningham, Charlotte (Mrs Joseph Hart Clinch) 145n
Cunningham, John 116, 145nn1, 4
Cunningham, Perez 145n, 154, 154n, 155n, 185n, 188, 188n
Cunningham, Richard 145n
Cunningham, Sarah 145n
Curry, Wm 106n
Cutler, Ebenezer 34n
Cutler, Edward H. 34, 34n, 265

Dalhousie, Earl of. *See* Ramsey, George
Daniel, Mr 267
Darwin, Charles 179, 219n
Darwin, Emily Catherine 219n
Darwin, Susan Elizabeth 219n
Darwin family 179
Davies, John 74
Davies, Samuel 74
Davies, William 28, 29n, 47
Davis, Charles Augustus 79n
Davis, Susanna (Francklin). *See* Haliburton, Susanna
Davoust *versus* Doucett 33
Dawes, Mrs 156, 156n
Dawson, Peter 81n, 85
De Grey, Lord (Thomas Philip, Earl De Grey) 139, 139n
De Monts, Pierre du Gua, sieur de 40, 44n
Derby, Lord. *See* Stanley, Edward
Deuchar, Alexander 124n
Deveau family 34n
DeWolfe, Benjamin 55, 56nn1, 2, 81n

Dickens, Charles 267n
Disraeli, Benjamin 190n
Doucet family 34n
Dublin University Magazine 182, 212, 229, 229nn1, 2, 230, 231n
Duffis, Mrs (Susannah Murdoch) 18, 18n
Duffis, William 18n
Dundonald, Lord (Thomas Cochrane) 234, 235n
Durham, Earl of (John George Lambton), *Report on the Affairs of British North America* 89, 106, 107n, 109, 110n

Easson, John 32n
Eddis, Eden Upton 88, 101, 102, 102n
Edinburgh Review 198n
Elgin, Lord (James Bruce) 152, 153n, 190n
Elliott, Mrs, *Narrative of the First French Revolution* 210, 211n

Fairbanks, Charles 87–8, 102n; *Journal* 98n, 99n
Fairbanks, Samuel P. 60, 60n
Fales, Abigail 51, 70, 71n, 110, 111nn1, 2, 3
Fales, DeCoursey, *Fales Family of Bristol, Rhode Island* 71n
Fales, Eliza Ann 111n
Fales, Haliburton 110, 111nn1, 4
Fales, Lucy Ann 111n
Fales, Samuel 71n, 111nn1, 3
Fales, Samuel Bradford 111n
Fales, Susanna Maria 111n
Falkland, Lady (Amelia FitzClarence) 153n, 184, 189; *Chow Chow* 114, 153n, 189, 189n

Falkland, Viscount (Lucius Bentinck Carey) 114, 115, 126, 133, 135, 142, 144, 146, 152, 167, 174, 177
Fearon, Henry 164n
Feild, Bishop Edward 154, 155n
Fielding, Mrs 67
Fielding, William 59, 59nn2, 3, 66, 67
Fingard, Judith 14n
Finnis, Thomas Quested 183, 192n, 193n
FitzClarence, Lady Amelia. *See* Lady Falkland
FitzClarence, Lady Mary. *See* Mrs Mary Fox
Fletcher, Mr 245
Fletcher, Mrs 245
Fletcher, W.G. Dimock, *Historical Handbook to Loughborough* 164n
Forrester, Thomas 25, 26n
Fox, Colonel Charles Richard 86, 94, 94n, 98, 99n
Fox, Mrs Mary 94n, 99n
Francatelli, Charles, *Cook's Guide* 241–2, 242nn2, 4
Francklin, Michael 3
Francklin, Michael Nickelson 16, 18n
Fraser, Margaret ('Halli') 53n, 57n
Fraser's Magazine 110n, 115, 142, 142n, 149
Free Press (Halifax) 32n

Gallenga, Antonio (pseud. Luigi Mariotti) 3; *Episodes of My Second Life* 6n, 125n
Gardiner, John B. 262n
Gardiner, Robert W. 262n
Garrick Club 87, 99, 114, 130
Gateway to the Valley 117n, 152n
Gauci, M. 101, 102n
Gavasa, Antonio 9, 10n

Gebhard, Rosa 164n
General Mining Association 28, 29n
George IV (King of England) 107n
George, Sir Rupert D. 60n, 113
Gesner, Abraham 29n
Gilbart, James William 254, 254n
Gilpin, Rev. Alfred 116, 151n
Gilpin, Edwin 116
Girdlestone, Rev. Edward 187n
Gladstone, William Ewart 190n, 257, 257n
Glenelg, Lord (Charles Grant) 99, 99n, 104nn1, 2
Glode, Charles 37, 38n, 46
Goldsmith, Henry 13, 14n, 17, 18, 34
Gordon House 179, 180, 182, 184, 185n, 188, 190, 190n, 196n, 202, 202n, 215, 231n, 245n, 255
Gormley, James 61–2, 62n
Gormley, Mrs James 61–2
Gould, Nathan 99n
Graham, Michael 74
Grattan, Thomas Colley *Civilised America* 222, 222n
Gray, Thomas, 'Elegy Written in a Country Churchyard' 17n, 140, 141n
Great Exhibition (1851) 240n
Grey, Sir George 100n
Grigor, Dr William 78, 78n
Guthmin, Miss 117, 156n
Gypsum trade 4

Hagerman, Christopher Alexander 169, 170n
Haliburton, Alexander Fowden (son-in-law) 116, 186, 187n
Haliburton, Alfred Fales (cousin) 140, 141n
Haliburton, Amelia (daughter) 116

Haliburton, Arthur Lawrence (son) 71n, 115, 184, 185nn7, 8, 193, 194n, 206, 207n, 240n, 241

Haliburton, Augusta (daughter) 116

Haliburton, Emma (daughter) 116

Haliburton, George Mordaunt (uncle) 141n

Haliburton, Georgianna (cousin) 70, 71n; *Short Account of the Haliburtons of Windsor Nova Scotia* 103n

Haliburton, James (formerly Burton) 87, 89, 99, 99n, 109, 119, 120n, 131n, 140n, 183

Haliburton, John Gustavus Peoples (cousin) 141n

Haliburton, Laura (daughter) 116, 145, 145n, 188n, 206, 206n

Haliburton, Mrs Louisa (first wife). *See* Neville, Louisa

Haliburton, Lucy (mother) 3

Haliburton, Robert Grant (son) 115, 209–10, 210n, 224, 240, 240n, 245n

Haliburton, Mrs Sarah Harriet (second wife) 117, 179, 183, 185nn3, 5, 190n, 194n, 194, 196, 199, 201n, 201–2, 202n, 202, 203, 207, 208n, 216, 226, 228, 231, 231n, 235, 245, 255

Haliburton, Susannah (daughter) 106n, 115, 116, 240, 240nn2, 3

Haliburton, Susannah Boutineau (Francklin) (stepmother) 3

Haliburton, Susannah (Otis) (grandmother) 246, 246n

Haliburton, Thomas Chandler
- personal: graduates BA 3; marries Louisa Neville 4; applies to take MA 4; appointed notary 4, 6–7; moves to Annapolis Royal 4; judge of the probate court at Annapolis 5; elected to House of Assembly 5; death of father 6; requests 'grape vines' 10; dealings with Walter Bromley 12–13; relates Halifax gossip 19, 25; poor health of father 19; introduces bill for Common Schools 36n; supports removal of Roman Catholic test oaths 37; reports to Abbé Sigogne 37; describes archaeological discovery at Annapolis Royal 39–44; president of Avon Bridge Company 49; president of local board of health 49–51; prepares to move to Clifton 79n; circulates print of himself 88; attends dinner at Richard Bentley's 90n; complains about Bentley as a correspondent 137–8; complains about *Bentley's Quarterly Review* 182; complains about error in *Bentley's Miscellany* 260; offers conditional resignation 92–3; discusses literary plans 94, 113, 119, 122; thanks judges of Lunenburg 95; requests coronation ticket 97–8; sends copies of *Clockmaker* to friends 98–9; sends copy of *Bubbles* to Henry Wood 103; declines invitation to Trollopes 100; has portrait painted 102; applies for post as registrar of hackney coaches 104, 113; visits Crokers 105; first 'dispersion' of children 106; praises Croker's attack on Lord Durham 106; builds Clifton 113; appointed supreme court judge 114; death of Louisa 114; visits England 114–15, 117; state of family in 1841 115; conflict with Rev. Al-

fred Gilpin 116, 149–51; as Victorian father 116; marriage of daughters 116; marries Sarah Harriet Williams 117, 179; denies authorship of *Times* article 122; confused with Brenton Halliburton 123; communicates with A. Deuchar 124; comments on article about himself 128–9; returns parcel of prints 129; visiting member of Garrick Club 130; depression of spirits 136; seeks position for Michael Wallace Porter 139; seeks publisher for son's music 140; sends autograph to Lewis Cist 141; death of son Tom 144, 144n, 173n; desires colonial edition of his works 148–9; desires uniform edition of his works 175; donates land for church 152n; death of John Stephen 156, 156n; anticipates visit of Miss Guthmin to NS 156; relations with Henry Colburn, 157–8; reviewed by William Jerdan 161–2; attends Royal Agricultural Society meeting 163–4; calls on S. Holme 168; personal dealings with Joseph Howe 173, 187, 241; tries to visit Howe's son 232–3; tenders resignation 178, 179; delivers speeches 181–2, 187, 189, 190, 191, 192n, 211n, 239n, 242nn1, 5, 269–70; MP for Launceston 182, 212, 222–3, 223n, 256–7; writes article for *Bentley's Quarterly Review* 182, 210, 217, 218, 219, 220, 220–1, 222; member of Indian Mutiny Appeal Fund 183, 194n; describes new life at Gordon House 184; praises son Arthur 184; declines invitation to Athenaeum Club 186; publishes work recommending NS to emigrants 187; invites Bentley to dine 192, 196, 198, 198–9, 204, 205, 209, 218, 236, 242, 255; advises Bentley on literary matters 199, 200, 236, 241–2; attends 'London Shoeblacks' annual treat 193n; dines on Lord Mayor's barge 193; suffers malaria 195; sends W.B. Watkins a prescription for sore throat 195–6; visits Gloucester 195, 235; suffers gout 197, 197n, 199, 201–2, 203, 232; visits Manchester 202, 202n; compliments Anthony Trollope 205; invites Trollope to Gordon House 205; writes letter of introduction for Trollope 206; attends centenary of Robert Burns's birthday 208, 211, 211n; seeks job for son Robert 209–10, 224; visits North America 212, 233n, 234; death of 215–16; attends lecture by Sir Richard Owen 225; offers Bentley MS 226, 228; approaches Sir William Jolliffe 227; lodges in London 228; assists Bentley's son 233; responds to 'foolish letter' from Bentley 238; visits Launceston 238; claims writing career is over 230; attends Maynooth Grant Bill division 239, 239n; meets with W.H. Merritt 240–1; meets with J.E. Bradfield 247; congratulates W.B. Watkins 246; remi-

niscences of HMS *Shannon* at Halifax 249–53; witnesses devastation of *Chesapeake* 252–3; book dedicated to 255, 258; meets C.F. Berkely 259–60; on family illness 260–1; dines with Decimus Burton 262; declines to purchase engravings 262
- friendships: with G.K. Nichols 5; with Peleg Wiswall 5; with Abbé Sigogne 5; with Trollope family 88, 130–1, 132; with John Wilson Croker 89; with Lord Falkland 114; with Robert Parker 114, 261; with Richard Bentley 116, 155, 182; with Sir John Beverley Robinson 143–4; with Joseph Howe 179–81; with William Schaw Lindsay 183; with Thomas Quested Finnis 183; with William Benjamin Watkins 183; with Edmund Hopkinson 183
- legal and business matters: gypsum mining interests 4; inquires concerning land at Digby 7; threatens writ of habeas corpus 8; on the appointment of a judge for Cape Breton 9; on Sissiboo registry office 11; addresses grievance to lt-governor 14; transacts legal business 10, 27–8, 32, 34, 47; discusses appointment of circuit judges 19; reorganizes probate office at Annapolis Royal 24; account of Cross trial 25; discusses Annapolis Iron Company business 31; concern over cost of lawsuits 33, 38; early years as a judge 49; on murder of Thomas M. Rudolph 52; on jail conditions at Windsor 53–4; urges dismissal of sheriff 53–4; reports on petition of Francis Pyke 55–6; reports on plans to build Cornwallis bridge 69–70; reports on case of Robert Barry 82; reports on complaints against Thomas Tupper 83–4, 95–7; reports on extra judicial services 72–5; seeks advice on fee collection 57–8; dispute with Garret Millar 60; dispute with Central Board of Health 71–2; intercedes for James Gormley 61–2; defends sentencing of Mrs Corcum 62–4; urges clemency for Mrs Corcum 67–8; investigates Kilfoil case 66–7; transacts Avon Bridge Company business 79–80, 84–5; complains against magistrate 81–2; on non-receipt of fees 91; describes state of courts in NS 133–4; protests half salary while on leave 133–4, 162–3, 165–7, 168–70, 170–3; certifies absence on shore circuit 152; writes to Society for Propagation of the Gospel concerning land at Windsor 153–4; describes legal career 166–7, 177–8; denies petition of Dugald McNab 176; discusses pension problems 146–8, 174, 177–8, 187, 197, 240, 242–3; returns Bentley's prospectus 206; chairman of Canada Land and Emigration Company 212; champions business opportunities in North America 216; discusses Land Company business 237; discusses railway business 243–4; sells shares to J. Sandfield Macdonald 254; appoints commissioners of streets at Digby 264; writes reference for Elkanah Morton 268; pens letter (for Bentley) on the Shillibeer case 266–7

Index

– opinions: on publishing in NS 15–16; on emigration 16; on relations with US 16–17; on Thomas Ritchie 28; on politics in NS 28–9; on British colonial policy 30; on Mrs Ritchie's funeral 30; on schools 35–6; on the plight of the Indians 36; on politics 77–8; on life at forty 79; on Aunt Abigail 110–11; on Lord Elgin's policy 152–3; on state of Anglican Church in NS 154; on the booksellers *v.* publishers dispute 158, 159; on Richard Cobden 189; on launching of *Great Eastern* 197, 197n; on present state of English politics 223

– letters of, to: Aberdeen, Earl of 138–9; Archibald, Charles 105; Baker, Barwick 163–4; Barham, Richard 97–8; Barry, John 45; Bates, Mrs 101–2; Bentley, Richard 90–1, 98–9, 102–3, 107–8, 108–10, 111–12, 117–18, 118–20, 122–3, 125, 126, 127, 128–9, 135, 136–7, 137–8, 140, 143, 155, 157, 157–8, 159–60, 160–1, 162, 175, 189, 192, 194–5, 195, 196, 198 (154), 198 (155), 198–9, 199, 200, 200–1, 201–2, 202, 204 (163), 204 (164), 205, 206, 206–7, 207, 208, 209 (172), 209 (173), 210–11, 216–17, 217, 218, 218–19, 219, 220, 220–1, 221, 222, 224, 225, 226 (191), 226 (192), 227, 228 (195), 228 (196), 229, 230–1, 233–4, 234–5, 235, 235–6, 236, 236–7, 238–9, 239, 241–2, 245, 254–5, 260; Berkely(?), C.F. 259–60; Bradfield, J.E. 247; Broke-Middleton, Sir George 249–54; Browne, Dr William Alexander 191; Campbell, Sir Colin 79–80; Chipman, W.H. 76–7; Cist, Lewis 141; Clinch, Rev. Joseph Hart 144; Cranewich, Dr 244; Croker, John Wilson 106–7; Croker, Mrs 105–6; Cunningham, John 144–5; Customs, Lords Commissioners of 268; Dawson, Peter 80–1; Deuchar A. 124; Fales, Samuel 70–1, 110–11; Falkland, Lady 152–3; Finnis, Thomas Quested 192–3; Fletcher, Mrs 245; Gardiner, Mr 262; 'Gentlemen' 190; George, Sir Rupert D. 60, 61–2, 64–6, 66–7, 67–9, 69–70, 71–2, 72–5, 81–2, 84–5, 91, 92–3, 95–7, 120–1, 263, 264; Gilpin, Rev. Alfred 149–52; Girdlestone, Rev. Edward 186–7; Glenelg, Lord 104; Grey, Sir George 99–100; Guthmin, Miss 156; Haliburton, Arthur 240; Haliburton, George, Sr 140–1; Hawkins, Rev. Ernest 153–5; Henderson, Major 126–7, 129; Hill, William 52–3, 53–4, 55–6, 56–7, 57–8, 59, 264–5; Hodgson 243–4; Holme, Samuel 168; House of Assembly 177–8; Howe, Joseph 77–8, 146–8, 168–70, 170–3, 173, 174, 175–6, 176–7, 184–6, 187–8, 232–3, 241, 242–3, 265; James, T.W. 76, 82–3, 83–4 ; Jeffrey, Thomas N. 75–6; Jerdan, William 161–2; Jolliffe, Sir William 227; Kempt, Robert 255–6, 258; Launceston, Electors of 222–3, 256–7; Lea and Blanchard, Messrs 128, 148–9; Le Marchant, Sir John Gaspard 178; lieutenant-governor 46–7; Lunenburg, Judges of 95; Lytton, Sir Edward Bulwer 209–10, 224; MacDonald, J. Sandfield 254; Mariotti, Luigi 125; Marshall, John George 34–5; Merritt, W.H.

240–1; Millar, Garret 62–4; Montgomerie, Hugh 237–8; Newcastle, Duke of 162–3, 165–8; Nichols, G.K. 7, 8, 9–10, 10, 11–12, 21, 27–9, 34, 47, 47–8, 259; Nickisson, George 142; Northumberland, Duchess of 228–9; Owen, Sir Richard 225; Parker, Robert 79, 106, 136, 260–1, 261, 261–2; Porter, Asa 8–9; Power, De Witt 123–4; Ramsey, George (Earl of Dalhousie) 6–7; Robinson, John Beverley 143–4, 231–2; Shillibeer, H.W. 266–7; Sigogne, Abbé 33–4, 35–6, 37–8, 38–9; Sitwell, Lady 164; Smith, Lambert 247; Stanley, Lord 133–5; Tilley, Cecilia 130–1; Trollope, Anthony 205–6; Trollope, Mrs Frances 132; Trollope, Thomas Adolphus 100; Watkins, W.B. 189–90, 193–4, 195–6, 196–7, 203–4, 231, 246; Wiswall, Peleg 9, 12–14, 14–18, 18, 18–21, 21–4, 24–7, 29–32, 32; Wood, Henry 103; Young, George Renny 39–45

– letters of, to unidentified correspondents: 152, 197–8, 208, 225, 262, 268 (244, 245)

– published works: *Address on the Present Condition ... of British North America* 185n, 187, 191, 191n, 226n; *Americans at Home* 116, 157; *Attaché* 3, 94, 94n, 110, 113, 114, 115, 119, 122, 125, 125n, 127, 127n, 128, 128–9, 131n, 134n, 143, 143n, 148, 183; *Attaché* (Second Series) 98n, 115, 119, 127n, 135, 135n, 136, 136–7, 137, 138n, 140, 148; *Attaché* (combined edition) 149n; *Bubbles* 88–9, 90, 102, 103nn1, 3, 103, 103n; *Clockmaker* 78n, 86, 87, 90n, 90–1, 108, 109, 119, 122, 143, 143n, 148, 162, 181; *Clockmaker* (Second Series) 86, 87, 90, 91, 94, 94nn4, 5, 109, 119, 148; *Clockmaker* (Third Series) 90, 109, 111, 113, 118, 118–19, 119–20, 122, 123n, 126, 148, 181; *English in America* 113, 114, 116, 119, 120n, 154; *General Description* 5, 12–13, 14nn4, 5, 6, 17, 20n, 23nn1, 2, 32, 33, 34n, 34–5; *Historical ... Account* 5, 6, 12, 13, 14–15, 16, 17nn3, 6, 7, 19–20, 20nn7, 10, 21n, 21–3, 23n, 24n, 24, 26n, 29–30, 32n, 35, 45, 45nn2, 3, 47–8, 48nn2, 3, 54n, 111–12, 112n, 113, 119, 120–1, 122, 168n, 181, 244; *Letter-Bag* 89–90, 107–8, 108nn1, 2, 108–9, 110n, 111, 112, 117, 118, 118–19, 120n, 143n; *Nature and Human Nature* 176nn2, 3, 226n; *Old Judge* 110n, 113, 115, 122, 123n, 137, 142, 142n, 148, 149, 149n; *Reply to the Earl of Durham* 89, 90, 122, 123n; *Sam Slick's Wise Saws* 116, 117, 157, 159, 160, 161, 162n, 187n, 226n; *Season Ticket* 182, 212, 228n, 229, 229n, 230, 230n; *Traits of American Humour by Native Authors* 157, 158n

– sources of previously published letters: *Acadian Recorder* 253; Bennett, Raymond M. 131; Brighton, Rev. J.G., *Admiral Sir P.B.V. Broke, Bart, K.C.B., &c: A Memoir* 253; *Canadian Magazine* 79, 94, 106, 136, 261, 262; *Canadian Notes and Queries* 35; *Catalogue of the William Inglis Morse Collection at Dalhousie* 173, 175; Chittick, V.L.O. 8, 17, 23,

Index

26, 29, 33, 47, 78, 141, 174, 175, 188, 253, 259; Fales, DeCoursey, *Fales Family of Bristol, Rhode Island* 70, 111; *Hants & King's County Gazette* 76; Hall, N. John, ed., *The Letters of Anthony Trollope* 206; *Journals ... of the House of Assembly* 91, 93, 174, 178; *Launceston Weekly News* 223, 257; Morse, W.I., ed. 91, 99, 102, 108, 109, 112, 120, 123, 125, 126, 127, 129, 135, 137, 138, 140, 143, 155, 157, 158, 159, 161, 175, 189, 194, 199, 201, 202, 207, 209, 211, 217, 218, 219, 220, 221, 222, 226, 229, 230, 234, 235, 236, 238, 239, 242, 260; Murdoch, Beamish, *History of Nova Scotia, or Acadie* 253; *Novascotian* 44, 265; *Nova Scotia Royal Gazette* 95; *Report of the P.A.N.S.* 13, 17, 20, 23, 26, 31, 48; Robinson, C.W., *Life of Sir John Beverley Robinson* 144; Trollope, Frances Eleanor, *Frances Trollope: Her Life and Work* 132
Haliburton, Thomas (son) 115, 144n, 173n
Haliburton, W.H. (grandfather) 3, 246, 246n
Haliburton, William Hersey Otis (father) 3, 4, 9, 9n, 19, 20n, 60n, 110
Haliburton Museum (Windsor, NS) 86
Halifax Morning Chronicle 187, 188nn2, 3
Halifax Royal Gazette 82n
Hall, James 46, 47n
Halleburton, J. 247n
Halliburton, Sir Brenton 25, 26, 26nn5, 6, 27n, 123, 124n, 135n
Halliburton, Dr John 123, 124n
Halliburton, Rebecca 27n
Hallyburton, Lord (Lord Frederick Gordon) 184, 185n
Hamilton, Sir Charles 27n
Harker, Mr 193, 194n
Harris, John (John Elder) 47n
Harvey, Dr D.C. 18n, 52n
Harvey, Sir John 146, 148n
Harvey, Whittle 104
Hawkins, Ernest 154n
Henderson, Major John Alexander 127n
Hill, William 52n, 135n
Hodges, James 247
Hodgson, Richard 244n
Hodgson, Sir Robert 244n
Holdsworth, James B. 264, 264n
Holman (unidentified) 150
Holme, James 168n
Holme, Samuel 168n
Hook, Theodore 87, 90n, 161, 161n
Hopkinson, Edmund 131n, 183, 196n, 236n
Horace, *Epistles* 44n; *Odes* 108n
Howe, Joseph 17n, 27n, 51, 78nn1, 5, 18, 86, 87, 179-81, 185n, 188n, 216, 233n, 241n; *Speech ... on the Union of the North American Provinces* 175, 176nn1, 5, 185, 186n; *Letter to the Right Honourable William E. Gladstone, M.P.* 185, 186n, 188n
Howe, Julia Ward 217, 217n; 'Battle Hymn of the Republic' 217n; *A Trip to Cuba* 217n
Howe, Mary 173n, 181
Howe, Mrs 185, 233, 241
Howe, Sydenham 78n
Hoyt, Captain Jesse 34n
Hoyt, Jesse 34n, 47
Hoyt, Silas 34n, 47

288 Index

Hume, Joseph 175, 176n
Hurst and Blackett 117, 158n, 161, 161n, 175, 226, 226n
Huskins, Martin 74

Indian Mutiny Appeal Fund 183
Inglis, Bishop Charles 154, 154n, 155n
Inglis, Bishop John 150, 152n, 154, 155n, 199nn2, 6
Inglis, Mrs John 199, 199nn2, 6
Inglis, Sir John 199, 199n
Inglis, Lady, *Siege of Lucknow: A Diary* 199, 199n
International Exhibition (1862) 240, 240n, 245, 245n

James, Mr 60, 60n, 65
James, Thomas W. 76n
James, Rev. William J. 201, 201n
Jeffrey, Thomas N. 76n
Jeffreys, Lord Frances 197, 198n
Jennings, Sylvester 74
Jerdan, William 90n, 117, 162n
Jerrold, Douglas 211n
Jerrold, William Blanchard 211, 211n
Johnstone, James W. 77, 78n, 170
Jolliffe, William George (Baron Hilton) 227n
Jordan, Mrs 94n, 153n
Journals ... of the House of Assembly 27n, 38n, 85n, 93n, 174n, 188n

Kaulbach, John H. 63, 64n, 64-5, 66n, 68, 69n
Kavanagh, Lawrence 37, 38n
Kemble, Fanny (Fanny Anne Butler), *Journal* 109, 110n

Kempt, Sir James 11, 12, 12n, 13n, 14, 18, 18n, 19, 25, 36, 37, 38n, 81, 99, 263, 264, 265
Kempt, Robert, *American Joe Miller* 255, 255n, 256n, 258, 258n, 262n
Kennedy, Sir Arthur Edward 210, 210n
Kenyon, Mrs (unidentified) 201
Kilfoil, William 66, 67n, 73
Kilmorey, Earl of 185n
King, Harry 53n, 57n
King's College (Windsor) 3, 4, 20n, 116, 125n, 138, 139n, 185n, 259n; *King's College Board Minutes* 6n

Lambert, Mr (unidentified) 247
La Tour, Charles Etienne 43
Launceston Weekly News 239n
Lawrence, Captain James 251, 253, 254n
Lawson, John 75, 259, 259n
Lawson, William 26, 27n
Lea and Blanchard 99, 99n, 102, 103n, 109, 111, 112n, 120
Lea, Isaac 99n
Lebel 43
Leech, John 120n
Leigh, Percival, *Comic Latin Grammar* 118, 120n
Le Marchant, Sir Dennis 199, 199n
Le Marchant, Sir John Gaspard 168, 170n, 173n, 174
Lescarbot, Marc 40, 41, 44nn4, 5; *Nova Francia* 44n
Lewis, Sampson (bookseller) 244
Lindsay, William Schaw 183, 244n
Literary Gazette 117, 137, 138n, 162nn1, 2
Lockhart, John Gibson 197, 198n
Lockhart (unidentified) 102, 103n
Lockyer, Henry 30, 32n

Index

Longfellow, Henry Wadsworth 161, 161n
Longman, Thomas 161, 161n
Longman, William 161, 161n
Lovett, James R. 263, 263n
Lyell, Charles, *Travels in North America* 29n
Lytton, Sir Edward Bulwer 210n, 224n

Macara, Mrs Henrietta 29n
McCarthy, Charles W. 36, 36n
McCormack, Thomas 74
McCormick, Michael 57
McDermot, Michael 73
MacDonald, J. Sandfield 254n
McDougall, Alexander 126, 126n
MacIver, Charles 136, 137, 137n, 157, 157n
MacIver, David 136, 137, 137n, 157n
Macnab, Sir Allan Napier 237, 238n
McNab, Dugald 176
McNab, Dugald, Sr 177n
Magee, Henry 84n
Mahon, A. Wylie 94n, 136n
Mainwaring, Charles Kynaston 218n
Maitland, Sir Peregrine 46, 47n, 55, 56, 57, 58, 60, 61, 63, 64, 66, 67, 68, 69, 71, 81
Major Jack Downing 78
Manchester Athenaeum 181, 185, 185n, 186n
Manchester City News 183n
Manchester Review 230n
Mansion House 193, 194n
March, Colonel 42
Mariotti, Luigi. *See* Gallenga, Antonio
Marsh, Mr 230

Marshall, John George 22, 24n, 178n; *Patriotic Call* 24n, 35, 35n; *Industries and Resources of Nova Scotia* 24n; *Guide to Justices of the Peace* 24n; *Provincial Laws* 121n
Marshall, John Joseph 178n
Mason, James Murray 246, 246n, 262, 262n
Mauger, Joshua 27n
Maynard, Captain Thomas 26, 27n
Maynooth College (Ireland) 239n
Maynooth College Bill 239nn1, 2
Maynooth Grant 239
Medley, Bishop John 154, 155n
Merivale, Mr 163n
Merritt, William Hamilton 241n
Mildmay, Wm 43
Millar, Garret 60, 60n, 62, 64, 65, 69n
Millar, J. 137n
Miller, J.F. 137n
Minns, William 19, 20n
Money Market Review 216nn2, 3
Montgomerie, Hugh Edmonstone 238n
Moody, Colonel James 7n
Moody, John 7, 7n
Moorhouse, James 27-8, 29n
Moorhouse, John 27-8, 29n
Morning Chronicle (Halifax) 98n, 173
Morning Herald (London) 242
Morton, Elkanah 10, 10n, 34, 34n, 259, 259n, 264, 268, 268n
Mossman, Andrew 29n
Mossman *versus* Mossman 28
Mostyn-Owen family 211n. *See also* Owen, William Mostyn
Mudie, Charles Edward 236, 236n
Muir, W. 32, 32n, 259, 259n
Murdoch, Susannah. *See* Duffis
Murdoch, Thomas William Clinton 99, 99n

Murray, John 158, 158n
Murray, Admiral Robert 26, 27n

Nelson, Admiral Horatio 233n
Neville, Captain Laurence 4, 6n, 156, 156n
Neville, Louisa (Mrs Louisa Haliburton) 4, 26, 33, 51, 114, 115, 124n, 136n, 156, 173n
Neville, Captain William Frederick 6n
Newcastle, Duke of (Henry Pelham Fiennes Clinton) 163n
Nichols, George K. 5, 8n, 29, 264
Nichols, Mrs 8
Nickisson, George 115, 142n
North American Review 17n
North British Daily Mail 190n, 211n
Northumberland, Duke of (Algernon Percy) 185n, 223n, 226, 226n, 229
Northumberland, Duchess of (Lady Eleanor Grosvenor) 229n
Norton, Mrs Caroline 87, 99, 99n
Nova Scotia and New Brunswick Company 31, 32n
Novascotian 5, 6, 17n, 38n, 44nn1, 4, 51, 52n, 71n, 78nn18, 19, 79n, 85n, 181, 188n

Old Stone House (Avondale) 4
O'Neale, William 74
Owen, William Mostyn 179. *See also* Mostyn-Owen
Owen, Arthur 243, 244n
Owen, Mrs Frances 193, 194n
Owen, Sir Richard 225, 225n

Pall Mall Gazette 253
Palmer, Mrs 106n
Palmerston, Lord 190nn3, 4, 191n

Pardoe, Julia 208, 208n; *Episodes of French History* 208n; *A Life's Struggle* 208n
Parker, Abigail 47n
Parker, Charles Stewart 234n
Parker, James (London) 234n
Parker, James (Nova Scotia) 46, 47n
Parker, Rt Hon. John C. 234n
Parker, John William 158, 158n
Parker, Miss 70
Parker, Mr 233
Parker, Robert 3, 22, 24n, 79n, 114
Parker, Mrs Robert 262
Peachey family 228n
Peel, Sir Robert 107n, 134n, 187, 188n
Peninsular and Oriental Company 194
Piercy, Mrs Ann 3-4
Piercy, Captain Richard 4
Polehampton, Rev. Henry 200, 201nn5, 8; *Memoir, Letters and Diary of the late Revd Henry S. Polehampton, Chaplain of Lucknow* 207n
Polehampton, Mrs 201
Pontrincourt. *See* Poutrincourt
Pope, Alexander 129n
Porter, Asa 9n
Porter, Asa, Jr 9n
Porter, Dr Charles 138-9, 139n
Porter, Edward 233, 234n
Porter, Michael Wallace 139
Porter, Reginald 184, 185n, 187, 188n
Post Office Directory (London) 156n
Post Office Directory (Shrewsbury) 201n
Potter, Israel 32n
Poutrincourt, Jean de Biencourt, sieur de 40, 41, 42, 45n
Power, De Witt C. 124n
Prevost, Sir George 21, 249, 254n
Price, Stephen 87, 99, 99n

Punch 211
Pyke, Francis 55, 56

Quarterly Review 89, 107n, 125, 197, 198n, 208n

Ramsey, George (Earl of Dalhousie) 7n
Ratchford, James 56n
Reform Bill (1859) 256-7
Revised Statutes of Nova Scotia 12n
Ritchie, Mrs 30
Ritchie, Thomas 8, 19, 20n, 28, 29n, 31, 34, 34n
Roach, William H. 10, 10n, 28, 46, 47n
Robert Burns Centenary Festival 211n
Roberts, Abraham J. 237, 238n
Roberts, Eleanor 74
Robertson, Alexander 45, 45n
Robertson, James 265
Robertson *versus* Bonnell 28, 32
Robicheau family 33, 34n
Robie, Simon Bradstreet 25, 27, 72, 75n, 250
Robinson, Deborah 28, 29n
Robinson, John Beverley, Jr 212
Robinson, Sir John Beverley 89, 144n, 212, 232nn1, 2
Robinson, Lady 232
Robinson, Sir William 232n
Robson's Court Guide 99n, 106n, 247n
Robson's Liverpool Directory 168n
Robson's London Directory for 1838 99n
Royal Agricultural Society 163
Royal Gazette (Halifax) 29n
Royal Literary Fund 192n
Rudolph, Thomas M. 52, 52n, 53n, 53
Ruggles, Timothy 263, 263n
Rundle, Jno 106n
Russell, Lady Frances 245, 245n

Russell, Lord John 147, 148n, 245n, 257, 257n

Sadler, James 25, 27n
Saunders, John 10, 10n, 11
Scott, Sir Walter 197, 198nn4, 5; *Lady of the Lake* 25, 27n; *Rob Roy* 25, 27n; *Marmion* 27n
Sedgewick, Major 43
Sentell, Joseph 54, 54n, 55, 59, 59n
Shand, Gwendolyn, *Historical Hants County* 6n, 80n; 'The Cunninghams of Hants County' 145n
Shaw, Moses 31, 32n
Sheridan, Richard Brinsley 99n
Sherman (unidentified) 199
Shillibeer, Miss 159, 266-7
Shillibeer, Mr 267n
Shillito, Benjamin 54n
Shirley, Governor 42
Shrewsbury Chronicle 117n
Shrewsbury Peerage Case 195n
Sigogne, Abbé Jean-Mandé 5
Sitwell, Edith 164n
Sitwell, Lady (of Barmoor Castle, Northumberland) 164n
Sitwell, Lady (of Ferney Hall, Craven Arms, Shropshire) 164n
Sitwell, Lady (of Renishaw Hall, Derbyshire) 164n
'Slick, Sam' 77, 78, 86, 108, 118, 122, 123n, 128–9, 137, 141, 182, 230
Small, Thomas 264
Smith, Benjamin 155n
Smith, Bennett 155n
Smith, Francis 46, 47n
Smith, Lambert (unidentified) 249n
Smith, Mr (unidentified) 154
Smith, Richard 155n
Smith, Seba 79n

Smith (unidentified) 34
Smyth, Major Robert Carmychael 99, 99n; *Letter from Major Robert Carmychael-Smyth to His Friend the Author of 'The Clockmaker'* 99n
Society for the Propagation of the Gospel 153, 154n
Specht, Anthony 9n
Specht, William 9n
Standard (London) 102n, 193n, 194nn5, 6, 195nn1, 2, 207n, 236n, 239n, 242, 242n
Stanley, Edward (Lord Derby) 115, 134n, 135n, 163, 165, 172, 256
Stanser, Bishop Robert 154, 155n
Stationers' Company 239n
Statutes at Large 39n, 58n
Stephen, Harriet 156n
Stephen, Henry 156n
Stephen, John 91, 91n, 156, 156nn2, 3
Stephens, James 135n
Stephenson, Andrew 122, 123n
Stewart, James 170, 170n
Stewart, Judge James 11, 12n, 22, 25, 26n, 28, 61, 62n
Stokes, Anthony, *A View of the Constitution of the British Colonies* 30, 32n
Stringer and Townshend 149
Sumner, Charles 124, 124n
Sydney, Alderman Thomas 193, 194n

Tandem Law 11
Thesiger, Frederick (Baron Chelmsford) 199, 199n
Tibedo, Joseph 38, 38n
Tilley, Cecilia (Cecilia Trollope) 88, 131n, 132, 132n
Tilley, John 88, 131, 131n

Times, The (London) 89, 90n, 117n, 120, 122, 123nn4, 5, 158n, 185n, 187, 188n, 194n, 199n, 204n, 211, 211n, 216, 217n, 219, 219n, 235n
Trefnel, Mr (unidentified) 144
Tristram Shandy 11, 12n
Trollope, Anthony, *Autobiography* 88, 206nn1, 2
Trollope, Frances Eleanor, *Frances Trollope: Her Life and Work* 90n, 132n
Trollope, Mrs Frances 88, 110n, 114, 115, 130-1, 131nn3, 4; *Domestic Manners of the Americans* 88; *Widow Barnaby* 88, 110n; *Michael Armstrong, the Factory Boy* 88, 100, 109, 110n, 112
Trollope, Thomas Adolphus 88
Trollope family 88, 109
Trotter, Rev. Mr 24n
Tupper, Thomas 83, 95
Twiss, Horace 120, 120n

Uniacke, Fitzgerald 25, 27n
Uniacke, James Boyle 19, 20n
Uniacke, Richard John, Jr 37, 38nn2, 4
Uniacke, Richard John, Sr 11, 12n, 27n, 30, 38n, 76n
Union Club 233, 234n
United Service Magazine 158, 158n
Urwin, Alan C.B., *Railshead Isleworth* 185n, 231n

Victoria (Queen of England) 98n, 201
Vinson, General 83n
Von Holtzendorff, Professor, *An English Country Squire* 164n

Walker, Alexander 95
Wallace, Michael 52, 52n, 53, 54n

Wallis, Provo Featherstone 254n
Wallis, Sir Provo William Parry 250–1, 254n
Walpole, Spencer Horatio 204, 204n
Watkin family 204n
Watkins, Mrs Ellen 117, 190, 190n, 193, 197, 203, 231
Watkins, Helen 190, 190n, 193, 194n, 195, 196n, 231
Watkins, William Benjamin 117, 183, 190n, 196n, 197n, 202n
Waugh, Francis Gledstanes, *Members of the Athenaeum Club, 1842 to 1887* 234n
Webber, Mr (unidentified) 262
Weekly Chronicle (Halifax) 20n
Weeks, Mr 98n
Weldon, John Wesley 116, 240, 240n
Wellington, Duke of (Arthur Wellesley) 107n, 234, 235n
West, Samuel C. 184, 185n
Westminster, Marquis of 229n
Whibley's Shilling Court Directory (London) 247n, 248n
White, Thomas 10, 10n
White, William 74
Wilcox, Mr 53, 54n
Wilcox, Mrs 53
Wilkins, Lewis M., Jr 185n, 240, 240n
Wilkins, Lewis M., Sr 54, 54n, 115, 133, 135nn5, 6, 146, 147
William IV (King of England) 94n, 153n, 184
Williams, Sarah Harriet (Owen). *See* Haliburton, Mrs Sarah Harriet
Willis, Rev. Robert 154, 155n
Wilson, Henry 83
Wilson, Sydney 84n
Winniett, George Gilbert 10, 10n
Winniett, William 10n, 11, 12, 13, 13n, 21
Winston, James 130, 130n
Wiswall, John 5
Wiswall, Miss 13, 26
Wiswall, Mrs 13, 18, 20, 26, 29
Wiswall, Peleg 5, 10, 11, 18n, 28, 29n, 34, 47, 62n
Wolfe, General James 249, 254n
Wood, Emily 103n
Wood, Helen 103n
Wood, Henry, *Change for the American Notes* 103n
Wood, Mrs 103
Wood, Rose 103n
Wright, Patrick 55, 56nn1, 3, 59, 59n
Wynne, John Lloyd 211n

Young, George Renny 44